The Campus History Series

The Art Institute of Pittsburgh

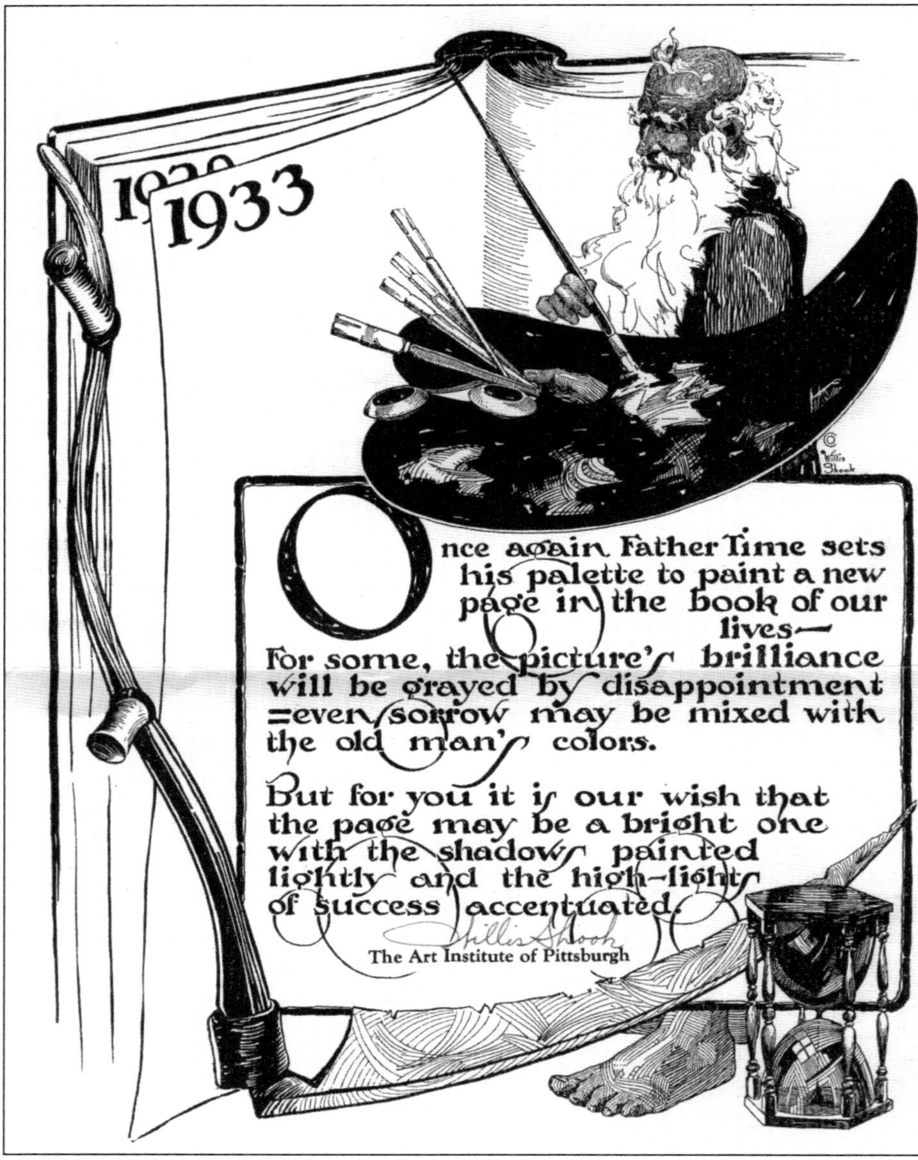

Willis Dresdale Shook, founder of the Art Institute of Pittsburgh, designed this New Year's greeting card, demonstrating his work both as an artist and writer. His paintings were used to demonstrate technique to students and formed a large personal collection. Other literary works included "I am Pittsburgh the Mighty!" apotheosis, included in a mural painting in the corridor of Pittsburgh's Stanwix Shops Building, a former location of the school, and numerous articles published in trade publications. (Courtesy of Willis D. Shook III.)

On the cover: Attending school in the Golden Triangle of downtown Pittsburgh, often called the City of Bridges, the students of the Art Institute of Pittsburgh have access to endless inspiration. This class in the 1980s sketches the beautiful scenes from the Sixth Street Bridge, also known as the Roberto Clemente Bridge, over the Allegheny River, with guidance from their instructor Henry Koerner, shown on the bicycle with his dog Piglet riding in the basket. (Courtesy of Morris Berman, Pittsburgh Post-Gazette.)

The Campus History Series

THE ART INSTITUTE OF PITTSBURGH

JACQUELYN FELIX FISHER AND E. W. GOODMAN

ARCADIA PUBLISHING

ISBN 978-0-7385-6554-5

Published by Arcadia Publishing
Charleston SC, Chicago IL, Portsmouth NH, San Francisco CA

Printed in the United States of America

Library of Congress Control Number: 2009923282

For all general information contact Arcadia Publishing at:
Telephone 843-853-2070
Fax 843-853-0044
E-mail sales@arcadiapublishing.com
For customer service and orders:
Toll-Free 1-888-313-2665

Visit us on the Internet at www.arcadiapublishing.com

CONTENTS

ACKNOWLEDGMENTS

Many people have contributed to this book, from its conception through production. We thank George Pry, president; Carrie Butler, director of public relations; and the members of the Education Management Corporation Scholarship Foundation for their input and belief in this project.

We especially thank Willis D. Shook III, M.D., whose grandfather, Willis Shook, was the founder of the Art Institute of Pittsburgh. Dr. Shook's enthusiasm for this project has enabled us to write the story of his grandfather's vision and the 41 years that he led the school. Dr. Shook has given us glimpses into the past through personal stories and artifacts, including ledgers, personal correspondence, diaries, photographs, artwork, and an amazing 72-year-old color movie reel.

Joseph A. Hajnas, a personal confidante of Willis Shook, first as a 1953 graduate, then as a member of the faculty and a successful Pittsburgh artist and designer, has become a special friend to us. It has been our pleasure to learn from him and have him write the foreword to our book.

Patricia A. Nagle provided us with her technical expertise, scanning hundreds of photographs and photographing artifacts, transforming our history into digital images.

We are grateful for the searching in attics, boxes, drawers, albums, and scrapbooks for photographs that had not been seen in years. We have laughed at many stories from the people who created those historic moments and from people who knew those no longer with us. We heard the stories of these students and of those who taught the students. In our research, we read newsletters, newspapers, press releases, and notes that describe the accomplishments of thousands of graduates. Only a limited number of these could be included in this book; there are so many more equally tremendous stories of the impact that has been made by the Art Institute of Pittsburgh.

We thank all the staff, faculty, alumni, and former employees who have contributed photographs, reminisced, and told us many stories that, when woven together, form the fabric that is the history of the school.

We have noted with each image, the names of those who have generously and enthusiastically searched for and shared their photographs. All other images appear courtesy of the Art Institute of Pittsburgh.

FOREWORD

Welcome to the Art Institute of Pittsburgh! This book is intended to refresh the spirit that lives in memories of school days and to present the opportunities that await the dedicated student of an artistic endeavor.

From its early and modest beginnings, the Art Institute of Pittsburgh has focused on the quality of education provided to students from across the United States and around the world. Fifty-five thousand alumni have enjoyed successful careers in art-related pursuits.

The founder, Willis Shook, was a delightful gentleman and a personal friend. Students and faculty were always his concern. He especially appreciated the deeply committed student. During my student days, Willis Shook frequently expressed interest in my progress and offered encouragement when the challenge exceeded my limits. He knew that intense energy was required to achieve the goals that a student aspired to. I am indebted to Willis for his friendship and his guidance. I also remember other faculty members (and later my colleagues)—Vincent Nesbert, John Jellico, Carol Schott, Sally Watkins, Peter Wassum, Lee Gilbert, Betty Beal, and, more recently, John Johns, Jesse Hager, Tom Helwig, and Tom Kouris—who were patient in their wait for a student to blossom.

Today's faculty members continue the founder's example of dedication to the need of the student—one student at a time. Clear communication, competency in subject matter, and the ability to awaken the senses to beauty are the marks of the Art Institute's faculty. Each member knows that an art- or design-related career enriches our lives and those who see, touch, taste, or think about the well-executed work of the mind and the hand. As the faculty stimulates creativity, the Art Institute of Pittsburgh accomplishes its goals of preparing graduates for service to their families, communities, the business world, and allied professions.

Today's professionally focused art and design programs are each a proven career opener. These are presented in an environment that enables students to share ideas, concepts, and understandings—this interface energizes the creative spirit under the guidance of observant professional faculty sharing knowledge gained from their experience.

As you walk through these pages of history, with their memories, I wish you a joyful journey. In keeping with its tradition of friendliness and concern for the student, the Art Institute of Pittsburgh extends this welcome to visit and see what is happening today in preparation for an art or design career of tomorrow.

—Joseph A. Hajnas

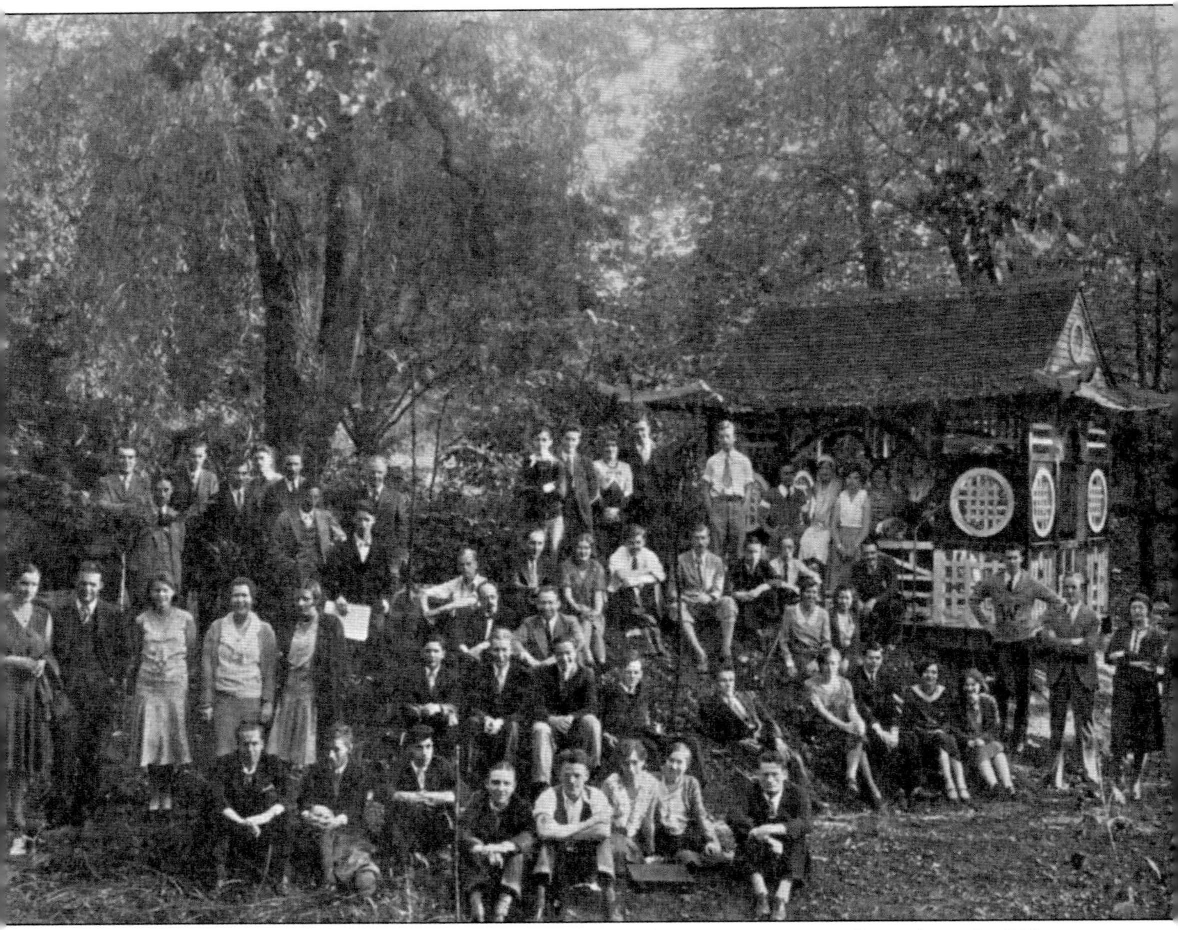

This is the earliest-known photograph from the Art Institute of Pittsburgh. Fifty-seven students and faculty pose in the oriental garden at Willis Shook's home in Sewickley, on October 11, 1930. Shook designed the garden to be a secluded place where "those fortunate people who were born with the yearning to squeeze paint tubes on to palettes find real delight in the charming vistas and novel scenes." The *Sewickley Herald* reported events of this day as "many canvasses were enthusiastically started but later forgotten as the artists turned their attention to a wiener roast with its accompanying delicacies of cider and cookies." Students in the photograph include Martha Beeler, Betty Bond, Jane Kunkle, and Amelia Drynan. Other Sewickley students who attended in the previous two years are also named: Martin Flora, Catherine Lowery, Marie Ward, Elizabeth Wehrum, Harriet Hyde Lyon, Louis Wolfe, Robert Boyd, Jean Morrison, Rachel Mather, Roger Taube, and Raymond Green. (Courtesy of the Sewickley Valley Historical Society and the Sewickley Herald.)

INTRODUCTION

Nearly 90 years after the founding of the Art Institute of Pittsburgh, we take a look back at the students, faculty, and staff who have made its history. The success of the Art Institute of Pittsburgh is because of the 55,000 alumni and the countless faculty and staff who have mentored them. Our history began even before the first nine students registered for classes in 1921, when a Pittsburgh artist, Willis Shook, recognized the need for a two-year school dedicated to commercial art, where artists could learn the skills needed to earn a living.

Born in Wilkinsburg, Shook studied art at Stephenson Art School in Pittsburgh, the Art Institute of Chicago, and the Chicago Academy of Fine Arts. He started his career as an artist at N. W. Ayer and Son, in Philadelphia, the first American full-service advertising agency. After returning to Pittsburgh and working as an artist at Harvey Blodgett and Barron Collier, Shook opened his own advertising firm, Willis Shook and Associates, specializing in letterhead and booklet design. He located his offices in the Pittsburgh Typefounders Building, just a block away from the current home of the Art Institute of Pittsburgh on the Boulevard of the Allies.

Then just 27 years old, Willis Shook placed an advertisement in the *Pittsburgh Press* to gauge interest in a commercial art school. The next day, potential students flooded his office. He named the school the Artists League of Pittsburgh, rented a room in the Fulton Building, and held the first class on October 1, 1921. In attendance were the school's first nine students: Olene Crist, Ruth Collins, Sara Zoeller, Dorothy Thompson, Dorothy Diamond, Robert Zoeller, Harold Phillips, Glen McCabe, and Barney Moore.

The location of the school changed several times as it expanded, adding more students, faculty, and courses. Just a few months after the first class started, the U.S. Veterans Bureau selected the school to provide education in commercial art to World War I veterans. In January 1922, 30 veterans began their studies. The school moved that year to a building at the corner of Grant Street and Fifth Avenue, expanding from 500 to 3,000 square feet. With the rapid popularity of the school, Shook sold his advertising firm to devote the next 41 years to the Art Institute of Pittsburgh.

With the additional space, a new program in fashion illustration began. Drawing upon his expertise in advertising, Shook placed advertisements in fashion magazines, including *Vogue*, *Harper's Bazaar*, *Cosmopolitan*, and *Redbook*, to attract students for the fashion illustration program. The Art Institute of Pittsburgh continued to attract students to its commercial art program with advertising in printers' magazines and publication of the school's annual fact book. Despite difficult financial times, Shook pursued his vision, borrowing against his home in Glenshaw, his furniture, and even his wife's diamond ring.

By 1925, the school relocated to its third location at 545 Sixth Avenue, a building that was situated between Wylie and Fifth Avenues, then referred to as the Art League Building. Within five years, the school, now renamed to the Art Institute of Pittsburgh, moved to its fourth location, the third floor of the Stanwix Shops Building on Stanwix Street, across the street from the Joseph Horne Company department store.

In 1940, with continued growth, the school moved its quarters to the fourth floor of the Smithfield Building, at 610 Smithfield Street, with space for modern offices, a reception room, and classrooms. But by the end of 1941, the start of America's involvement in World War II, enrollment diminished for the first time, when young men were drafted for military service.

The end of World War II brought the most significant event in American history to impact the growth and evolution of the Art Institute of Pittsburgh. Pres. Franklin Delano Roosevelt signed into law the Servicemen's Readjustment Act of 1944. Commonly known as the GI Bill, the law provided for a college education, among other important benefits, for veterans returning from the war. The Art Institute of Pittsburgh counted many of these veterans using the GI Bill among its students. In August 1946, to accommodate the hundreds of GIs seeking professional art training, the Art Institute of Pittsburgh moved across the street to 635 Smithfield Street. The new quarters comprised eight floors with 40 studios, and enrollment exceeded over 800 students. Two new courses, photography and advertising, were added to the school's eight professional courses in commercial art, fashion illustration, dress design, millinery, interior decoration, negative retouching, show card writing, and photograph retouching. The faculty expanded and included professional artists, fashion artists, and dress designers.

Throughout the 1950s, Willis Shook, founder and director, added prestigious artists to the faculty while he also personally taught five days and three evenings per week. He boasted of the success of his students and of the businesses where they worked after graduation. School catalogs list prestigious jobs that graduates gained following their training. As seen in some of the photographs in this book, social life often centered around the students and faculty working together, even outside the classroom. Just as students had visited his home in Glenshaw in the 1920s, and in Sewickley since the 1930s, they were now invited to the Shooks' new home and property in Lawrence County, where they painted and sketched breathtaking nature vistas.

In 1962, Shook sold the school to Earl Wheeler, who was the founder of the Earl Wheeler Finishing School and the Pinkerton Secretarial School. As Willis Shook states in his memoirs of the school: "to watch that initial group of nine students grow to an annual student body of 1500 boys and girls who had come from all of the states and twenty one countries, was a satisfaction."

The late 1960s and early 1970s continued to bring changes to the Art Institute of Pittsburgh. Education Management Corporation (EDMC) purchased the school in 1970, and the school moved to the Jackman Building on Penn Avenue. Founded in 1962, EDMC focused on professional development education. The purchase of the Art Institute dramatically changed the direction of the company. Robert Knutson, who began at EDMC in 1969, played an instrumental role in this change. When he became president in 1971, the company started a long period of expansion. The Art Institute, over the next 15 years, added schools in Denver, Fort Lauderdale, Atlanta, Philadelphia, Dallas, Houston, and Seattle.

EDMC, in the 1980s and 1990s, was devoted to improving and solidifying its member schools. The company updated facilities, rewrote curricula, expanded student services, and embraced the computer technology revolution. New programs, including music and video production, explored new methods of artistic expression while new computer equipment found homes in classrooms. EDMC also introduced fashion merchandising as part of the Fashion Institutes, a division of the Art Institute schools.

The new millennium marked a period of academic transition. George L. Pry joined the faculty and staff as the president of the Art Institute of Pittsburgh in 1999. One year later, the Art Institute of Pittsburgh became the first residential proprietary school to be granted baccalaureate status by the Commonwealth of Pennsylvania and began offering bachelor's degree programs. The college moved into a historic landmark location at 420 Boulevard of the Allies, its eighth and current downtown location. This new location situates the school between Point Park University and Duquesne University, the academic corridor of downtown Pittsburgh. Inaugurated in 2000, the Art Institute Online emerged as the Art Institute of Pittsburgh's distance-learning division. In recent years, a number of new technology-based programs have emerged, including media arts and animation and game art and design. New programs, including an associate's degree in culinary arts and a bachelor's degree in culinary management were launched in 2002.

Even more recently, the school solidified its status as a good neighbor in the center of Pittsburgh. By the fall of 2007, nearly 900 Art Institute students had become year-round residents of downtown Pittsburgh, occupying three renovated buildings with landmark status: Shannon Hall, Miller Hall, and the Standard Life building. The buildings are within two blocks and a short walking distance of the college, a benefit to students as well as making a substantial impact on the economic revitalization of downtown and surrounding neighborhoods. In 2008, the Art Institute of Pittsburgh received the milestone achievement of Middle States Accreditation, an acknowledgment of academic reputation and peer recognition. Now with 14 bachelor's degree programs as well as associate's degree programs, an average of 90 percent of graduates find field-related employment within six months of graduation. The Art Institute of Pittsburgh also became one of the nation's leaders offering online education. The Art Institute–Online Division has grown to include 12,000 students from all over the United States and abroad, who earn their degrees online.

Despite years of change, new faces, new degrees, new technologies, and new surroundings filled with new ideas, one fact remains absolutely and decidedly unchanged. The Art Institute of Pittsburgh is a place where students come with a dream of pursuing a career in the creative commercial arts and where dedicated professionals assemble each day to ensure that those dreams can be realized.

This book of images, moments that were captured on film over the last 88 years, represents just a small series of glances into the history of the Art Institute of Pittsburgh. We hope that these images and their stories bring to life memories of your own experiences in the community of the Art Institute of Pittsburgh. For our current and future students, we hope that the story of our past will inspire you as you create your own history to tell future generations.

One

A Vibrant and Talented Family of Students

Students have come to the Art Institute of Pittsburgh from all over the world and from all walks of life. It is their talents, energy, and enthusiasm that make the community of the Art Institute of Pittsburgh so vibrant. From 1921 through today, over 55,000 alumni have earned awards, recognition, and jobs throughout Pittsburgh and the world in the art, design, fashion, and culinary industries. The energy and enthusiasm of the students has always extended beyond the classroom, and students have made their presence known all over the city of Pittsburgh through working, living, and volunteering in the city's many neighborhoods. As written in the school's memoirs, students even added color to the downtown Pittsburgh scene: "Instead of conventional art smocks in grays and tans, our students wore two color smocks in orange, green, yellow, purple, and red, and wore berets to match." In this chapter are some glances of students as they prepare for their future careers, while always adding their personal styles and signatures to the city of Pittsburgh.

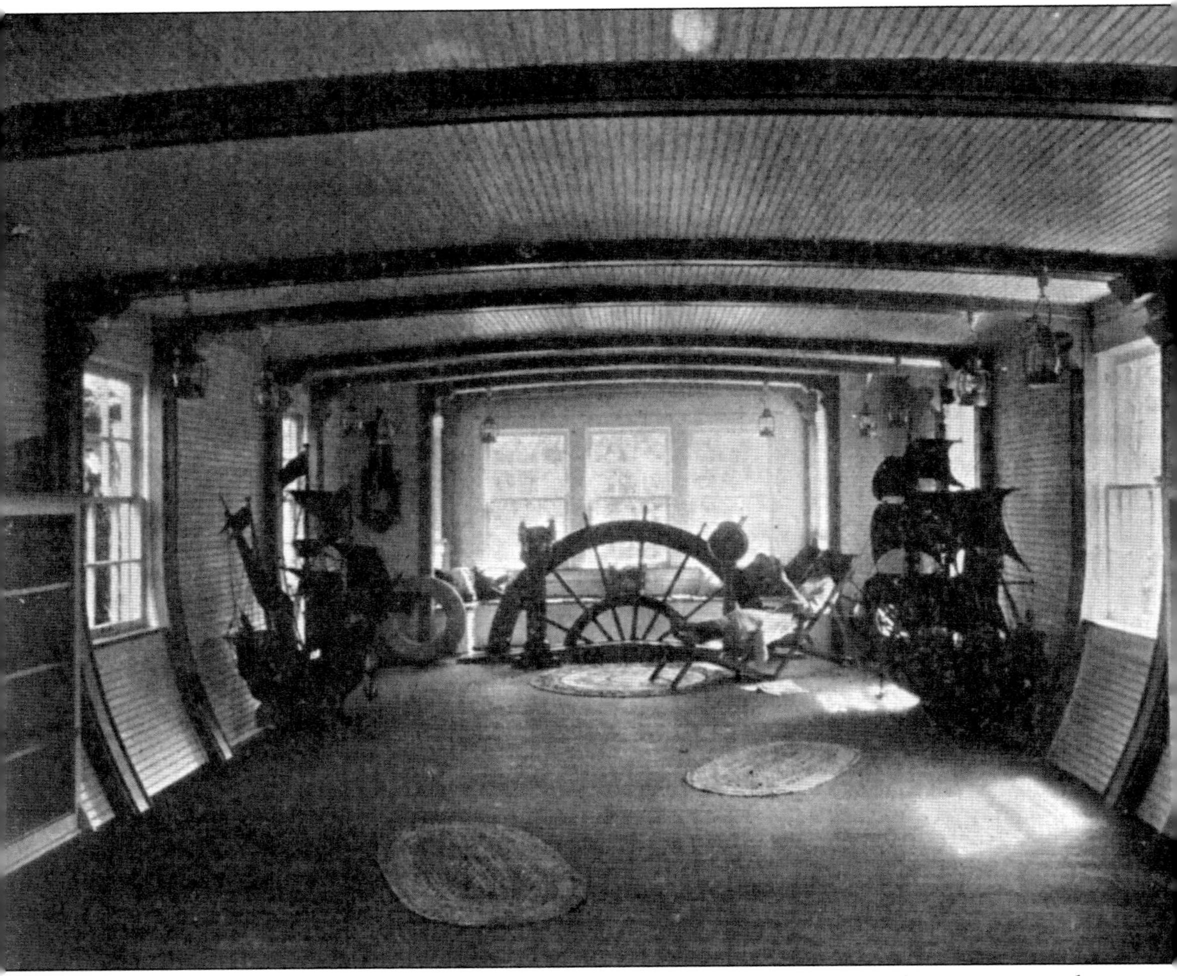

Willis Shook's home was the center of students' social life. In the 1930s, students celebrated the annual Halloween Ball in this unique ship room. Shook added this studio wing to his home, designed to resemble the interior of a river steamship, with curved walls, narrow clapboarding, and antiques, including the pilot wheel used on the old *Jim Brown*, the first river steamer to be equipped with electric lights. Also featured were an antique telegraph and compass that had made many voyages on the Great Lakes. (Courtesy of the Sewickley Valley Historical Society and the Sewickley Herald.)

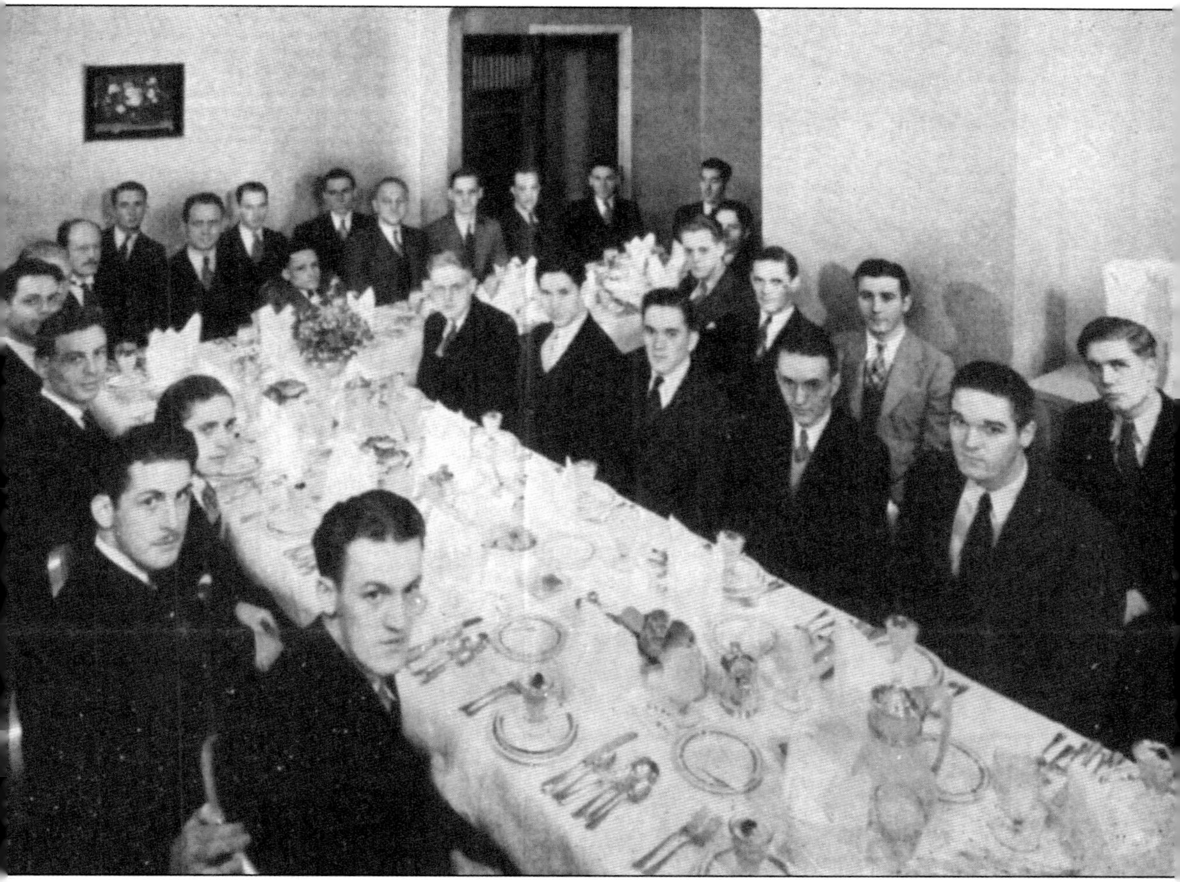

In the early years, fraternities and sororities were a big part of student life. In this 1935 photograph, the Gamma Chapter of the Omega Alpha fraternity honors incoming pledge members with a banquet at the Hotel Roosevelt, hosted by Willis Shook. The young pledges listened to speakers and famous illustrators discuss "Modern Engraving" and "What the Papermaker is Doing for the Artist and Advertiser." At another event, the *Pittsburgh Post-Gazette* announced in May 1935 the formal dance of the fraternity with the Iota Tau Delta sorority at the Hotel Schenley. The fraternity chair was Frank Soltez, with assistants Ken Smith and Norman Peterson, along with sorority chair Marge Sanera, assisted by Clarice Haudenshield and Connie Bell.

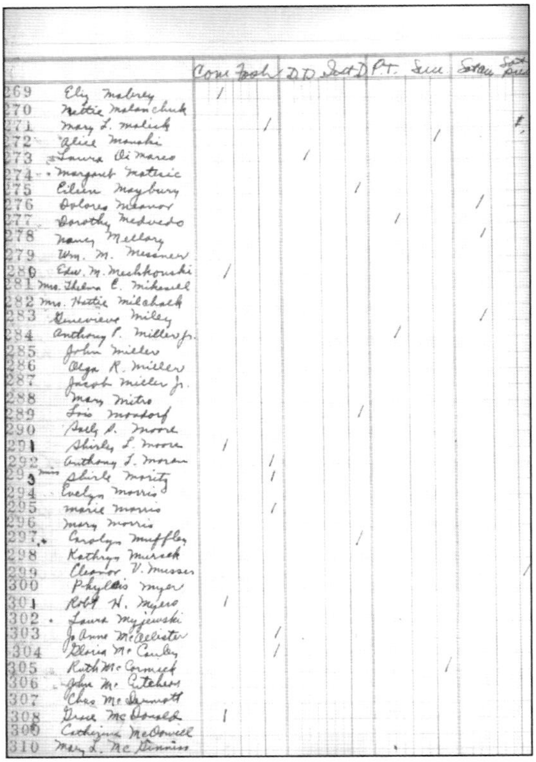

This bound handwritten ledger had long been forgotten when it was recently rediscovered by Willis D. Shook III. The ledger lists student names and their classes spanning the years 1941 through 1945, which are now recorded as a part of the historic school records. (Courtesy of Willis D. Shook III.)

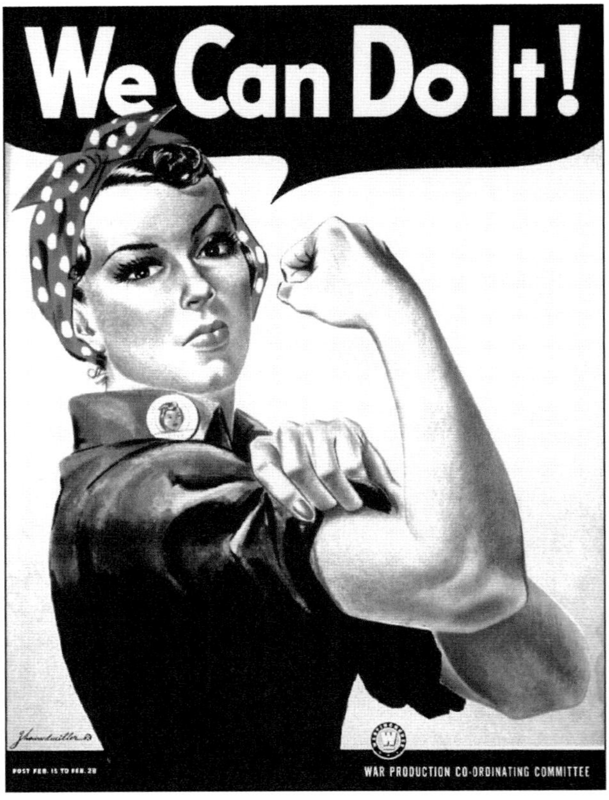

J. Howard Miller, class of 1939, created this famous poster as part of series for the Westinghouse Company. The image has become synonymous with Rosie the Riveter, the cultural icon representing the six million women who worked in manufacturing plants during World War II.

Fashion illustrator Ruth McCormick (left) visits Sueyoshi Iwamoto at Rockefeller Center in New York City during 1955. McCormick and Iwamoto were classmates in the 1943 fashion illustration program. McCormick had a successful career in fashion illustration at Gimbel's department store for 40 years. She continues to work as a watercolor artist, exhibiting her paintings of Pittsburgh and the many countries she has visited. Iwamoto, who has made his home in Manhattan, worked as a fashion illustrator and furniture artist for department stores, agencies, and art services. His artwork has appeared in the *New York Times* and other newspapers and magazines. Shown here in black and white, this colorful oil painting *Sunday Painter* of New York Park in Westchester is one of his extensive works of fine art, which he continues to exhibit and be honored for. (Right, courtesy of Ruth McCormick; below, courtesy of Sueyoshi Iwamoto.)

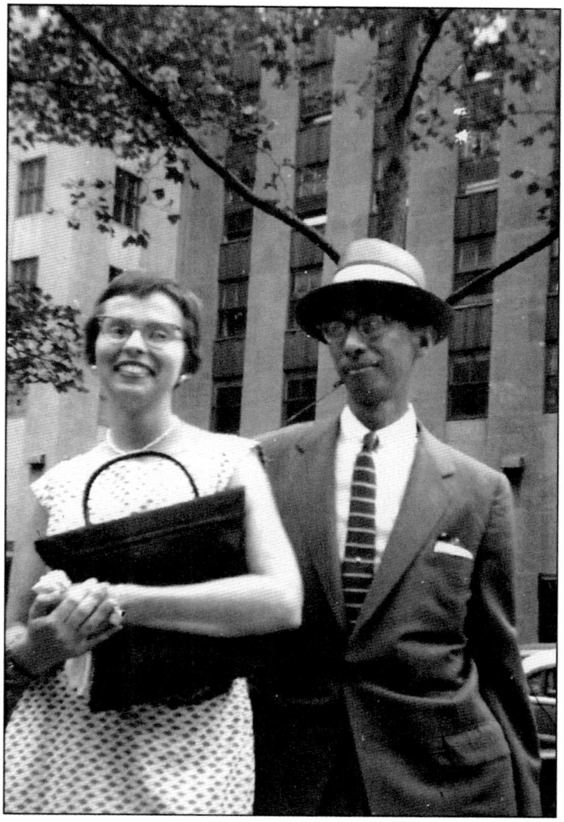

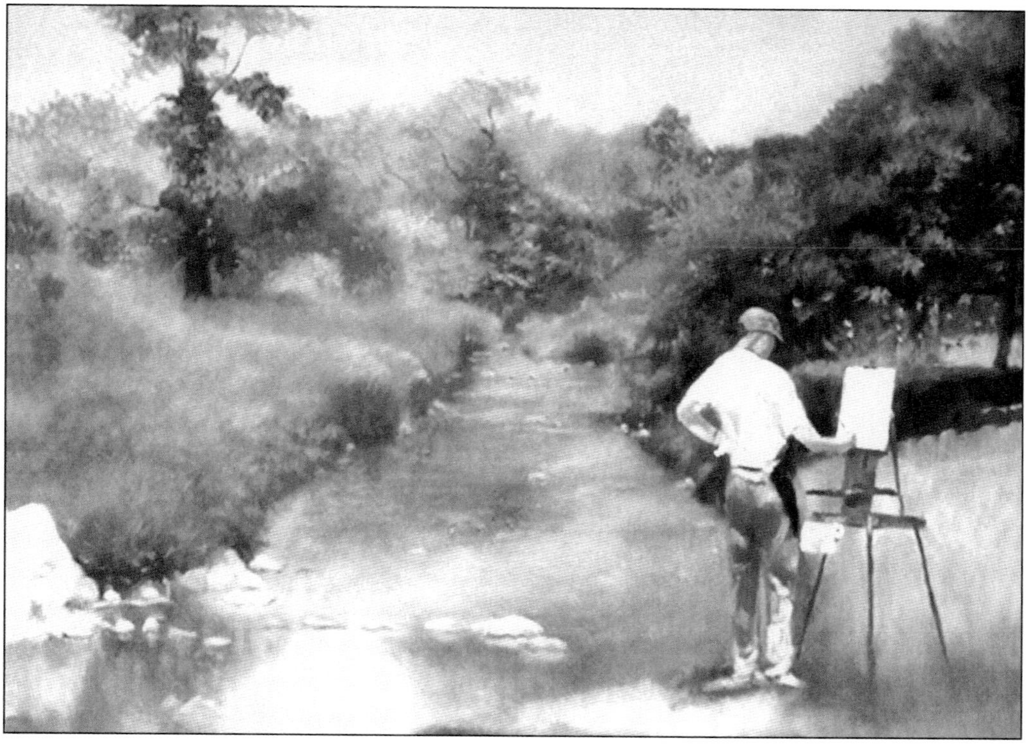

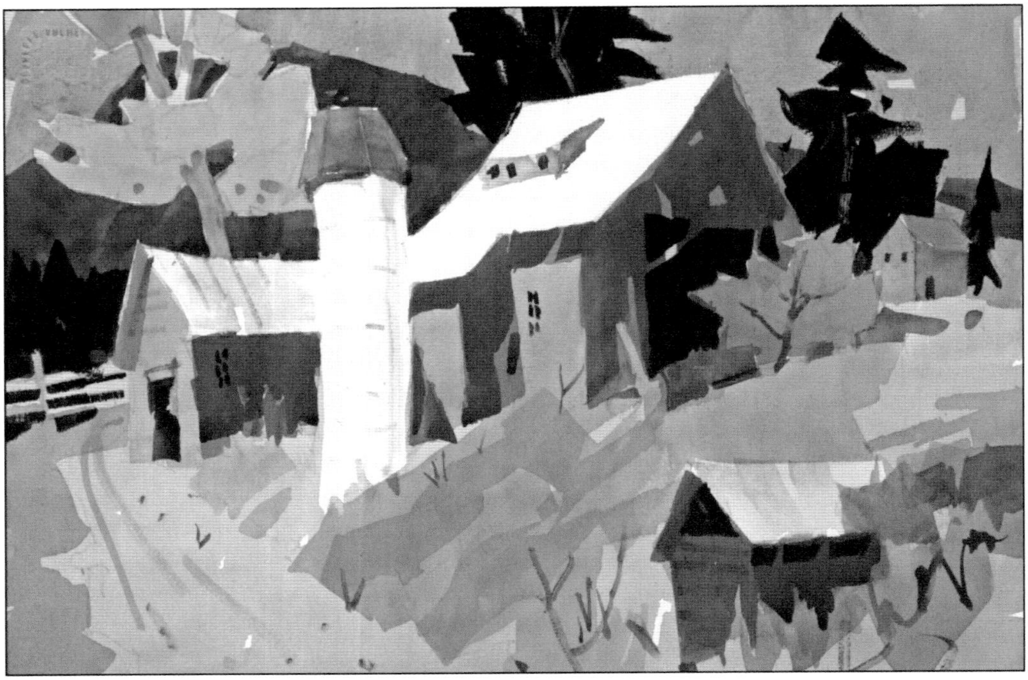

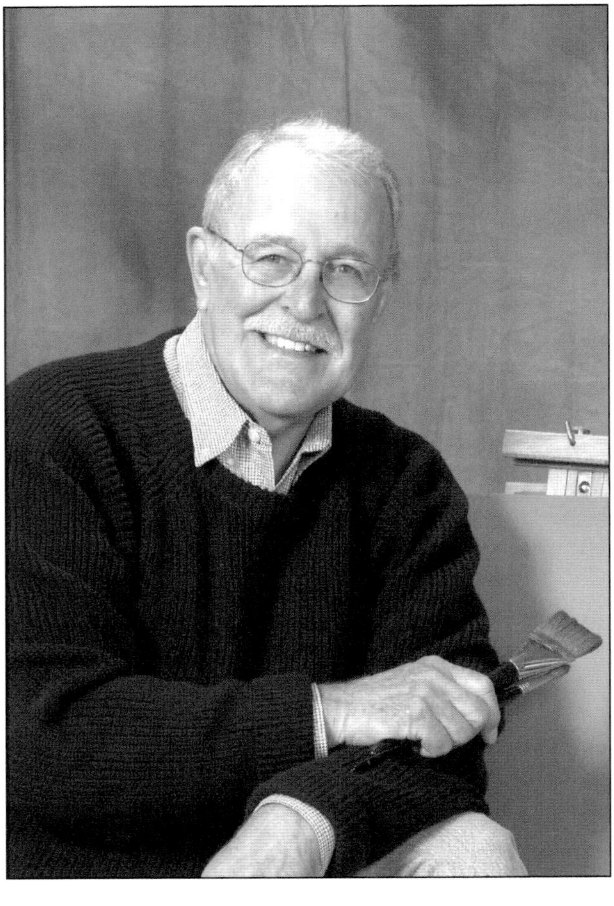

Skidmore Farm is just one work from Frank Webb's 60-year career in art. A 1946 visual communications graduate, Webb witnessed sweeping changes in the processes and tools used to produce art during his career. Reflecting on his time as a student, he credits his instructors and fellow students for teaching him his life's work. Life drawing, portrait painting, and lettering were the skills that enabled him to transition from a career in commercial art to his many works in fine art. Webb attended on the GI Bill after service in World War II and has many positive memories, including visits to Isaly's, Lack Zoom, and A&B Smith Company. Of course, his most significant event at school was meeting his future wife, Barbara Smith, while they studied side-by-side at easels. Webb continues to travel, teach, and exhibit his paintings around the world.

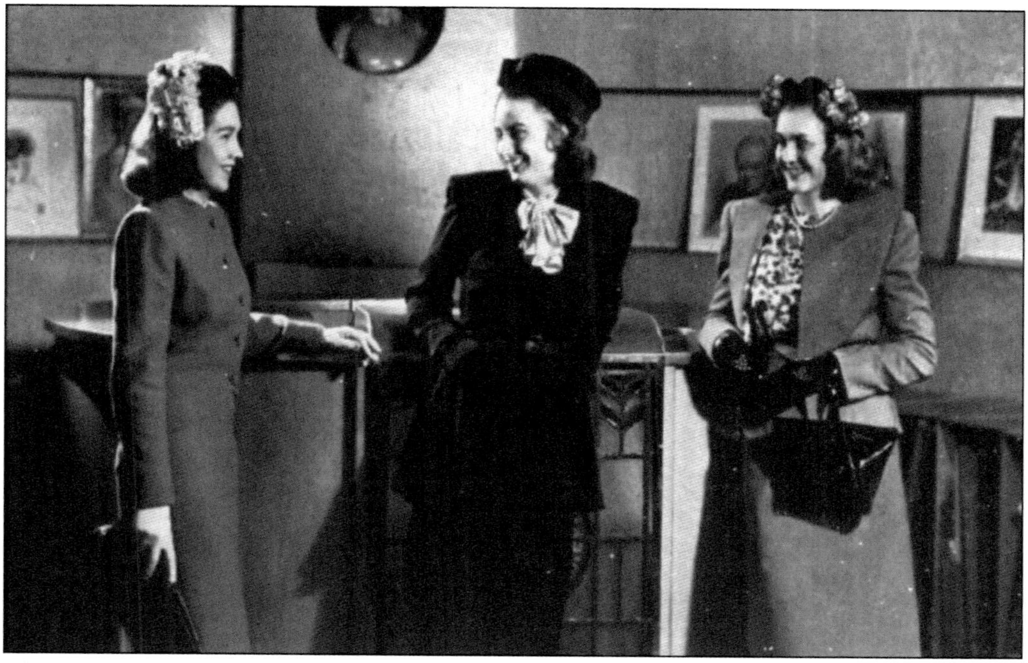

These three students model the stylish clothes they designed and constructed in the dress design and millinery program of the 1950s. From left to right are Margaret Jeanne Tyler with her spring suit, Wilma Virginia Harber modeling her tunic-type suit, and Charmaine Haller modeling her ensemble.

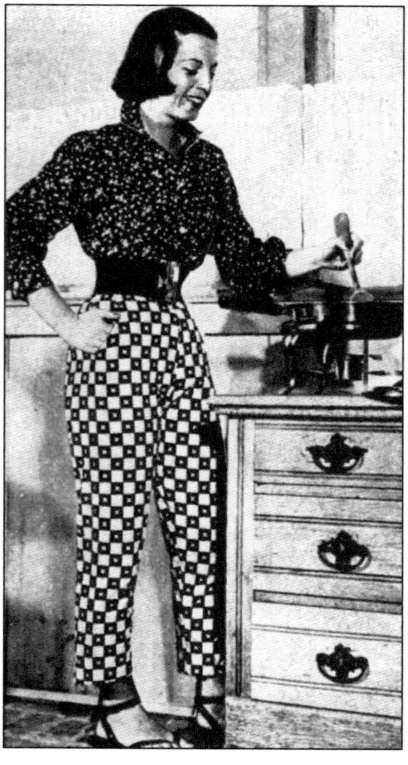

School catalogs are filled with lists of student awards. In the early 1950s, dress design and millinery student Jeanne Sanford Campbell won the Winnie, awarded by the Coty American Fashion Critics, the Oscar of the fashion world.

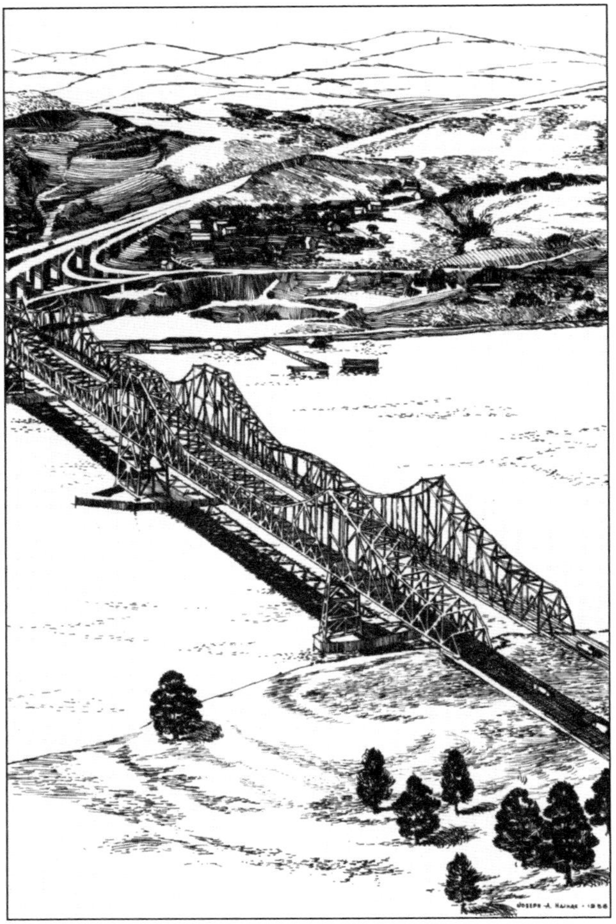

Joseph A. Hajnas, 1953 graduate and former faculty member, is featured in the 1962 catalog. Hajnas's career began with the United States Army, painting in Europe. Upon return, he created a series of bridge illustrations for the American Bridge Division of United States Steel, traveling across the country to set up his easel. Using pen and inkwell, he captured the finest details of the bridges and landscapes. The work appeared in advertising calendars, posters, and brochures, including the pen and ink of the Carquinez Straits Bridge in San Francisco Bay and the watercolor of the Shawneetown Bridge in Kentucky. United States Steel credited Hajnas with putting a feeling of sparkle and freshness into their promotional materials. Hajnas is an accomplished illustrator, fine artist, and registered landscape architect. He leads his firm, Joseph A. Hajnas and Associates, in Pittsburgh.

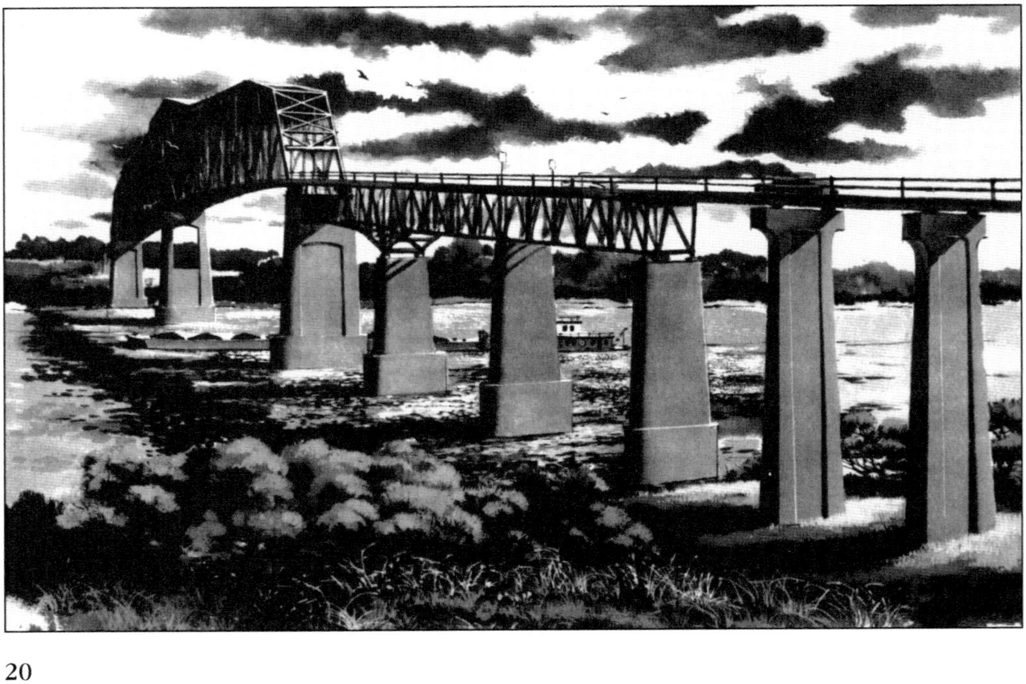

Logos changed over time and reflected the artistic styles of their eras. This hand-lettered and drawn logo appeared on letterhead that students would have undoubtedly seen on the correspondence they regularly received from the school. This photograph of Pittsburgh and the poem "I am Pittsburgh the Mighty!," written by Willis Shook in the early 1920s, appeared on a unique letterhead during the 1950s, located on the back of the page so that when folded it appeared on the front. "I am Pittsburgh the Mighty!" also appeared on a mural, painted by student Harrison Blass for a corridor of the Stanwix Shops Building. (Courtesy of Willis D. Shook III.)

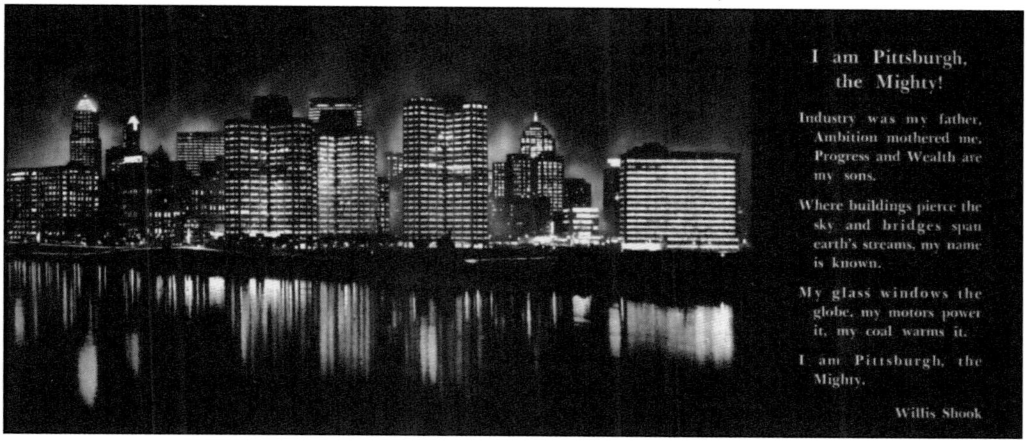

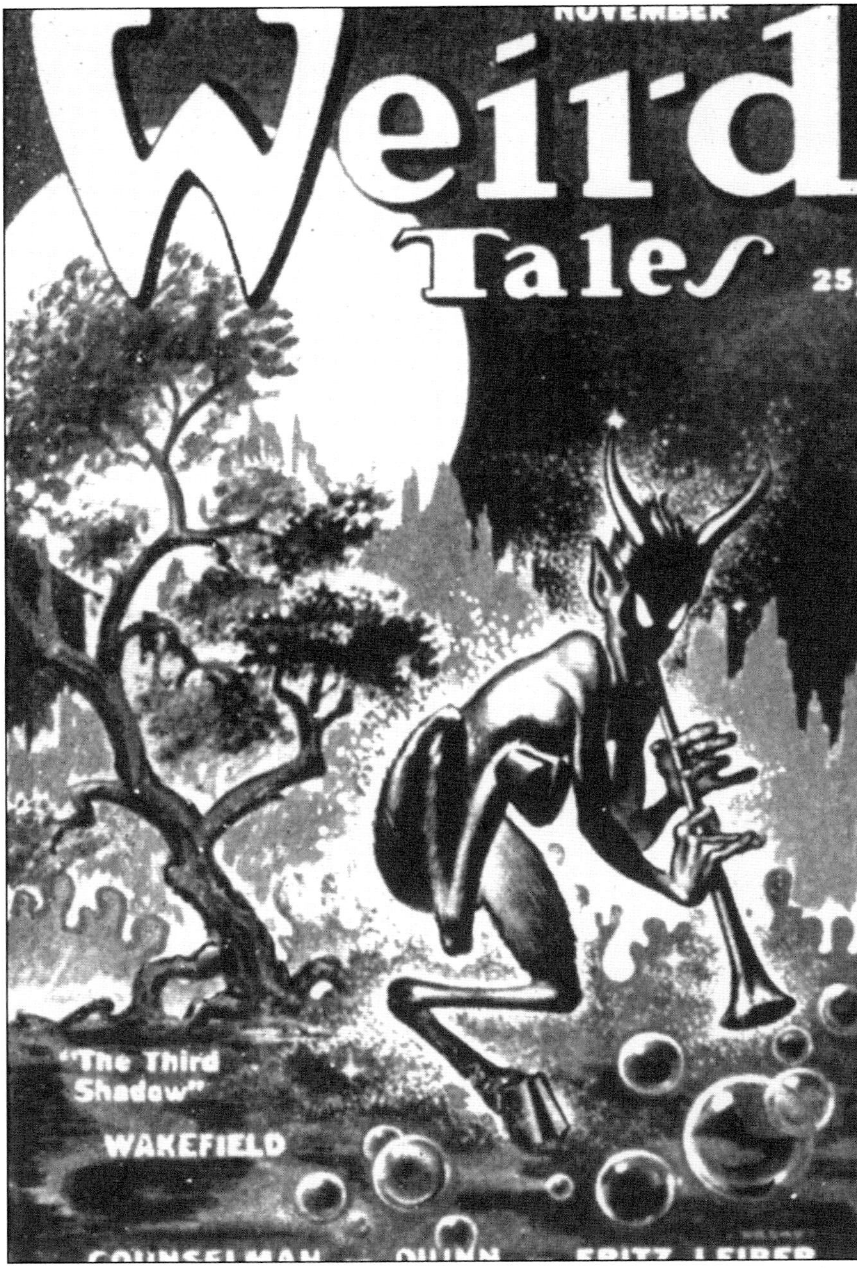

Since the school's early days, freelance work has earned money for students during their studies. Work has included letterheads, airbrush, logos, cartoons, caricatures, lettering, murals, and portraits. For a class assignment, Frank Kelly Freas created this science fiction illustration and sold the cover to *Weird Tales* magazine while he was a student in 1950. Freas is recognized as the most prolific science fiction illustrator of all time. He is also credited as a cocreator of Alfred E. Neuman for *MAD* magazine, the freckled, gap-toothed purveyor of the phrase, "What? Me Worry?," and for his illustrations of 30 *MAD* magazine covers from 1958 to 1962. Freas was also commissioned by NASA to develop a logo for Skylab I. Frank Kelly Freas was recognized with an honorary doctorate of the arts by the Art Institute of Pittsburgh.

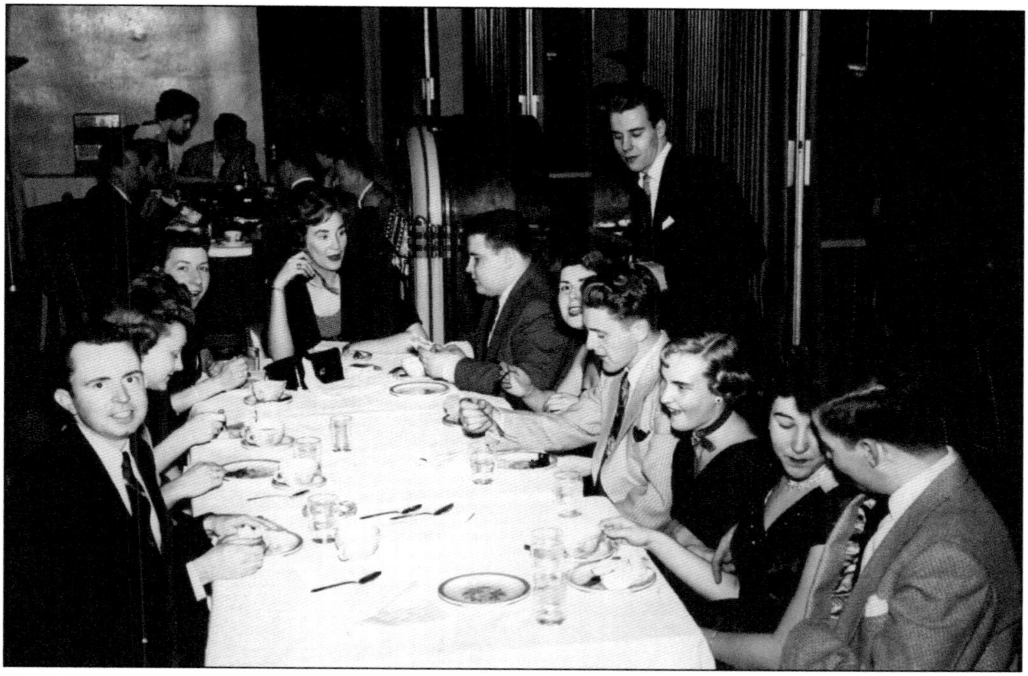

Student events and entertainment have always played an important part of student life. In this 1952 photograph, students are enjoying dessert and conversation at the annual Christmas Dinner Dance.

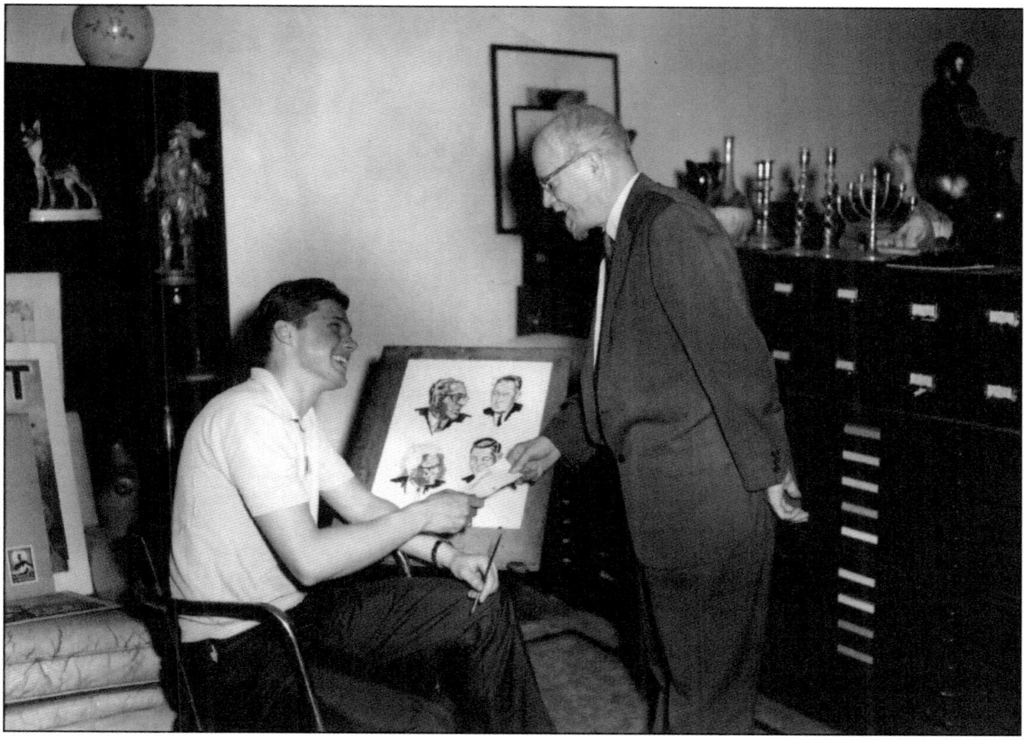

Willis Shook, in his office, presents a student with an award for his art. The photograph is estimated to have been taken in 1960–1962.

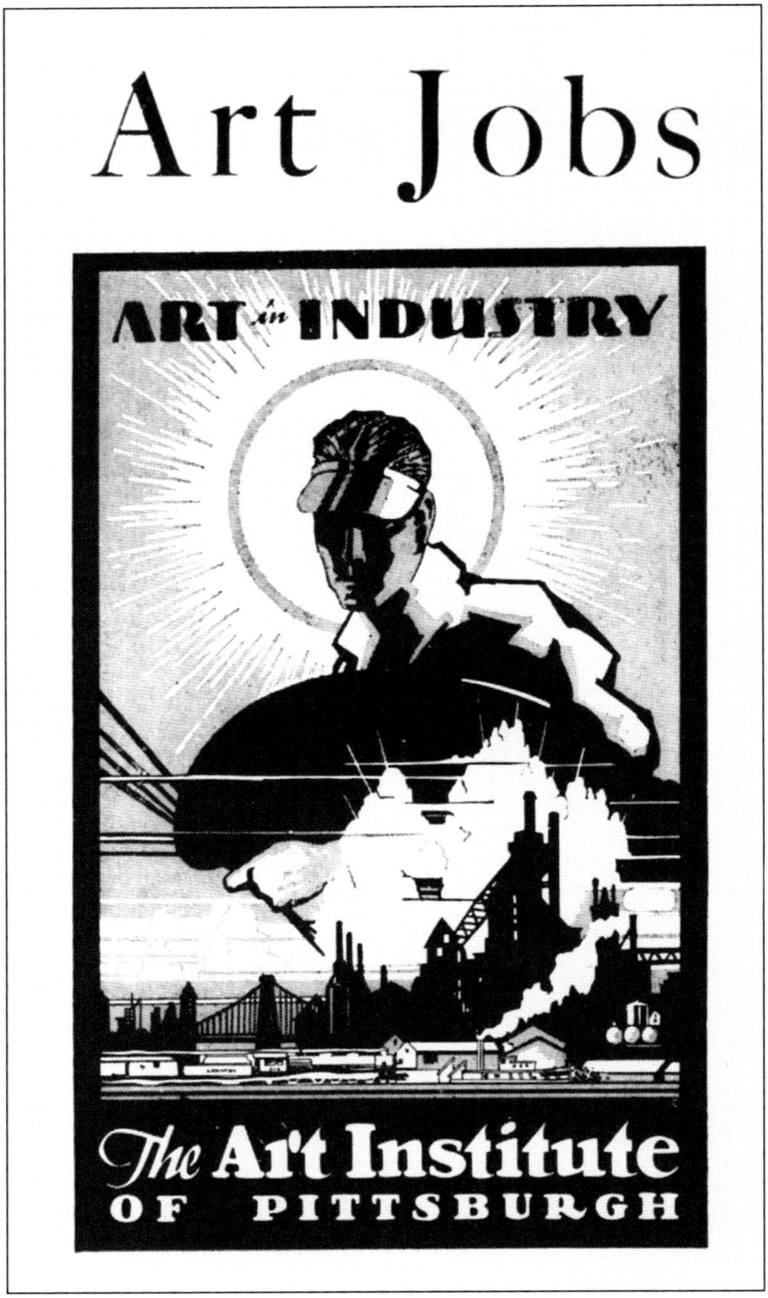

In 1950, Willis Shook authored *Art Jobs and How to Get Them*, a book that he personally presented to each graduate. Some advice may represent another era, such as recommendations for dress designers: "You will naturally wear a costume you have designed: suit, ensemble, dress, hat, complete and in good taste." Yet much advice in this 48-page book could still apply, in practical lessons on interviewing and freelancing, and in inspirational reminders. Shook was always proud to show off student work in publications. The cover of this book was designed and lettered by Joseph Eberle. Lettering on the title page was done by Kenneth Worstell, the foreword medallion by Walter Srocki, and the back cover drawing by Clair Cressler.

School catalogs, brochures, art magazines, and newspapers of the 1950s are filled with the successes of students and alumni. *Typo Graphic* and newspapers in 1957 published the winner of Miss Art Institute of Pittsburgh, Mary Lou Hast. Her title was given her by votes from a student body of more than 400. The contest was based on ability, appearance, and personality. Her prize was a portrait of herself by Vincent Nesbert, shown here presenting her prize.

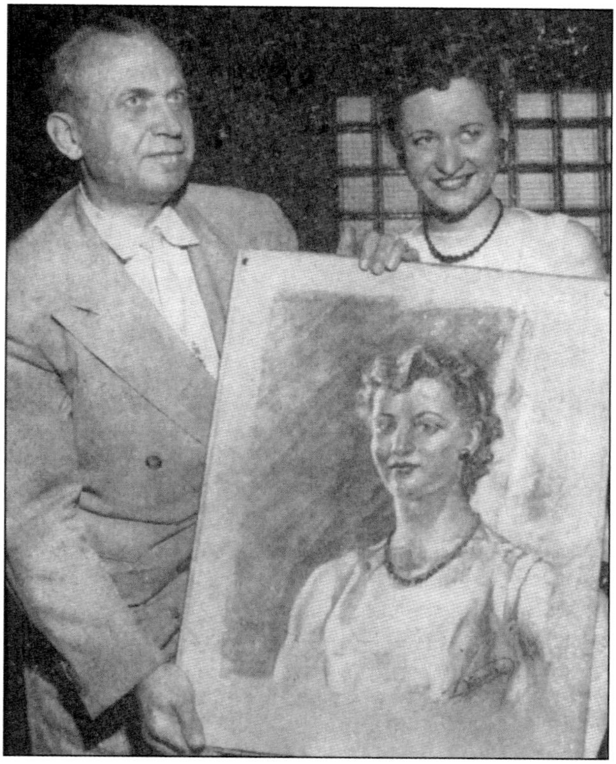

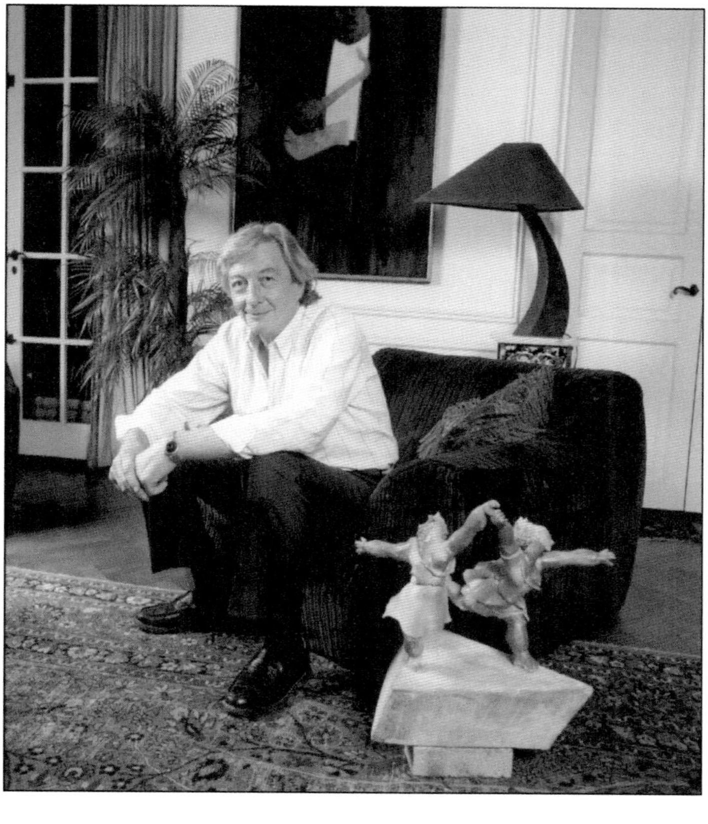

Tom Wilson is one of many graduate success stories. A 1955 graduate, Wilson is best known as the creator of Ziggy the bald little cartoon character with a heart of gold who greets the world in perpetual wonder. The character became a syndicated comic in 1971 and is still running. Today Wilson's son Tom Wilson Jr. pens and draws the strip.

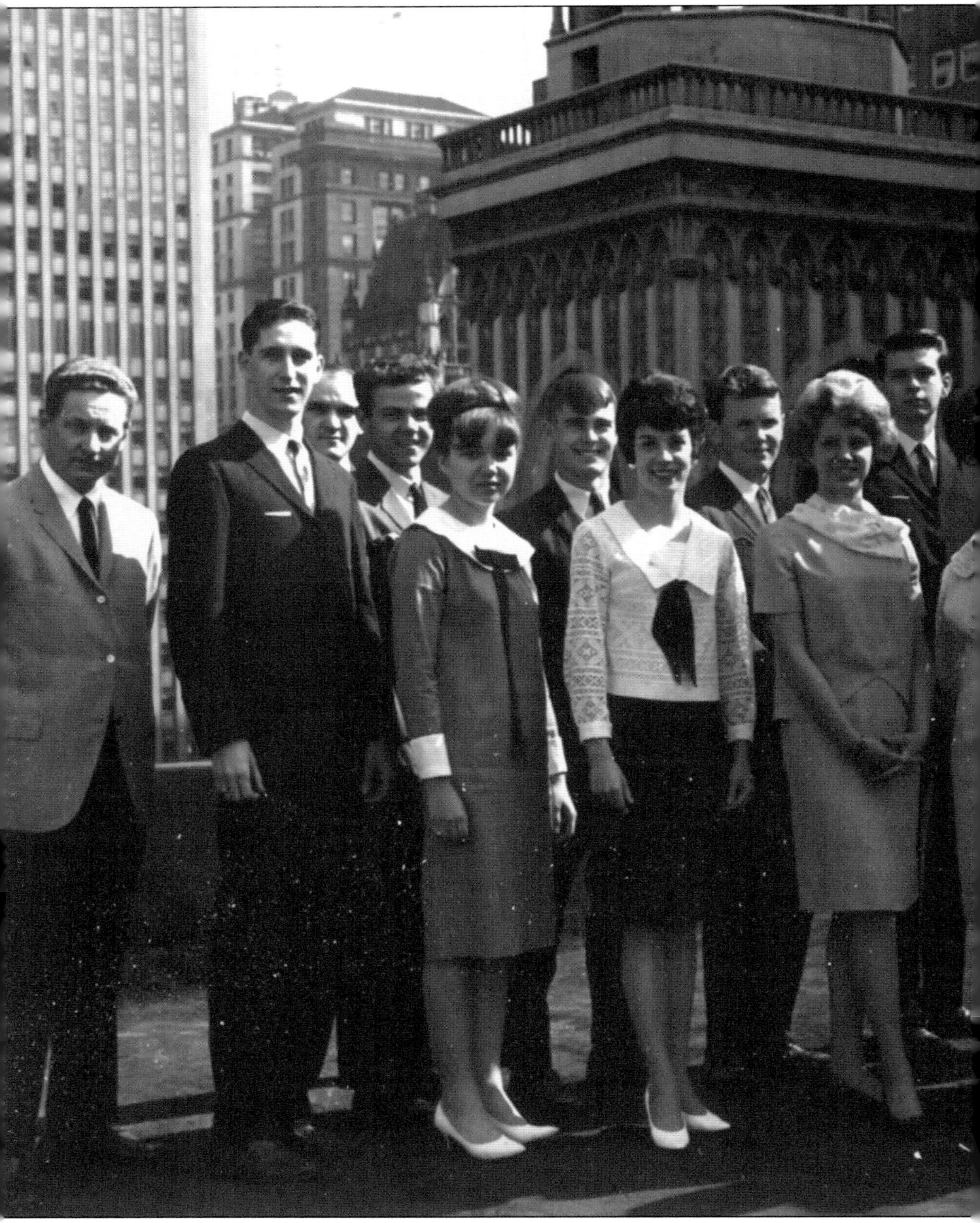

The graduating class of 1965 poses on the rooftop of the school with the city of Pittsburgh buildings in the background. In the 1960s, the school was proud to proclaim the "*Art Institute of Pittsburgh* is the art school of the Sixties in the City of the Sixties–the art

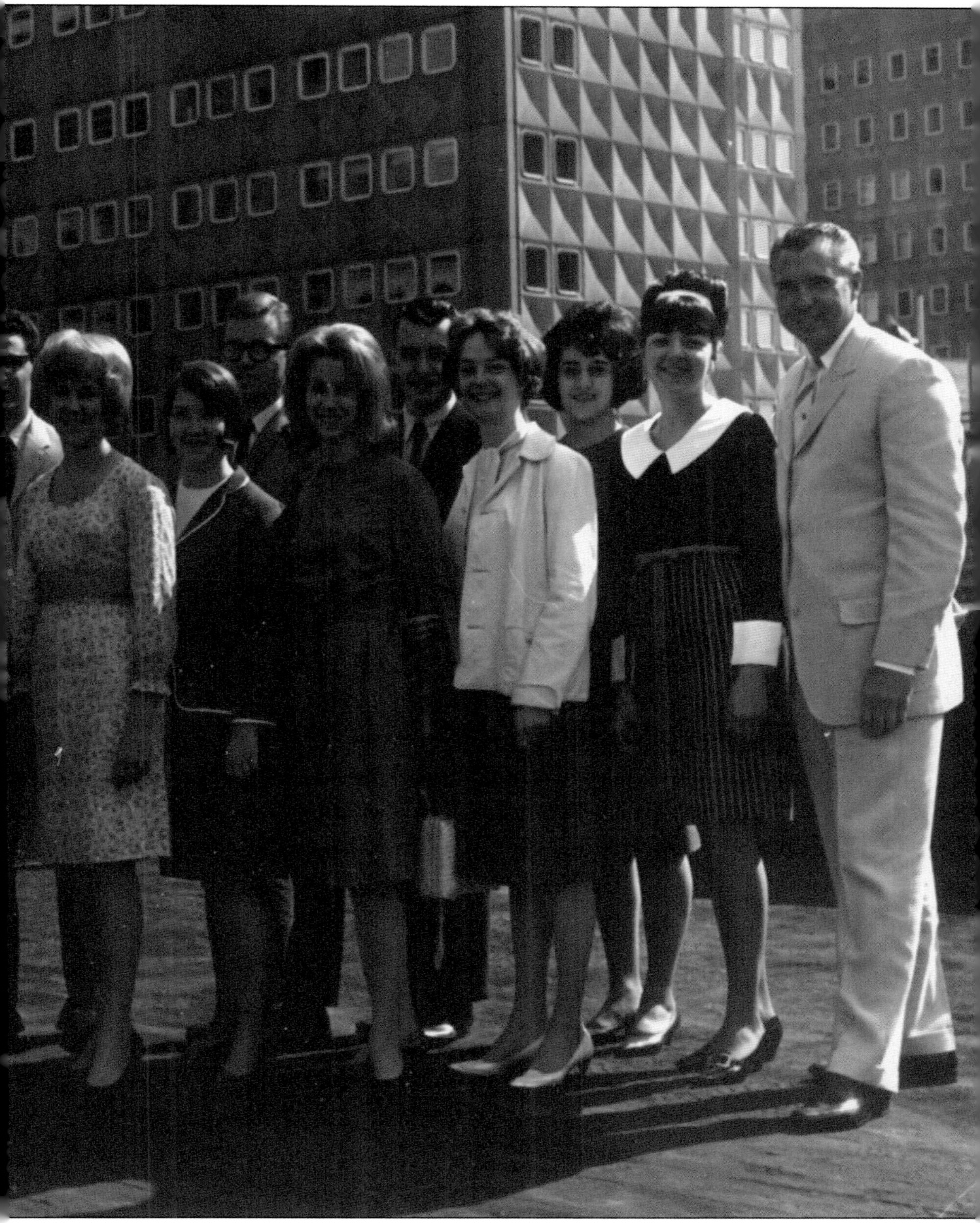

school for YOU! Pittsburgh is world-known as a City of Get-up and Go." Posing with the graduates are Ellis "Red" Matthews and Earl Wheeler. (Courtesy of Mary Jean Stabile.)

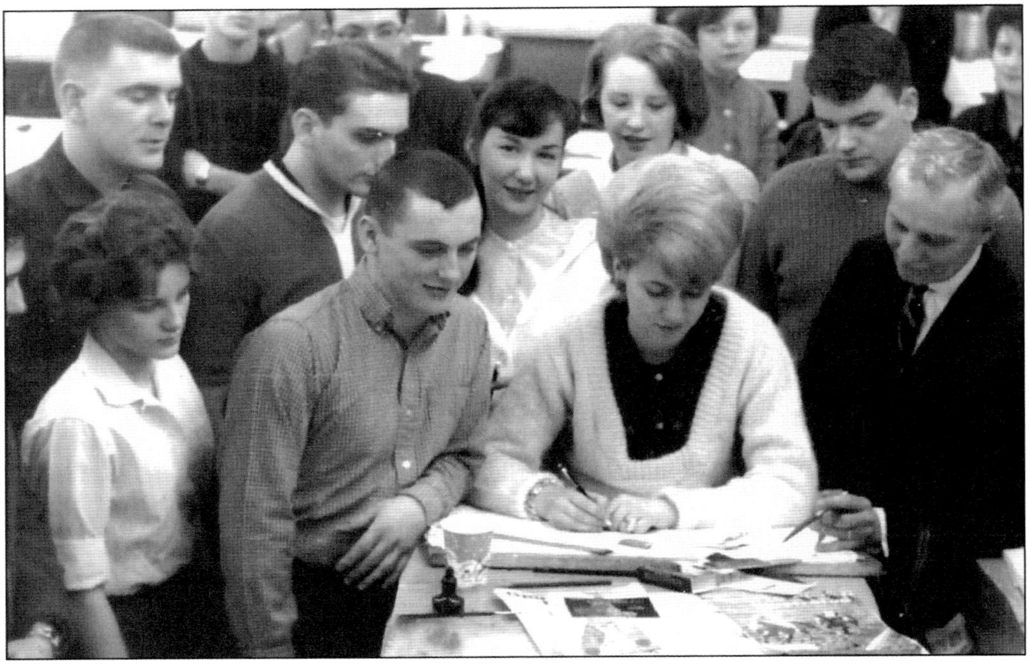

In this 1963 photograph, classmates watch as their instructor demonstrates and assists a student with her technique in a drawing class. From left to right are (first row) unidentified, Doug Caeser, unidentified, and unidentified; (second row) John Drugmand, Tom Connors, Mary Cunningham, unidentified, and unidentified. (Courtesy of Mary Cunningham Fisher.)

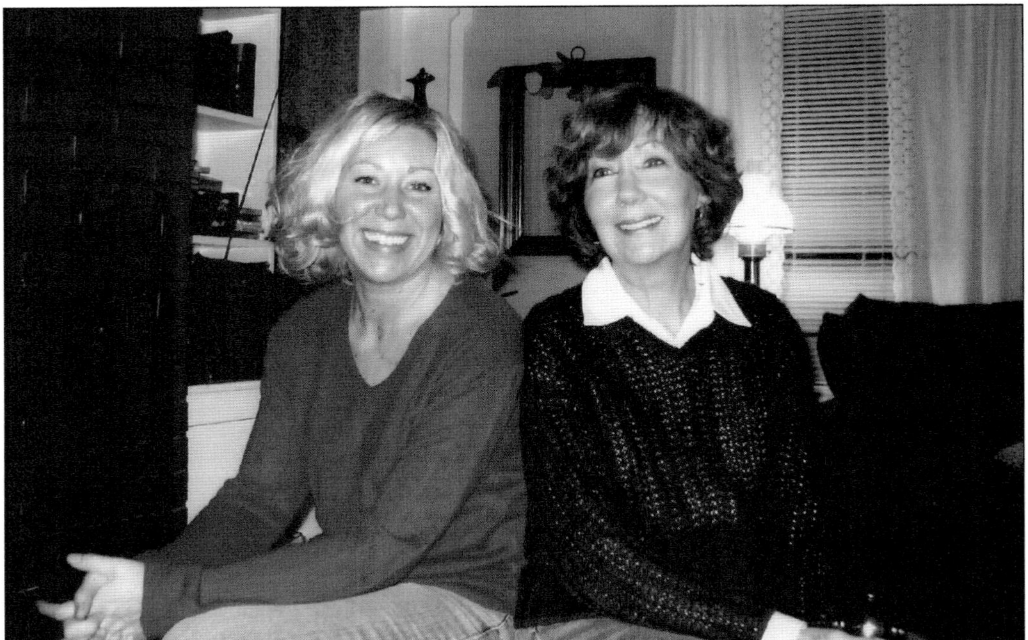

With an 88-year history, alumni include several generations of families. In this photograph are alumni Shana Fisher (left), 1988 interior design graduate, with her mother, Mary Cunningham Fisher, 1963 commercial art graduate.

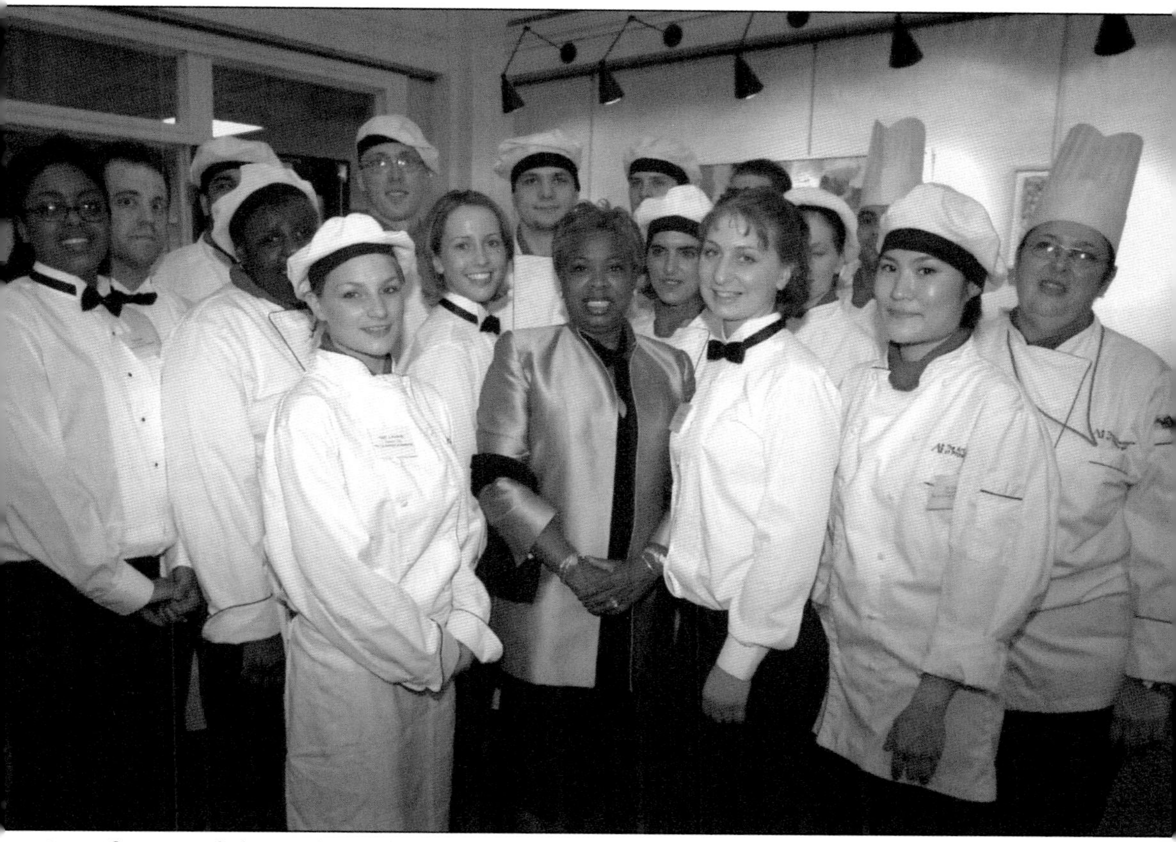

Jennifer Meredith Smith graduated in 1971 and pursued a career in fashion and news illustration. Her family roots and public service interests steered her to a political career, and she served as the first female premier of Bermuda, the country's highest elected position. Smith began the Masterworks Foundation in support of the arts in Bermuda and developed a scholarship program with the school after receiving an honorary doctorate degree from the Art Institute of Pittsburgh in 2003. Shown here, Dame Jennifer Meredith Smith is pictured with culinary students at a reception in her honor in 2003 preceding the conferring of her honorary degree.

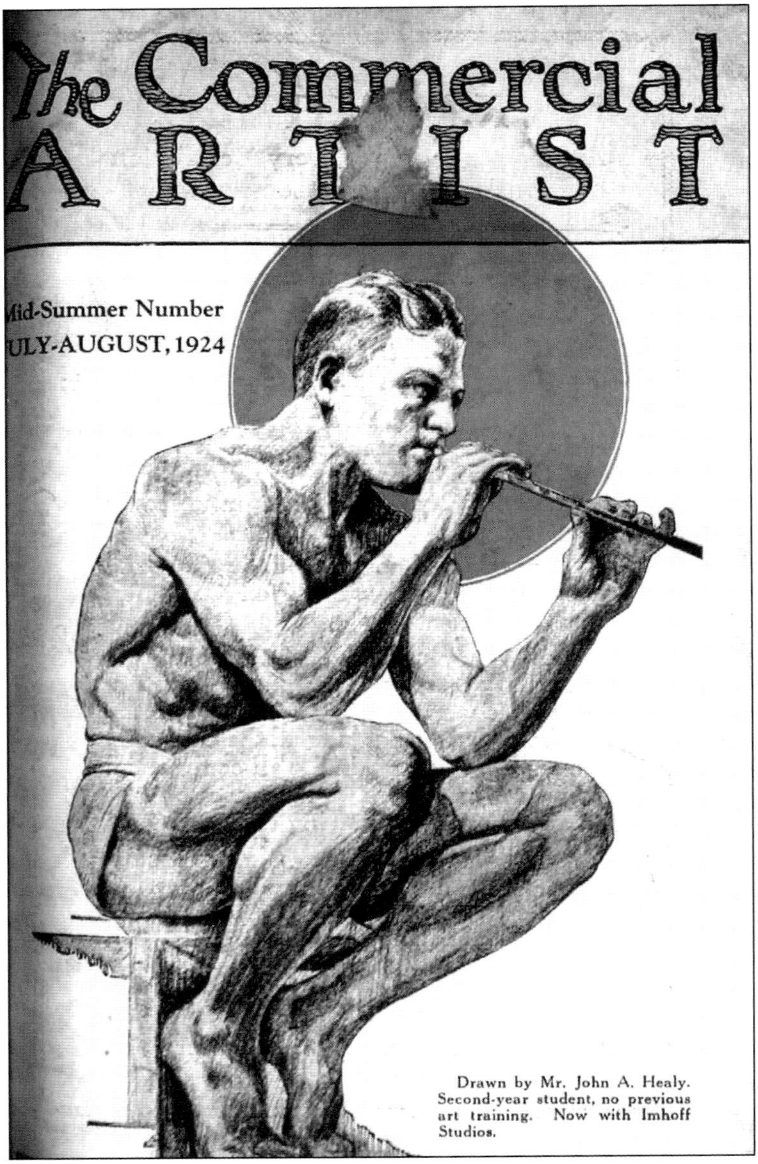

Over the years, students published several newsletters and college newspapers that featured student artwork, articles, and announcements for upcoming events. In 1924, students published the *Commercial Artist*. The *Bulletin Board*, published from the 1950s to the 1960s, and *Mixed Media*, in the 1970s, were two of the longest-running student publications. Other newsletters have included the *Informer* and the *Right Brain*. Today students often learn about upcoming events through digital monitors in the halls and e-mail. (Courtesy of the Carnegie Library of Pittsburgh.)

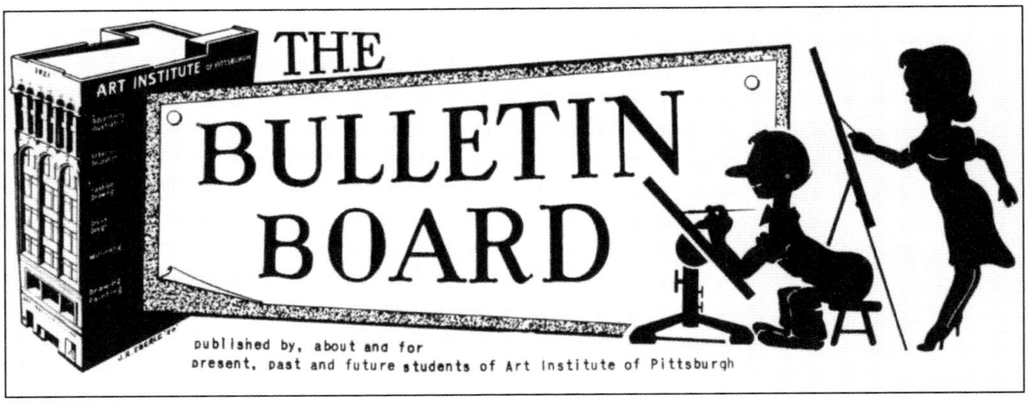

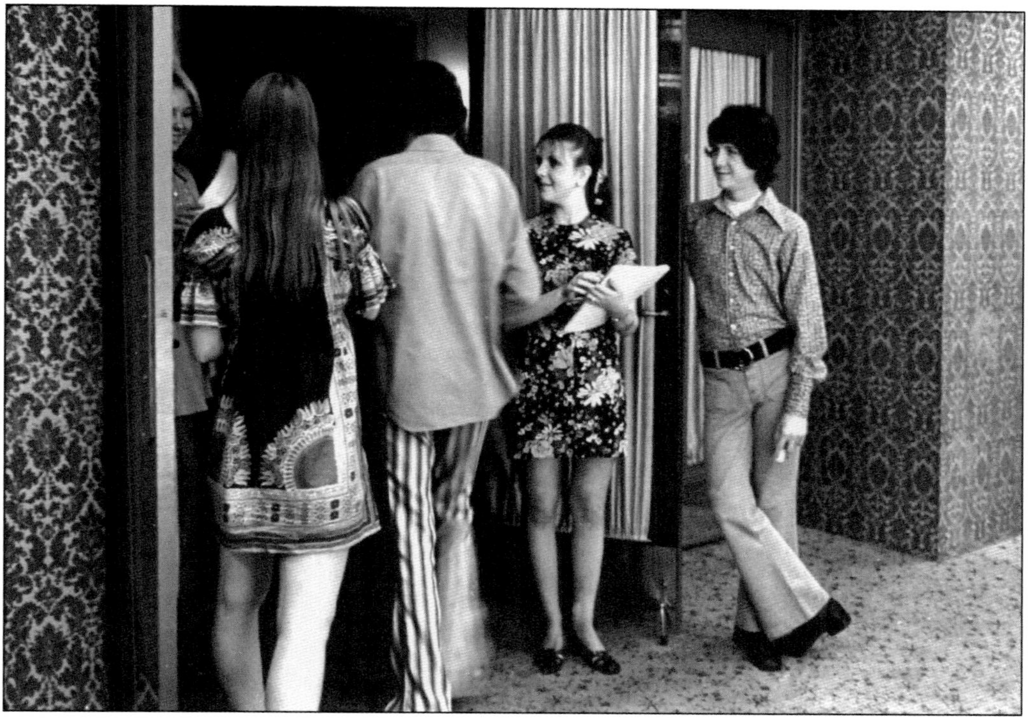

Students await the graduation ceremony at a local hotel in the early 1970s. Graduation ceremonies have been held in venues throughout Pittsburgh, including the Byham Theater, Hilton Hotel, Carlow College, Carnegie Music Hall, Soldiers and Sailors Memorial Hall, and most recently at the David L. Lawrence Convention Center.

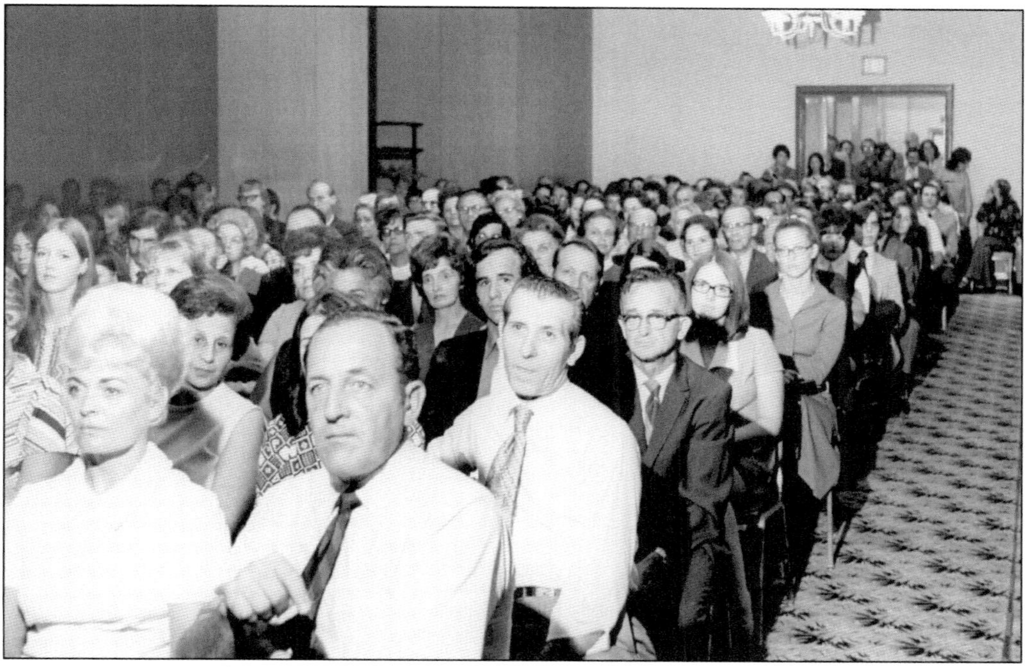

It is uncertain who or what was mesmerizing this audience at this September 1971 graduation!

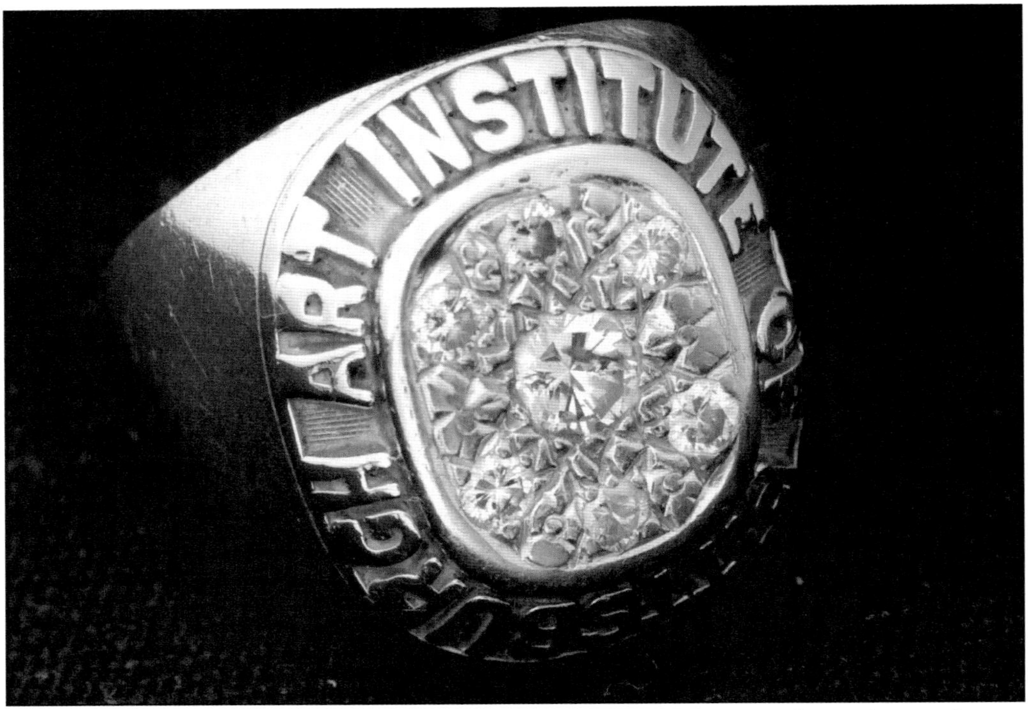

This class ring has been proudly worn by Vic Pugliano since completing his studies in the 1970s. Pugliano purchased the ring without a stone so that he could add his own seven diamonds. This tradition of class rings has disappeared but is anticipated to be returning to the school. Pugliano was an evening student and also worked as assistant director of admissions.

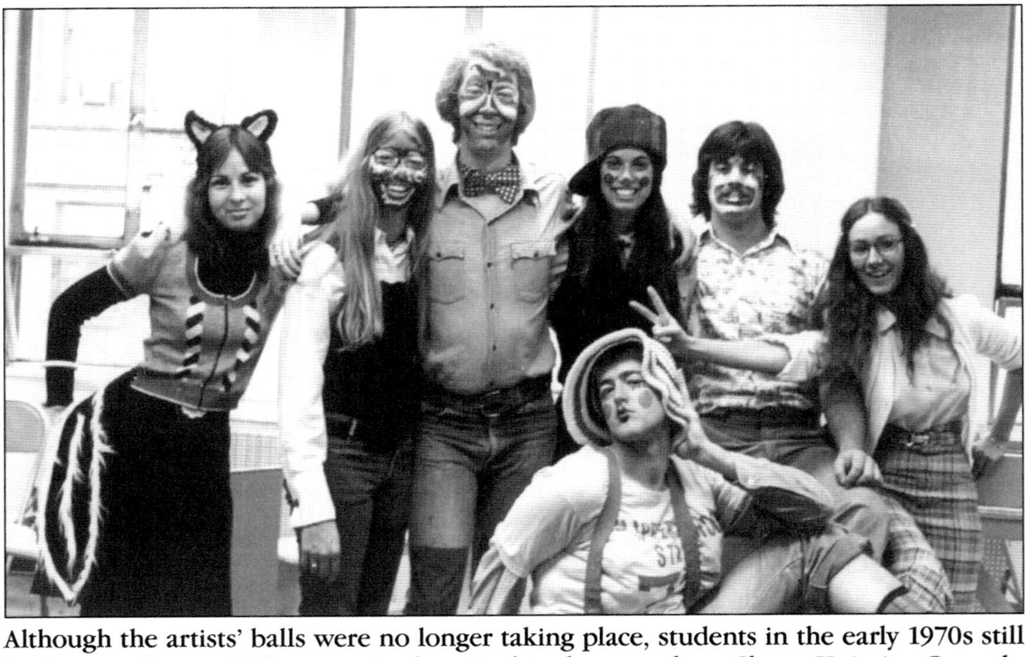

Although the artists' balls were no longer taking place, students in the early 1970s still had a great time on Halloween. Students in this photograph are Sherry Knierim, Carmelo Ferraro, Jan Anders, Carol Rederick, Glen Bicker, Wendy Walfe, and George Arnold.

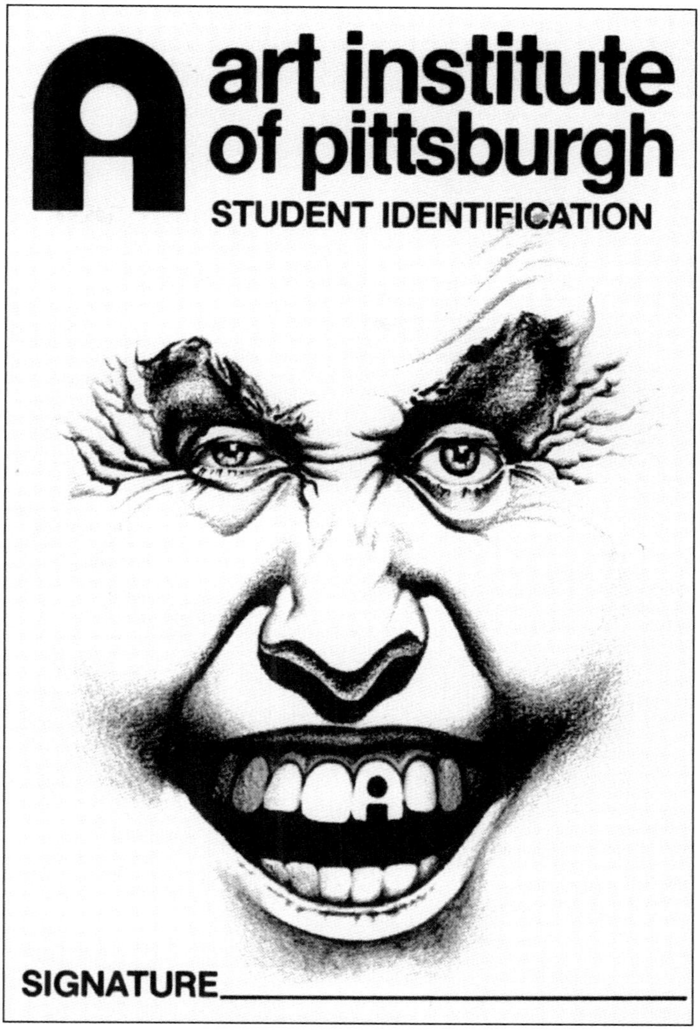

Faculty member Bert Gries illustrated this identification card for the Summer Teens program in the 1970s. Teens took Saturday classes in art and design fundamentals. Many of these teens enrolled following high school graduation and are now members of the alumni of the Art Institute of Pittsburgh. Teens can now participate in an intensive two-week course called Summer Studio. They stay in school housing and enjoy field trips to the city's many notable attractions.

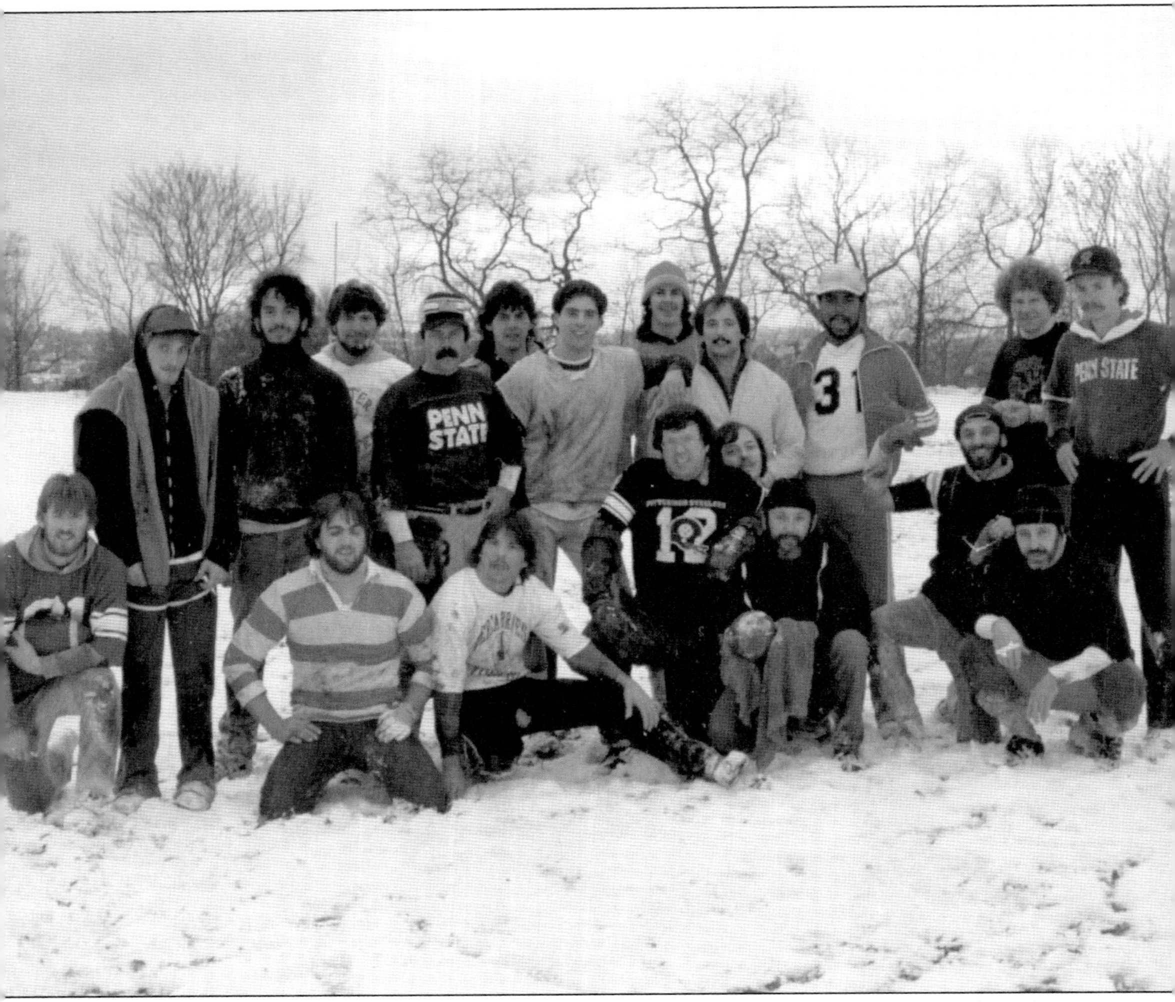

The final score was the faculty 49, students 7, on December 12, 1981, and in the years of flag football games in the 1980s, faculty bragged to have lost only one game to the students. These Saturday morning games in Schenley Park pitted the "young bucks" (and an occasional girl) against the "old guys." Even though game time was early, at 8:30 a.m., no one ever missed these. The football games were more than physical challenges—they built longtime friendships and respect among faculty and students. From left to right are (first row) unidentified (student), Jim Ivan (student), Chuck Yex (student), Ed Urian (faculty), Ken "Spike" Huber (staff), Mick "YA" Opalko (faculty), Rich Germinaro (faculty), and Dan Lafferty (faculty); (second row) unidentified (student), unidentified (student), unidentified (student), Bill McAnulty (faculty), unidentified (student), Dave Baron (student), unidentified (student), Jeff Porella (student), Marcus Jackson (student), David Bowers (faculty), and Greg Schooley (faculty). (Courtesy of Bill McAnulty and Mick Opalko.)

In 1981, the school celebrated its 60th anniversary with a special alumni invitational show, Art for Business Sake. This invitation also featured a pen illustration created in the 1920s as a school logo.

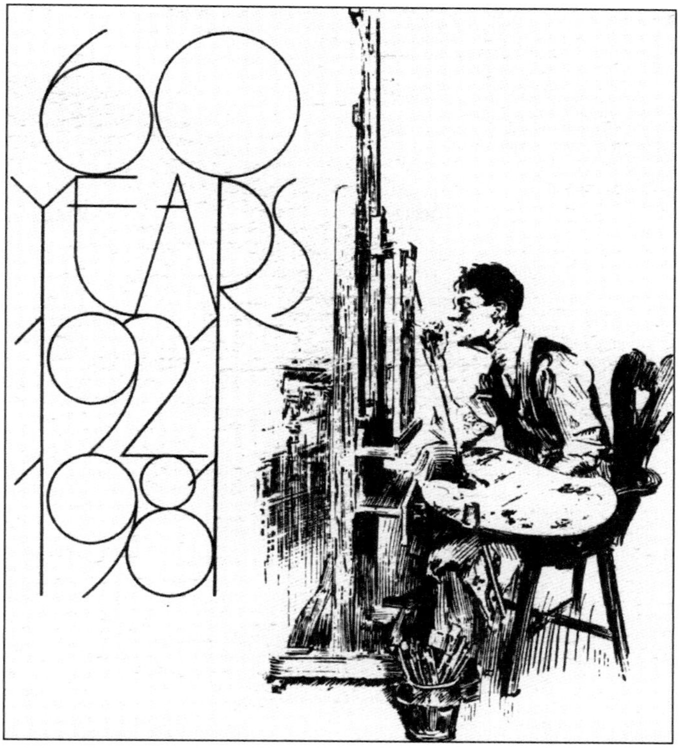

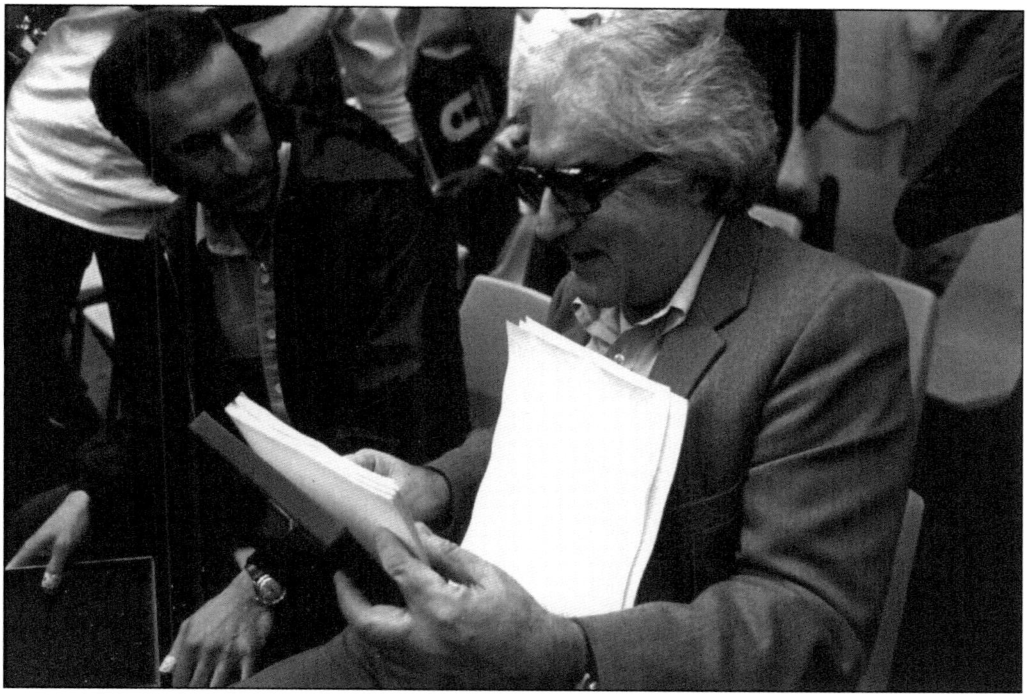

In this photograph from 1981, Cornell Capa reviews the photography of student Sergio Penchansky. Capa was a *Life* staff photographer, member of Magnum Photos, director of the International Center for Photography, and brother of famed photojournalist Robert Capa. (Photograph by Greg Ellis.)

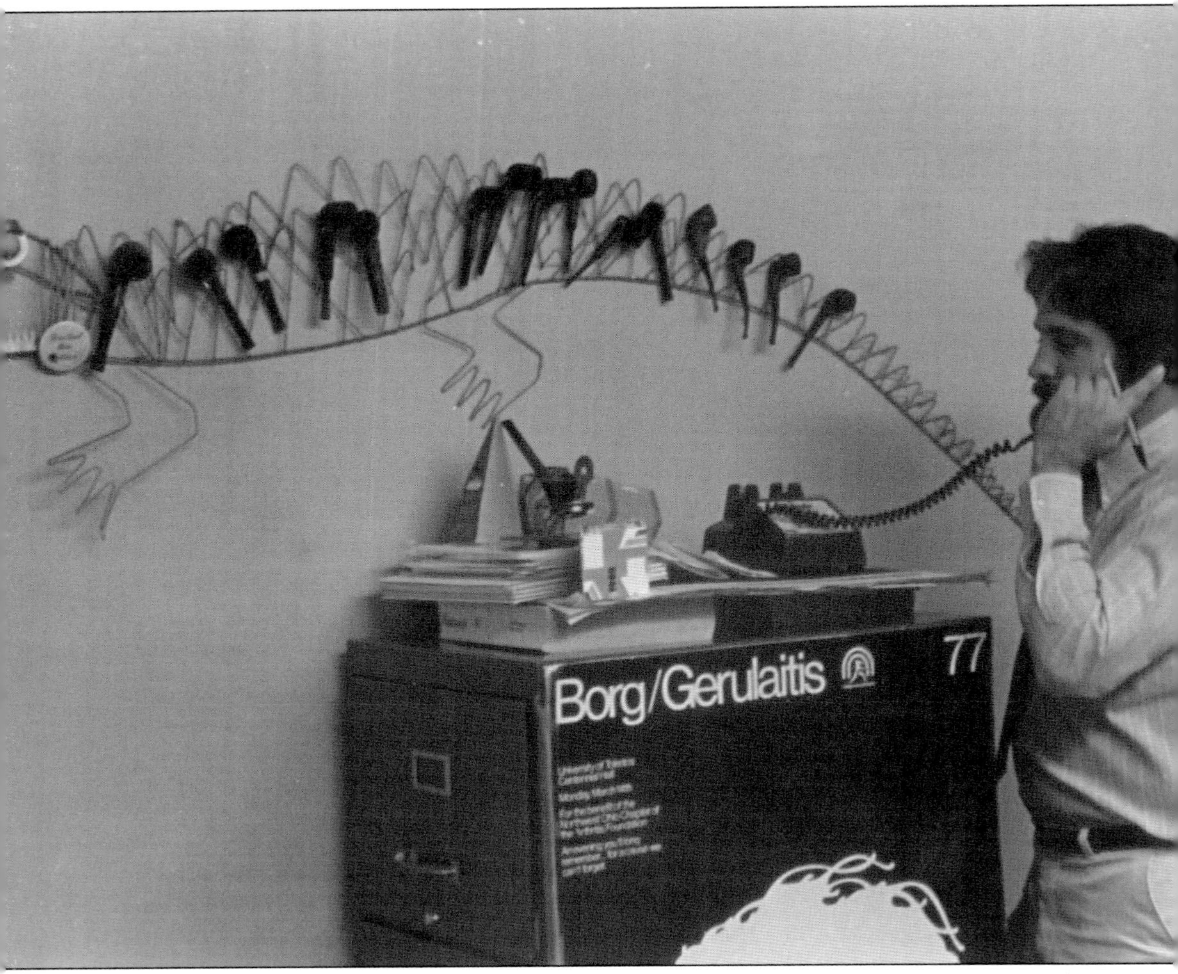

In this office in the 1980s, shared by pipe smoking directors Bill McAnulty and Dan Lafferty, this pipe rack adorned the wall. The rack was the creative work of maintenance supervisor Bob Chess, a construction of coat hangers and saw blades. Smoking habits have changed over time, and so have the rules about where to smoke. In 1943, a school rule stated: "One and a half hours after classes start, a recess bell rings, and for ten minutes you may walk, talk, buy supplies or smoke (in rest rooms only)." Now smoking is restricted to the outdoor smoke deck. Perhaps the smoke deck will disappear for future generations as habits change, but for now, it is a gathering place, rain or shine. (Courtesy of Bill McAnulty.)

This student handbook from 1988 reads a lot like the school's current handbook and enforces many of the same lessons, "In the real world of work there are no acceptable excuses for missing deadlines and it is extremely important that the student learns and establishes professional disciplines."

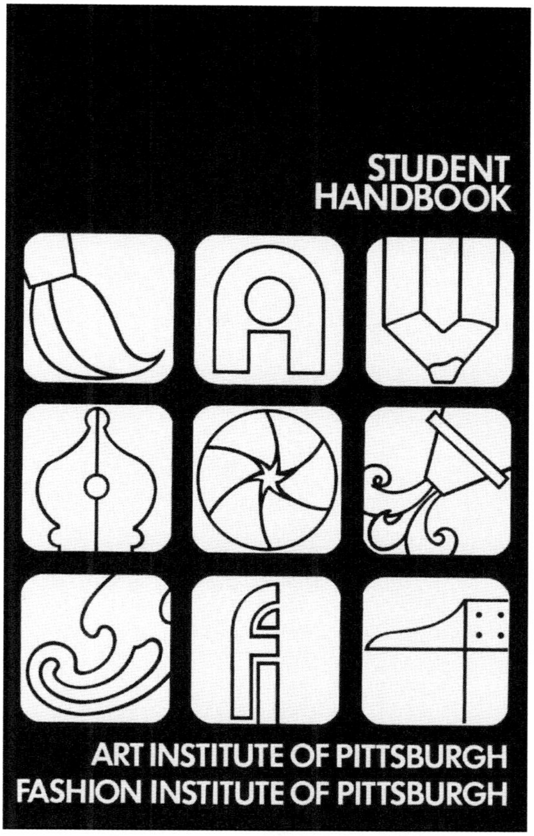

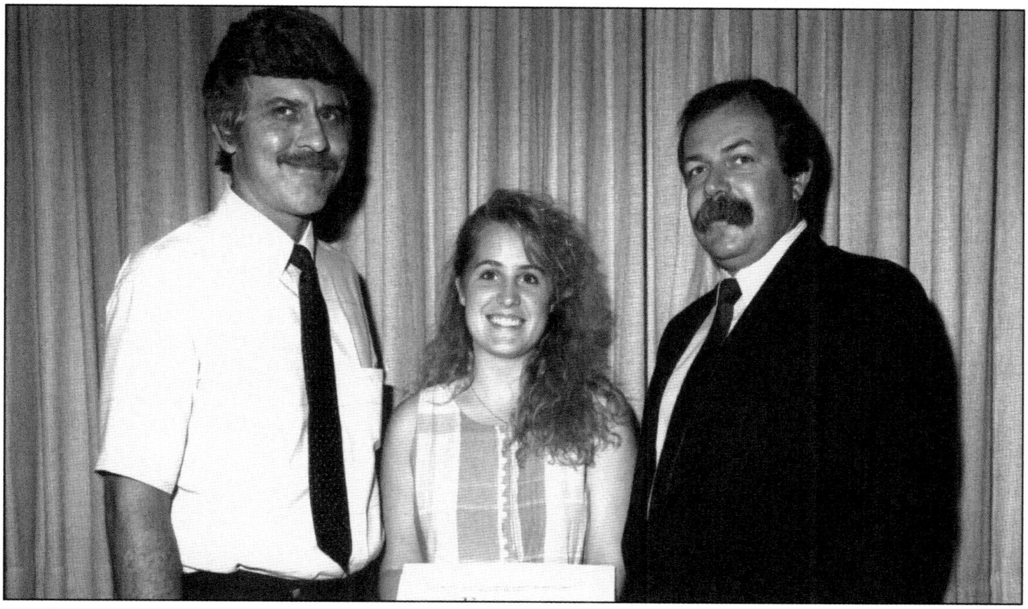

Students often compete in international design competitions. These competitions are a great opportunity for students to gain exposure in their field and to supplement their earnings. In 1989, Melissa Sleasman won the first prize national award of $500 at the International Design Conference. Ron Miller (left) and Bill McAnulty congratulate her.

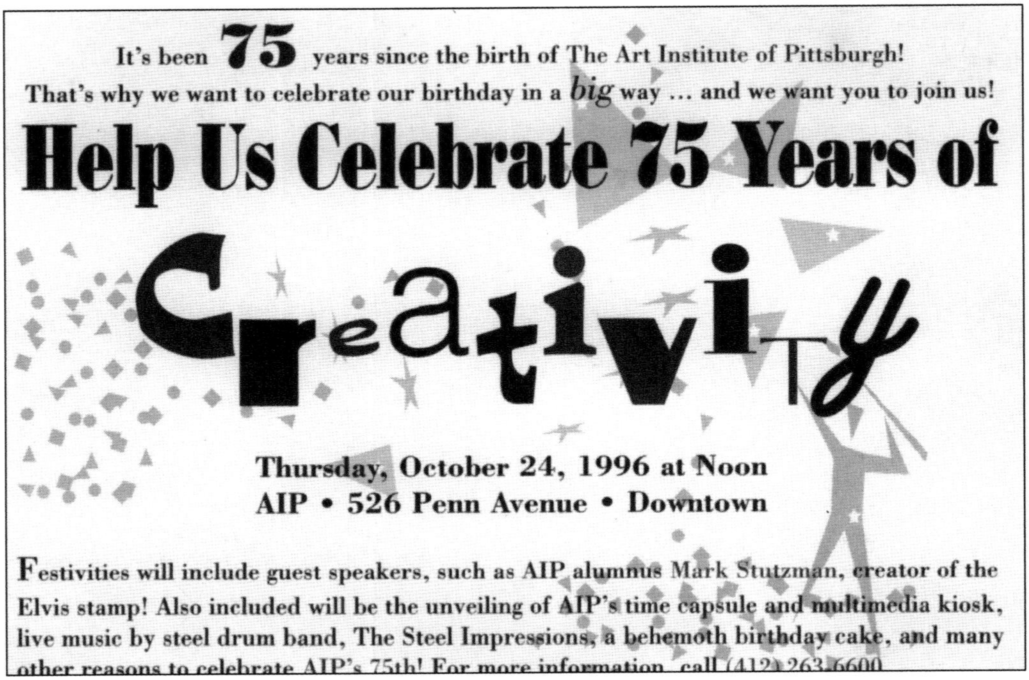

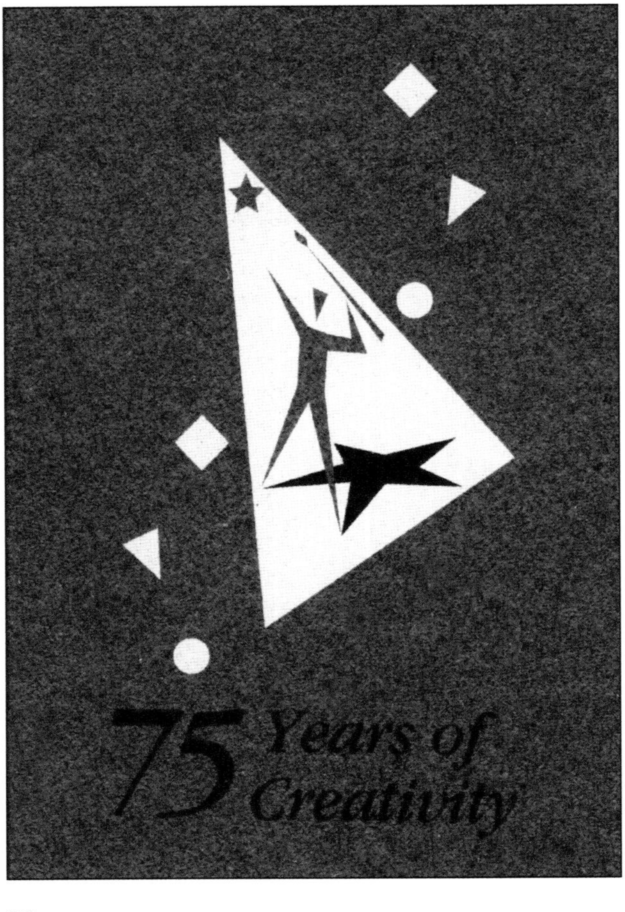

At its 75th anniversary in 1996, the school celebrated with great fanfare in a festive street party, complete with bubbles and balloons. Former president John Johns, who served from 1970 to 1982, was inducted into the school's hall of fame. Helping to celebrate was Mark Stutzman, an alumnus and designer of the Elvis stamp issued in 1993. Mayor Tom Murphy cut the ribbon around a time capsule that was reported to contain T-shirts, bubble containers, a 386 PC computer motherboard, a SyQuest computer storage disk, curriculum flow charts, and photographs. Freddie Chen, a fifth-quarter visual communications student, created the winning entry in the student contest for the anniversary logo design, shown left.

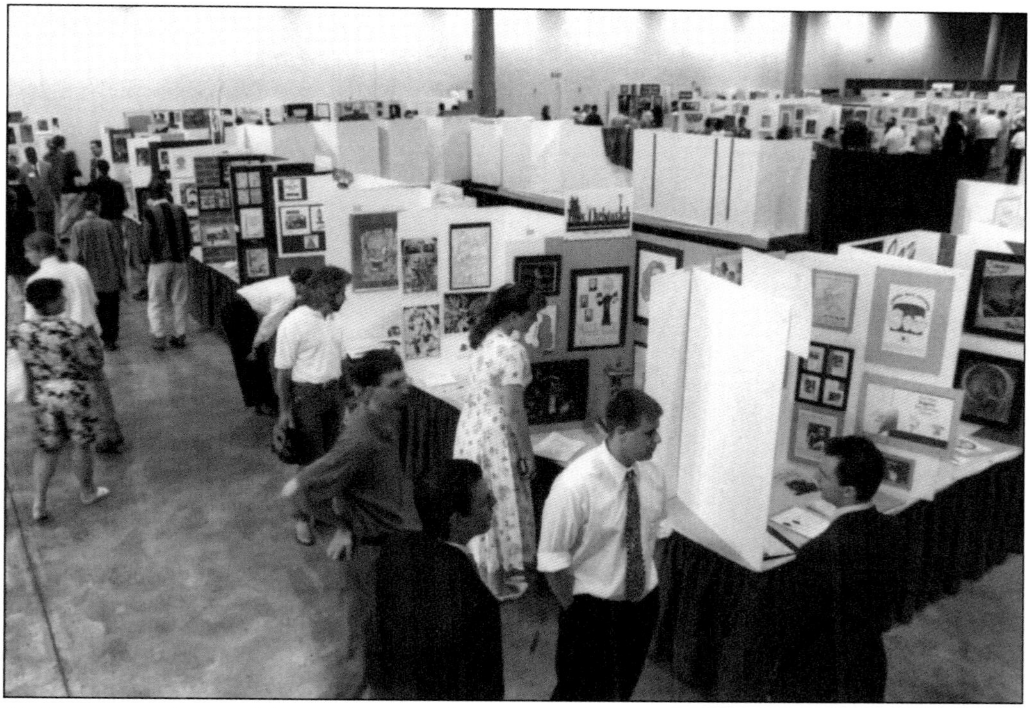

At the quarterly portfolio review, graduating students are invited to display their work for their peers, faculty, and prospective employers. Portfolio reviews have taken place at Soldiers and Sailors Memorial Hall in Oakland and more recently at the David L. Lawrence Convention Center, downtown. Over the years, displays have become more elaborate, incorporating technology, backdrops, and lighting. At each portfolio review, the Best in Show awards, a program developed by John Franke, are presented in each program to those students whose work is chosen by vote of the faculty. Sarah Shepard won the photography award for this elegant display in 2008.

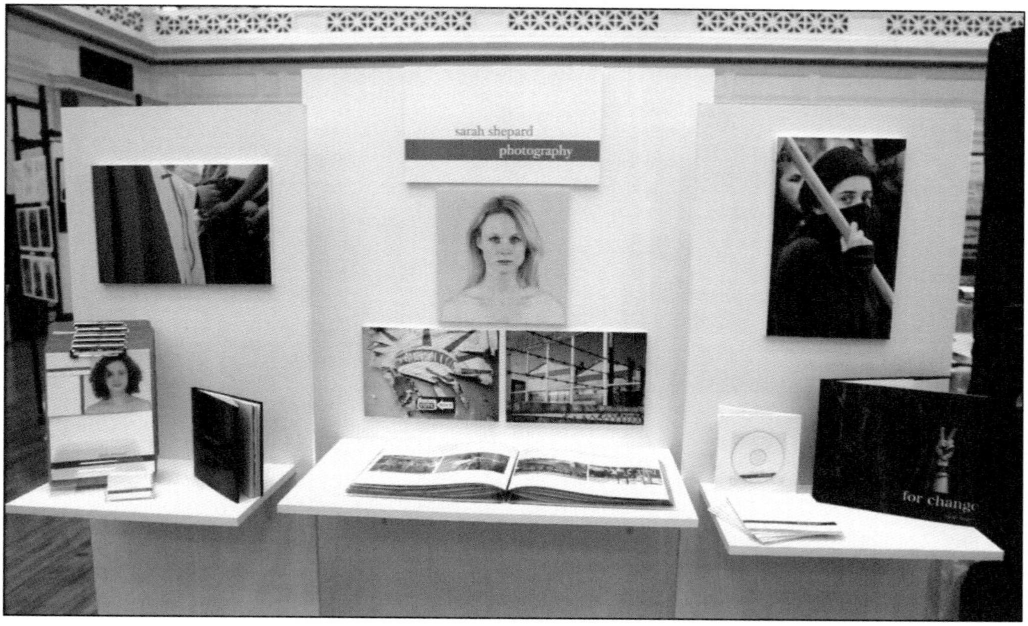

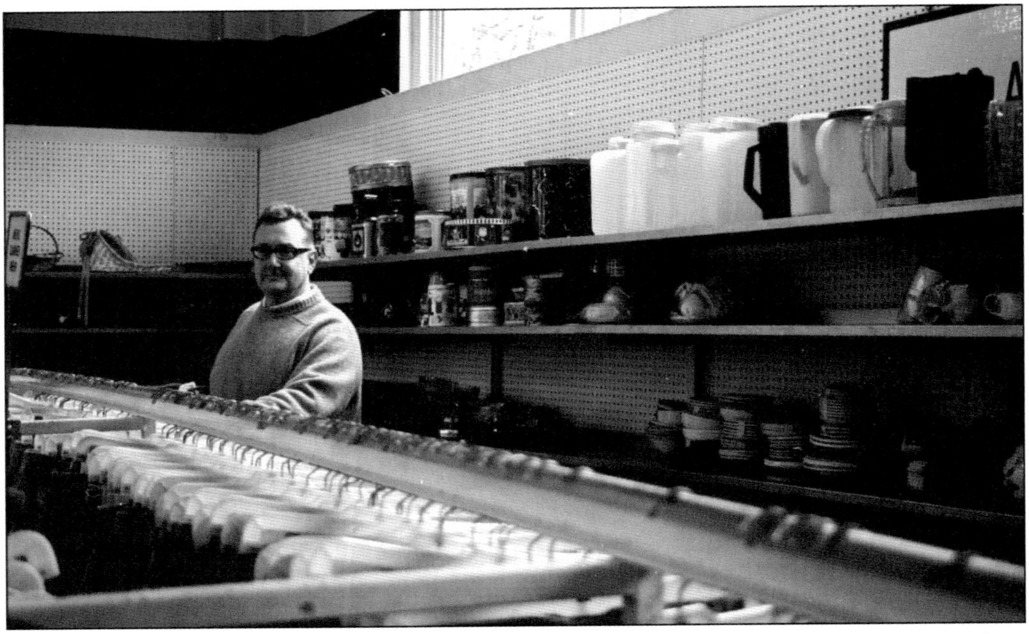

Quarterly workshops presented by faculty and staff give students opportunities to explore topics outside their fields of study. In the popular thrift shopping workshop, students visit and shop in thrift, consignment, and vintage shops throughout the Pittsburgh area. Students meet early on Saturday morning and set out on their mission for the best deals in the city, with faculty member John Franke as their knowledgeable guide.

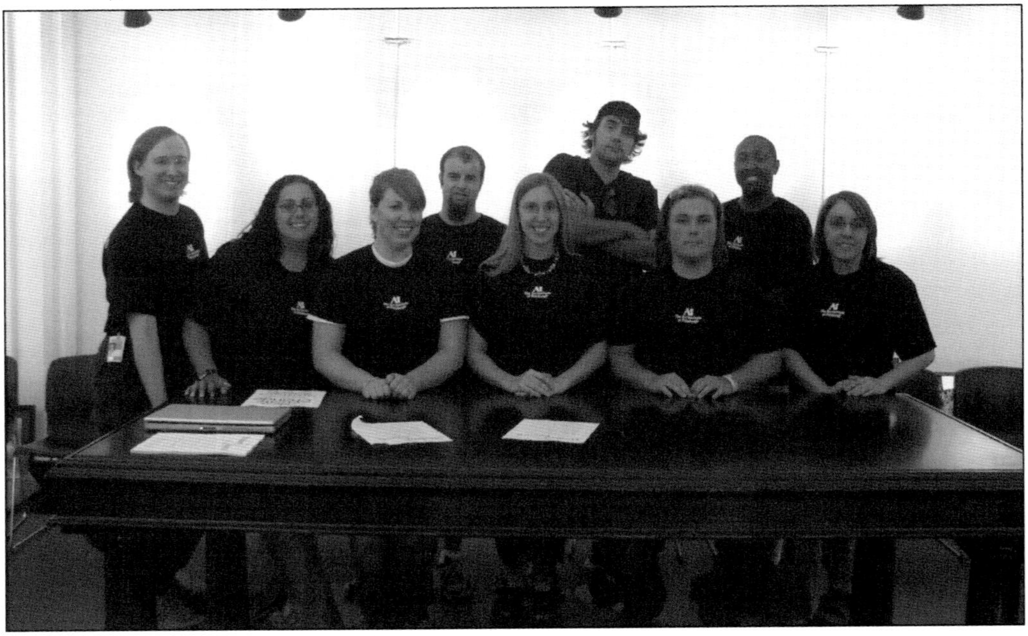

The student council began in the late 1990s to provide student input regarding events and to communicate student concerns. It grew out of informal student meetings and the Dine with the Dean lunches. This group from 2007 includes, from left to right, Michael Fulk, Rose Wasef, Emily Davis, Dale Capellanio, Tiffany Olejnik, Kai Deventich, Brandon Edwards, J. R. Poole, and Hillary Steiger.

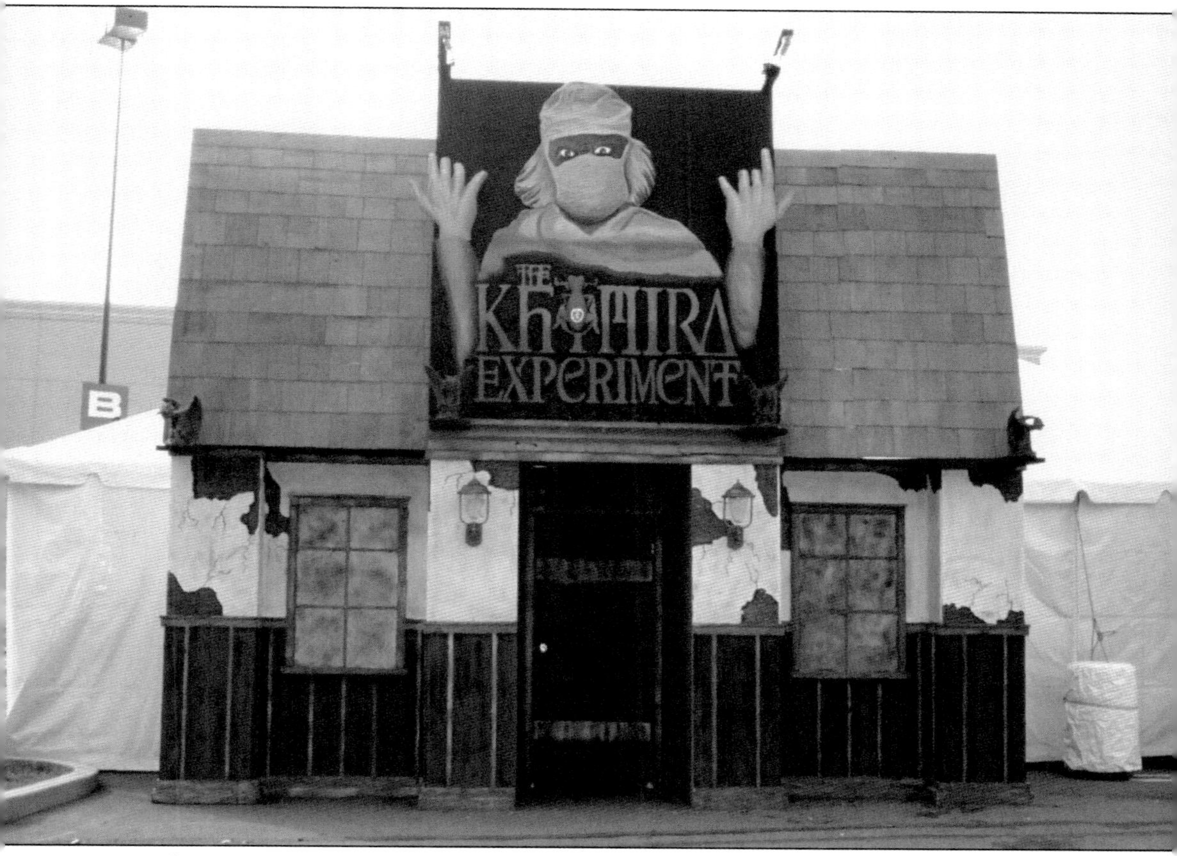

In 2003, there was something wicked in the parking lot of the Mall at Robinson. That something was the Khymira Experiment. Students, faculty, and staff from many departments worked together to create and build the haunted attraction. Behind that door were the type of frights and sights that make the Halloween season. The project was a benefit event for the EDMC Education Foundation.

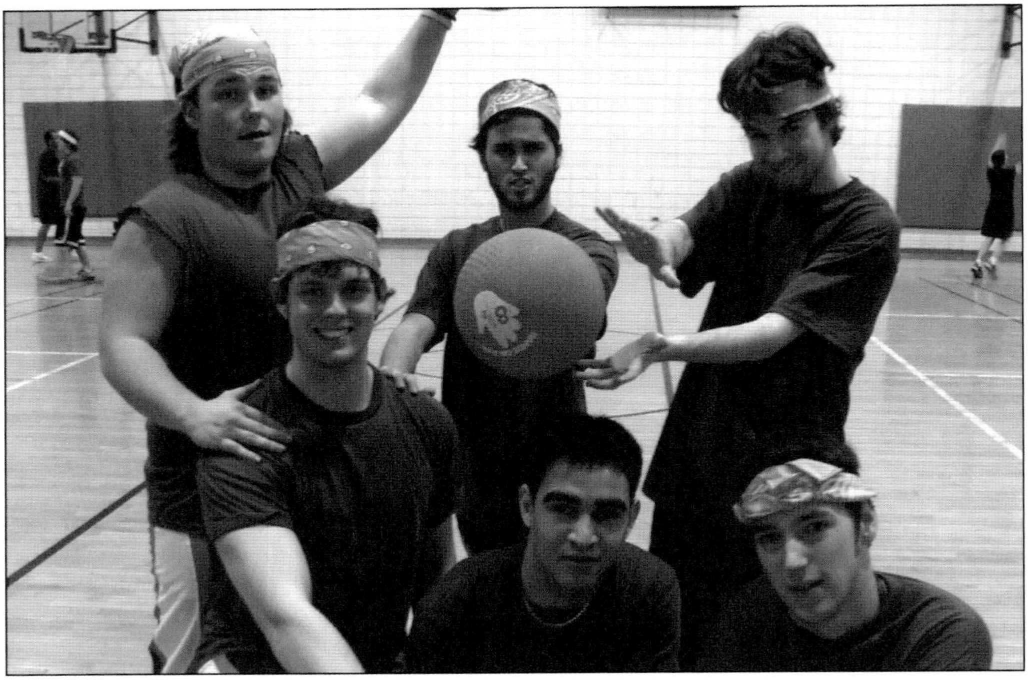

Director of student activities Sara Rathburn plans events to foster students' personal growth and create the campus community. This team of students was the winner in the winter 2006 dodgeball championship.

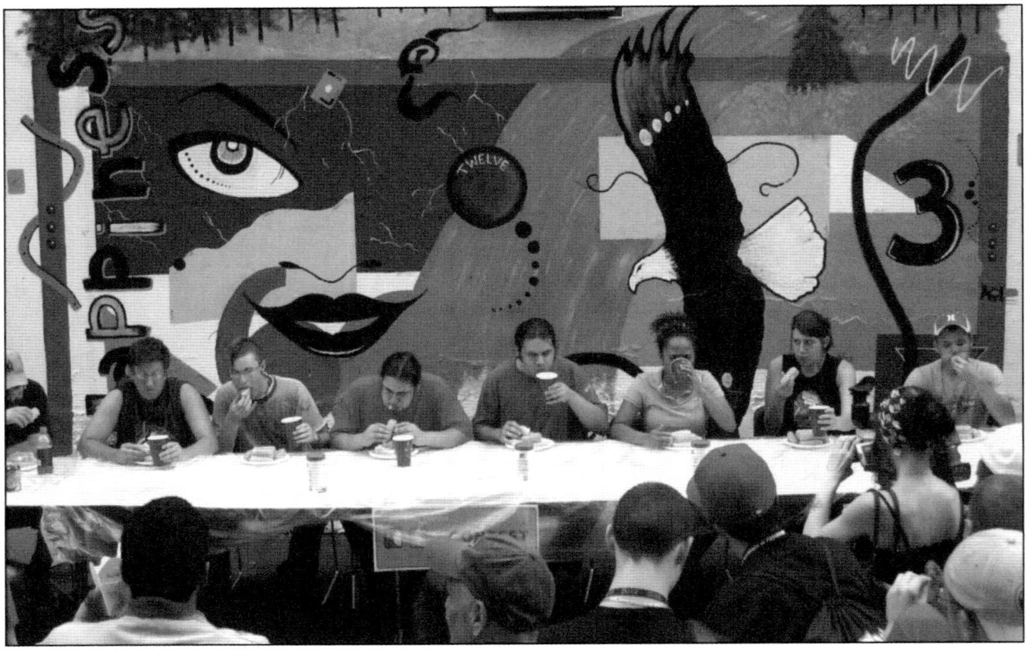

The annual Summer Carnival began when the school moved into the current facility on the Boulevard of the Allies. Since then, it has expanded from a simple picnic to an all-day event, featuring live bands, comedians, and contests. In this photograph, a group of students competes in the Twinkie-eating contest. Behind them is a mural designed by student Eric "Pops" Johnson.

Two

CAREERS IN THE MAKING

Technology has dramatically changed the way students are taught and the programs offered by the school. Willis Shook might initially be shocked by a tour of today's Art Institute of Pittsburgh. However, there is no doubt that he would soon recognize his vision in this modern version.

In many programs, the basic lessons remain the same. Graphic design replaces commercial art in name, but the fundamental education of typography, color, and layout continues. Interior design uses AutoCAD and computer programs to create environments, but students still need a thorough understanding of color, texture, and lighting. Photography is moving out of the darkroom and onto the computer screen, and industrial design technology's assortment of tools have grown and expanded; yet, both are still based in core competencies that are taught regardless of format.

Other programs also stay true to Willis Shook's vision of a school dedicated to training students for business. While fashion design and millinery have been discontinued, fashion and retail management continues the tradition and prepares students for jobs in the fashion industry. Advertising students learn essential business skills in a marketing-oriented program. Media arts and animation, game art and design, Web design and interactive media, digital filmmaking and video production, and culinary arts started as a direct response to the industry need for well-trained individuals. In this chapter are images from all programs of study as students prepared for their careers.

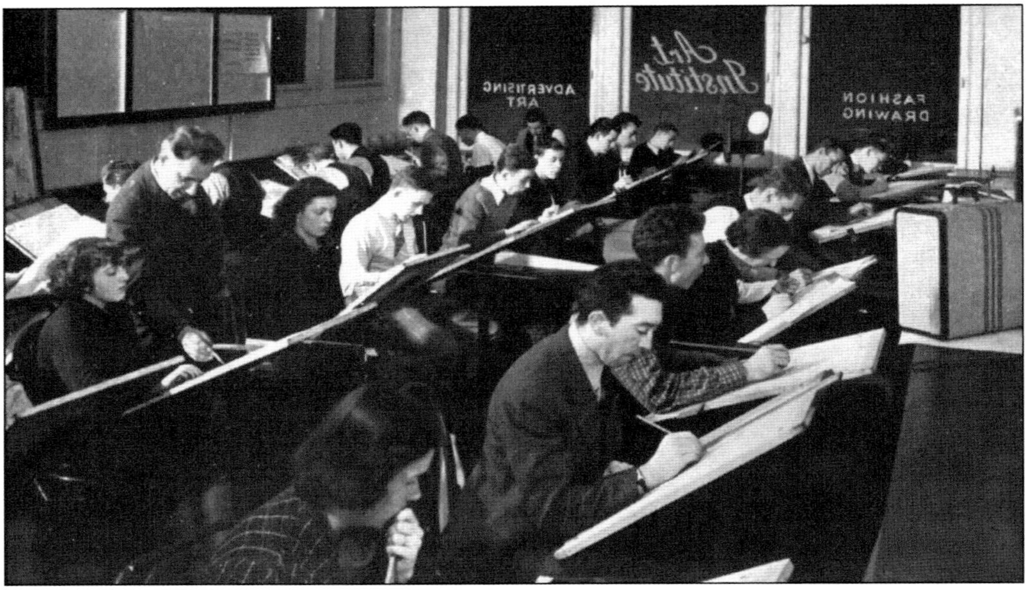

Willis Shook founded the Artist's League of Pittsburgh to teach commercial art, an 18-month course. First-year students practiced their illustration skills, learning the fundamentals of composition, layout, lettering, perspective, color, and advanced drawing techniques. Students produced advertisements, bulletin boards, signage, catalog illustrations, logos, and letterheads as part of their training for industry. In this photograph, students practice still life drawing.

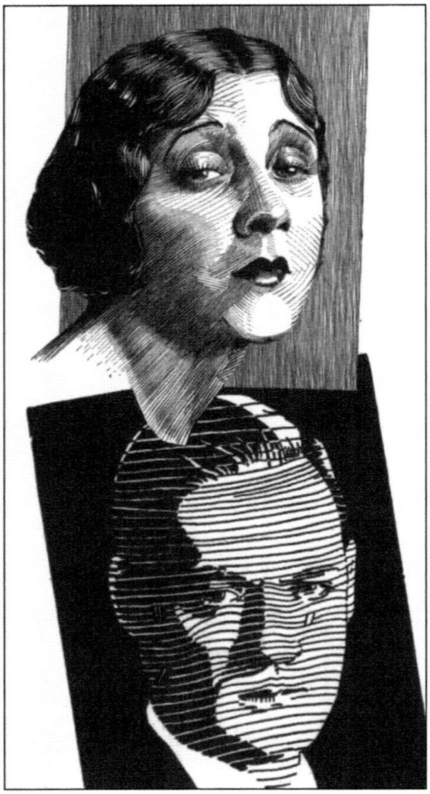

These movie poster illustrations are the work of first- and second-year students. In the 1920s, no phase of commercial art offered more remuneration than the moving picture industry. These illustrations demonstrate the unique methods learned in a course on movie poster drawing. Students in the course created posters for local theaters, including the Stanley, Rowland, and Clark Theaters.

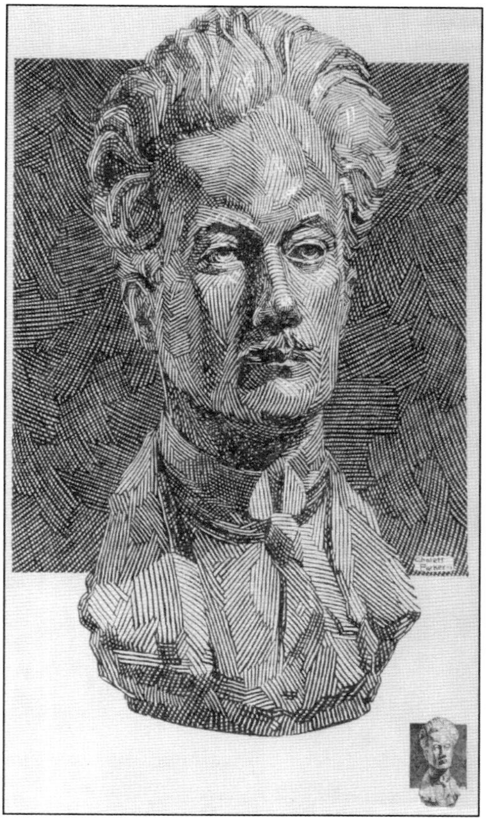

This illustration (right) appeared in many early school catalogs as an example of the fundamental lessons that students would learn. First-year student Cholett Parker drew this pen illustration in the early 1920s. Parker later served as a member of the faculty, while running his own successful design studio, Dahlpark Studios, in the city. The subject for this illustration was the bronze bust of Willis Shook (below), sculpted by Frank Vittor. Vittor had studied with Rodin in Paris and joined the faculty in 1922. He became one of Pittsburgh's most famous sculptors, creating over 50 statues and memorials all around Pittsburgh. (Photograph by Patricia A. Nagle, courtesy of Willis D. Shook III.)

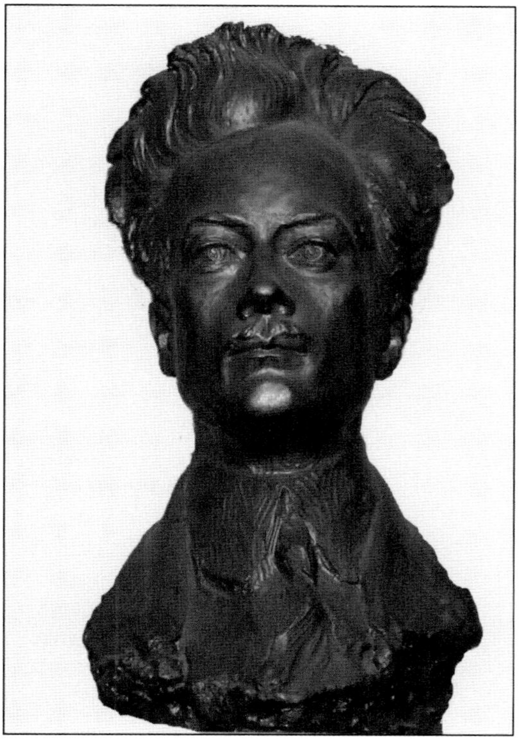

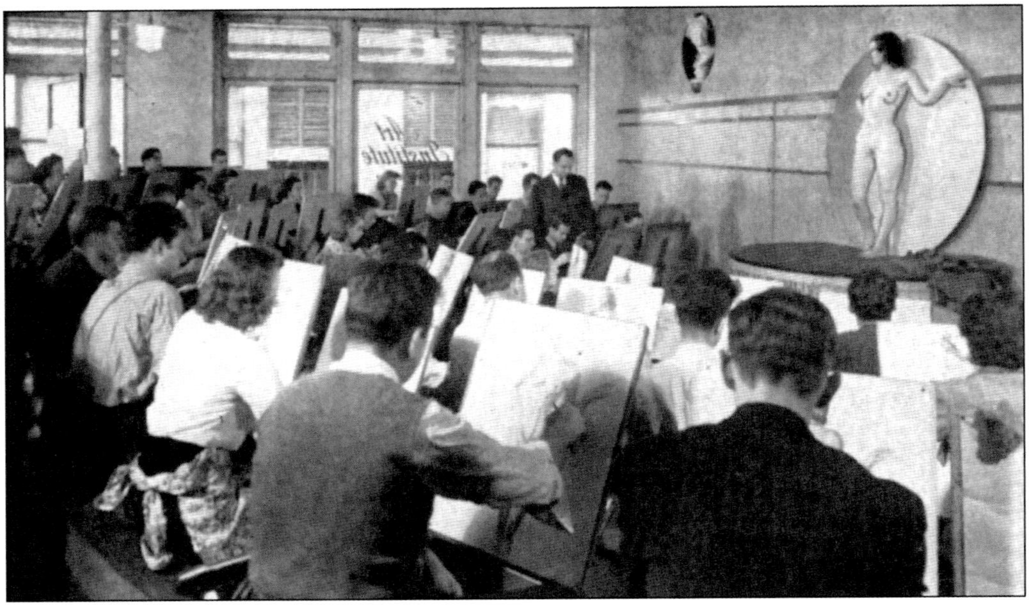

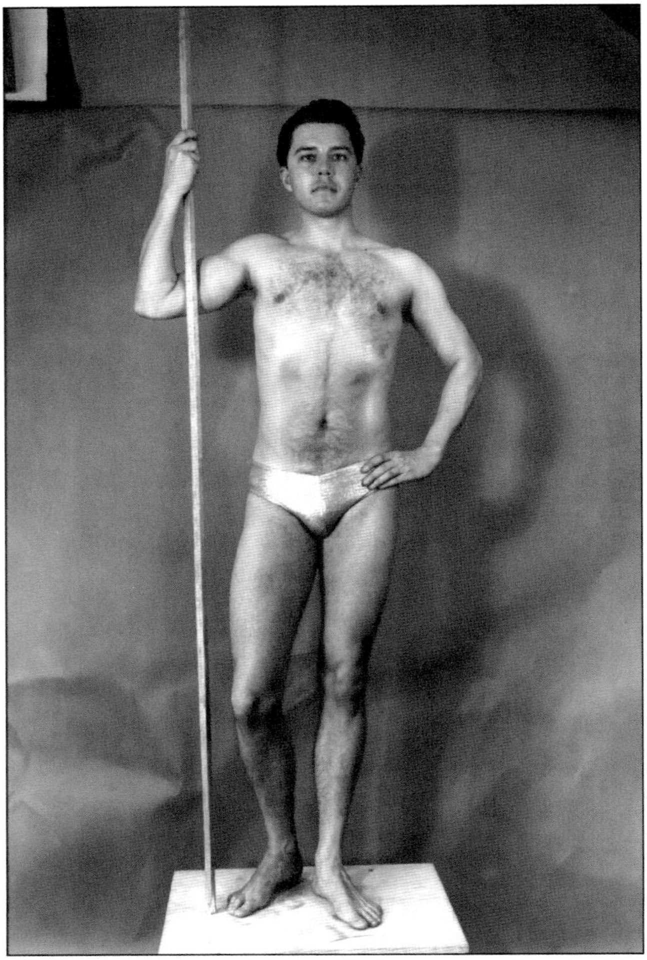

Models for life drawing classes from different eras, both nude and costumed, are shown here. A model posed for the first time "in the altogether" in the life drawing class on the fourth-floor studio of the Fulton Building in 1921. The story was told in the daily newspaper, "Last evening a citizen of the North Side was wending his way thoughtfully homeward over the Sixth Street Bridge, scanning the skies for a view of the Great Dipper. Suddenly he froze in his tracks and fellow travelers heard his startled cry, *Oh lookie*! In no time six hundred males jammed the bridge, as they stared upwards with popping eyes and rubber necks." When police stormed the classroom, Shook was admonished by these "valiant minions of the law" to see to it that all blinds were down in the future.

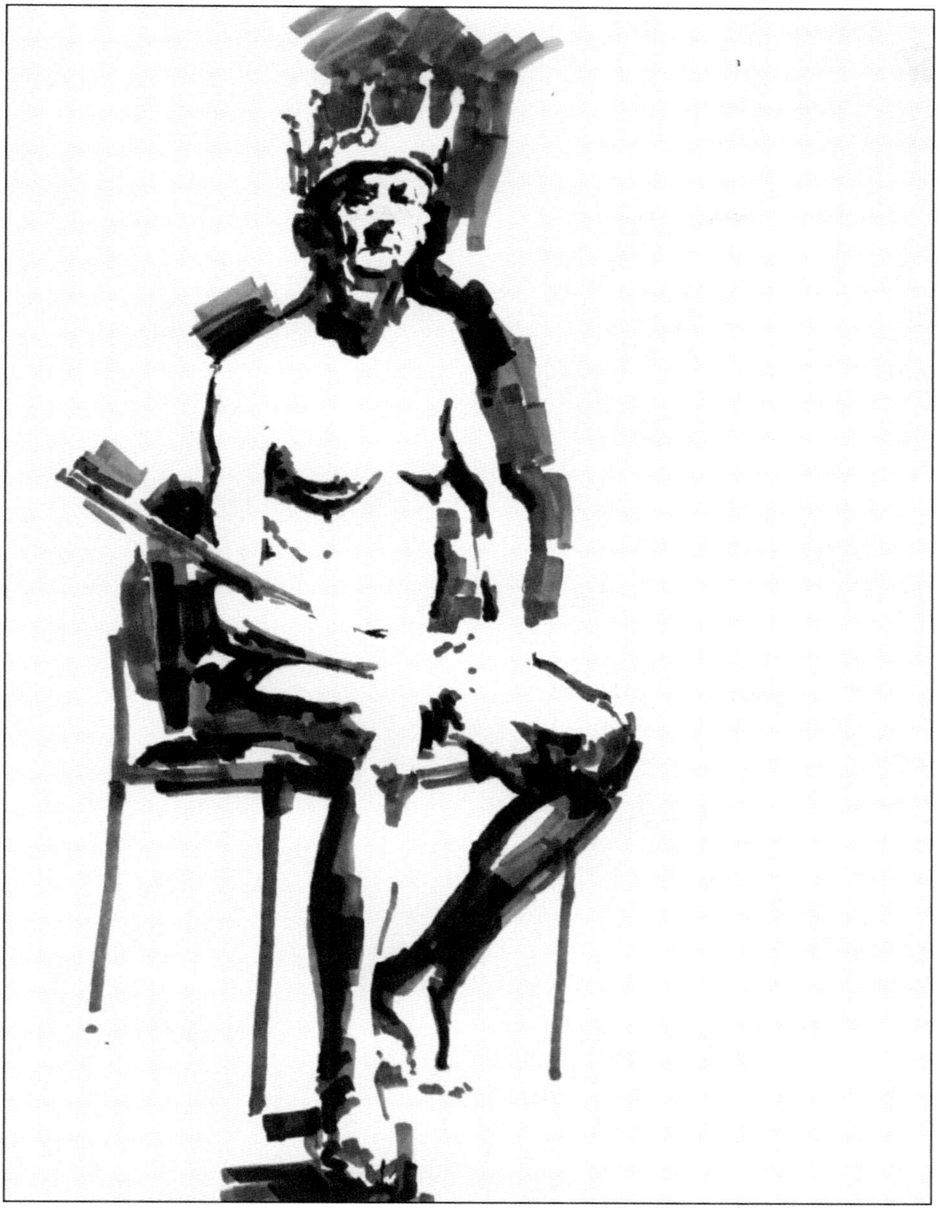

Into the 1960s, illustration of the human form was used extensively in advertising to show merchandising, on magazine covers, and in the magazine romance stories. The current commercial arts industry may be dominated by photography, but drawing the human figure and understanding anatomical function is still a fundamental art skill and now essential to the game design and animation industries. Life drawing instruction includes learning gestures, proportions, alignment, shapes, and tonal patterns. Models perform the difficult tasks of becoming motionless, frequently under hot spotlights. The interaction between the model and a class can take on theatrical qualities. This sketch by Helen Webster, member of the graphic design faculty, captures Ron Lessig recreating Camelot. The class painted to the soundtrack from the popular musical while Lessig donned a collection of kingly props. Ron Lessig is a popular model in life drawing classes today, performing his poses with the intensity of an athlete or dancer.

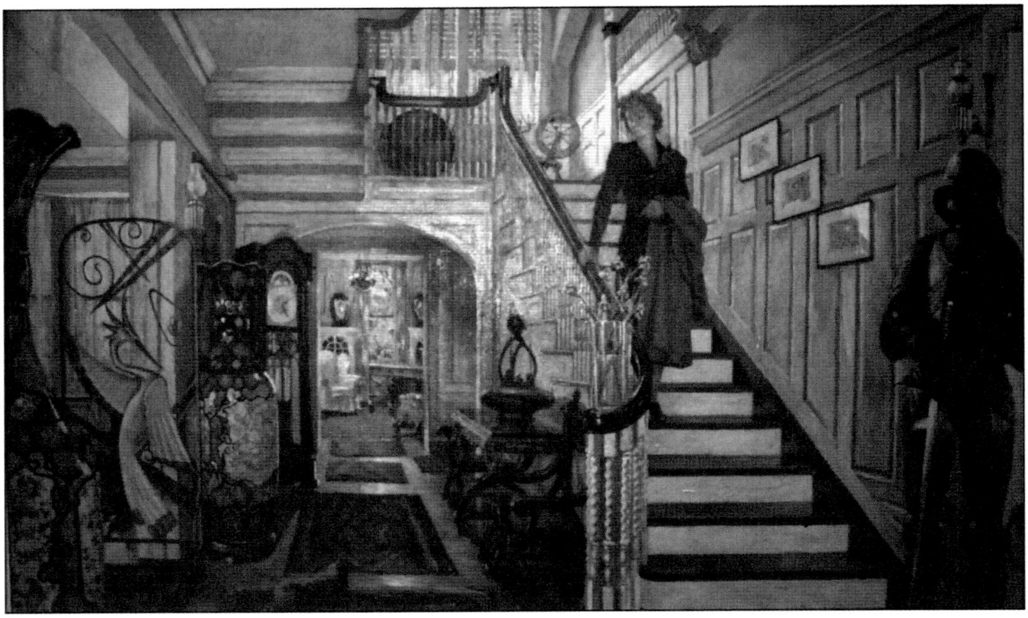

Woman Descending a Staircase: A Study in Perspective was an important work for students as they studied perspective under the instruction of Willis Shook. Shook painted the 31-inch-by-48-inch oil painting at his residence in Sewickley in the 1940s. Elizabeth Buckley Shook, his student, and later his wife, modeled for the painting. (Courtesy of Willis D. Shook III.)

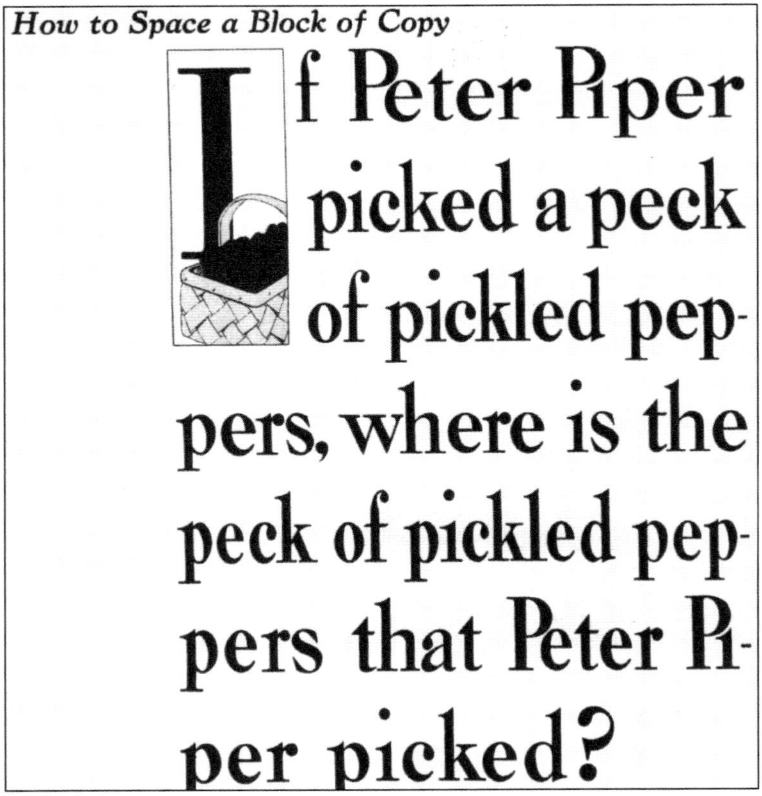

Lettering played a crucial role in good design work. Students used Willis Shook's book *The Art of Lettering for Reproduction* as their guide. Students were taught to trace type from lettering cards and books, letter by letter, designing, spacing, and kerning type by eye, first in pencil then in ink, paint, or marker. Hand lettering was used in advertisements, brochures, posters, magazine covers, and billboards.

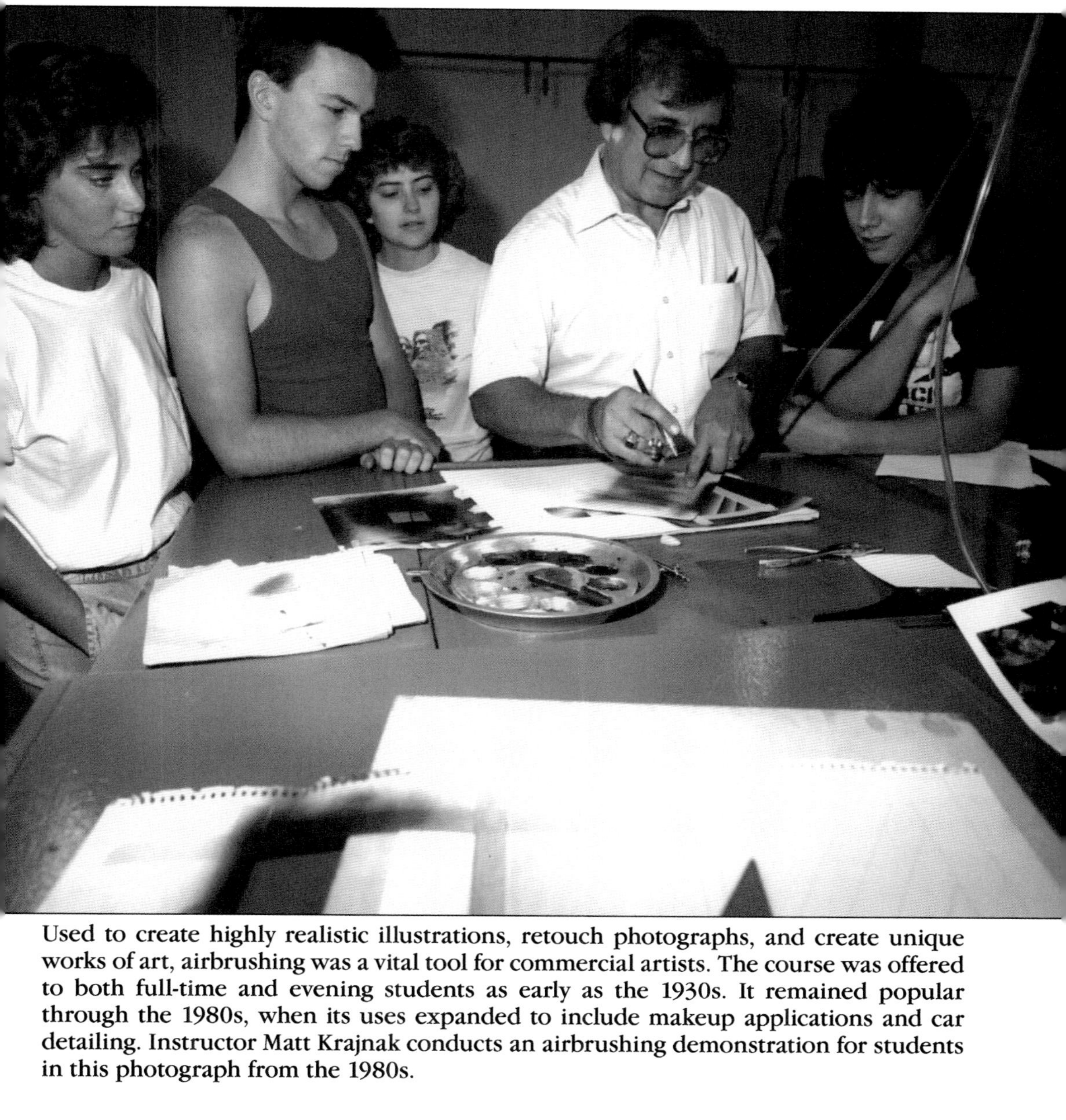

Used to create highly realistic illustrations, retouch photographs, and create unique works of art, airbrushing was a vital tool for commercial artists. The course was offered to both full-time and evening students as early as the 1930s. It remained popular through the 1980s, when its uses expanded to include makeup applications and car detailing. Instructor Matt Krajnak conducts an airbrushing demonstration for students in this photograph from the 1980s.

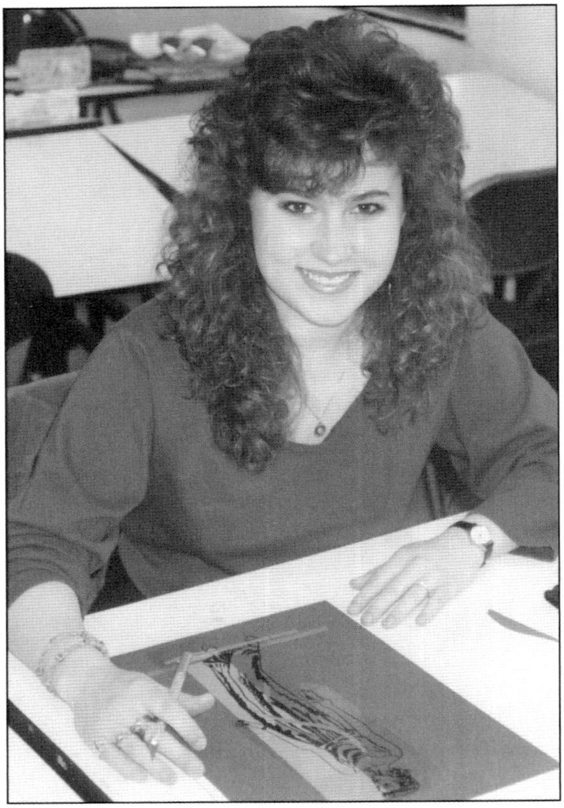

In the early 1970s, the program title commercial art changed to visual communications. Students and faculty began experimenting with mixed-media projects. Many classes utilized the photocopier, cut paper, and found objects to create highly realistic and unusual works of art. In this photograph, from the late 1980s, a student uses an X-ACTO knife to cut strips of canson paper to create this classically inspired collage.

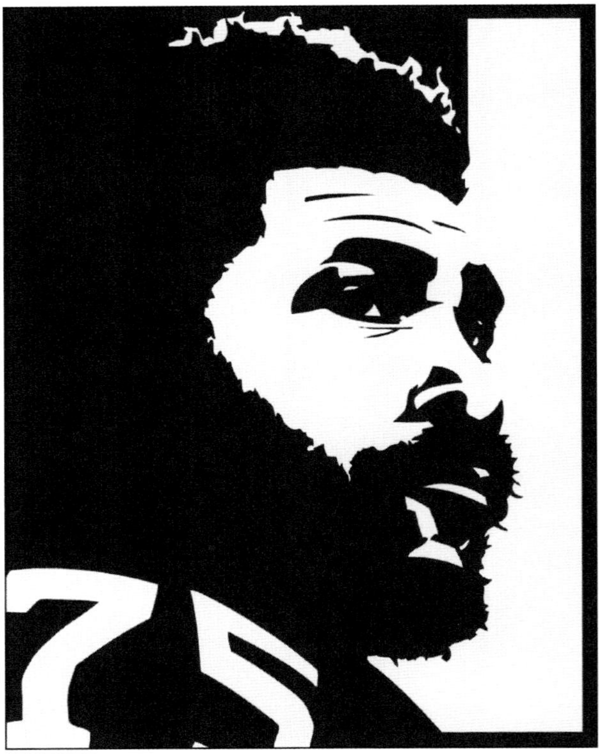

In 1997, the curriculum changed titles again. The new title, graphic design, reflected not only industry standards but the shift to a more computer-based artistic experience. Students combine traditional and computerized art, as in this portrait of Pittsburgh Steeler Mean Joe Greene by Jordan Bush. Originally drawn in pen on vellum, the illustration was then scanned and converted in Adobe Illustrator to create a vector graphic. (Courtesy of Jordan Bush.)

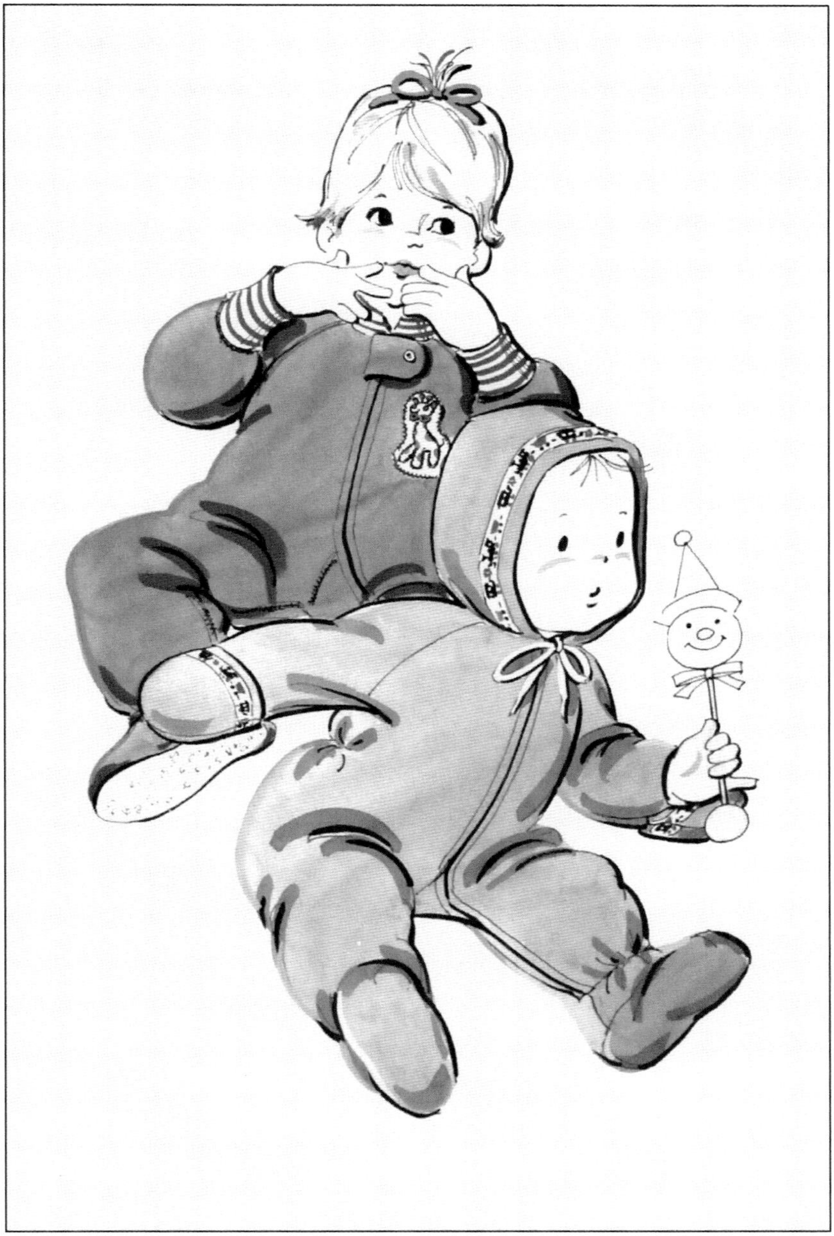

The school added fashion illustration as its second course in the 1920s. In fashion illustration, students focused on depicting the ever-changing array of styles and products that made their way into the market each season. Students learned to depict figures of all types: men, women, and children of all ages. Equal attention was given to fabric and texture; students learned techniques for rendering everything from cotton to mink. In addition to clothing, they studied jewelry, furniture, and housewares. Following studies in the fashion illustration program in 1943, Ruth McCormick enjoyed a 40-year career at Gimbel's department store. McCormick illustrated the advertisements that appeared in the daily newspaper and in store advertising. Illustrating children's clothing was McCormick's favorite work, as shown in her 1960s illustrated advertisement.

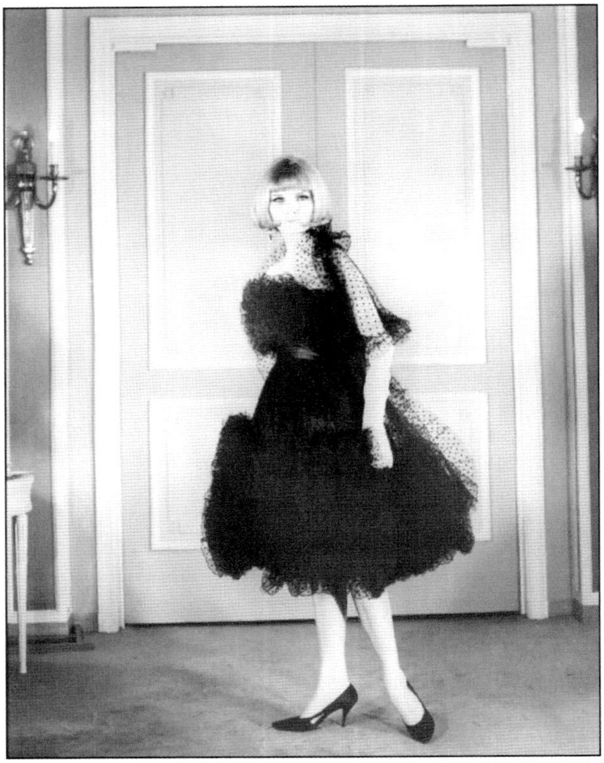

The fashion design and millinery programs were offered since the 1930s. Students designed and built their own clothing in the school's sewing machine–filled workrooms while learning the fundamentals of fabric, fit, and cut. Their designs often reflected the mood and style of their times. In this photograph from the late 1950s, the model exemplifies the formality and grandeur of that era in her black toile evening ensemble.

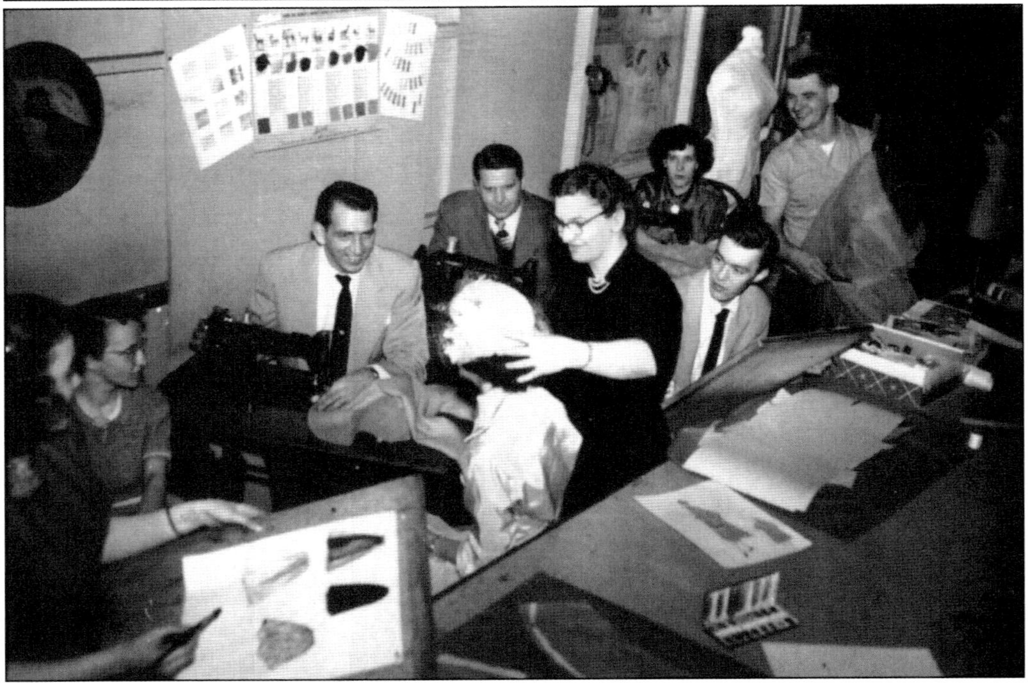

Back when it was proper to wear a hat when leaving the house, the millinery program was very popular with those seeking to create and design their own hats. The hands-on training and customer demand for hats made students attractive to department stores all over the city. Many students found work before even completing the program.

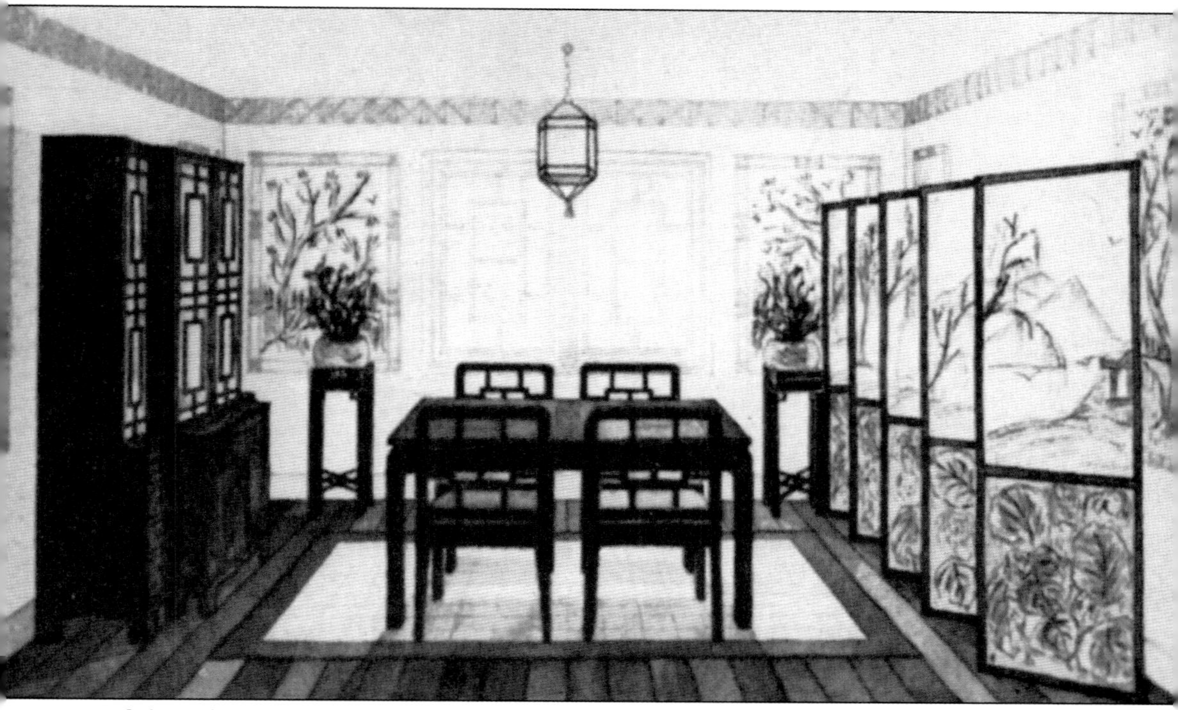

One of the school's longest-lasting programs is interior design; established in the late 1920s, its popularity continues into the present day. In 1954, the catalog describes the 18-month course, beginning with a foundation in "interior architecture, design, color theory and harmonies, color rendering, scale drawing, perspective, wall, window and floor treatments, arrangement of furniture, composition of decorative accessories, research into period decorations, and history and times of each period." Students focused on the nuances of each historical style. And finally, senior students worked on creating their own rooms. The certificate program was marketed as a hobby course for homemakers who wished to apply their expanded knowledge and refined taste to their own homes.

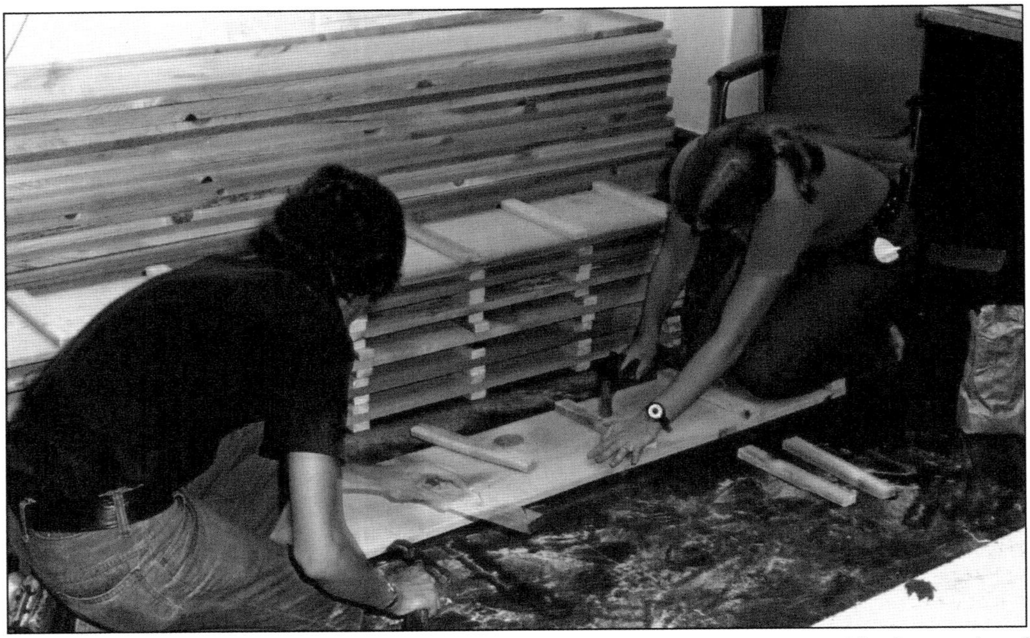

A crucial component of the interior design program is experience with the tools of the trade: paint swatches, fabric and material samples, drafting equipment, computer programs, and technology. Students have always had access to samples in wallpaper and fabric books. During the summer of 1974, members of the student chapter of the American Institute of Interior Designers redesigned the department's fabric room. Specially built shelving kept sample books organized and in easy reach while file cabinets kept items grouped and ordered. The room quickly became a favorite of students working on project boards.

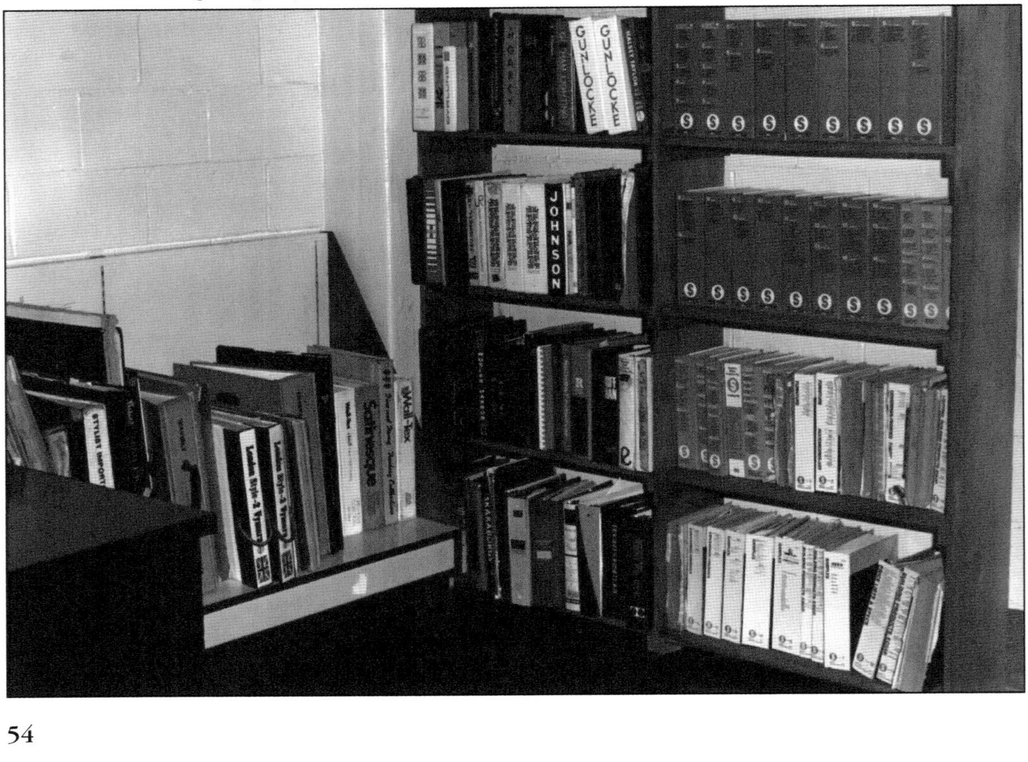

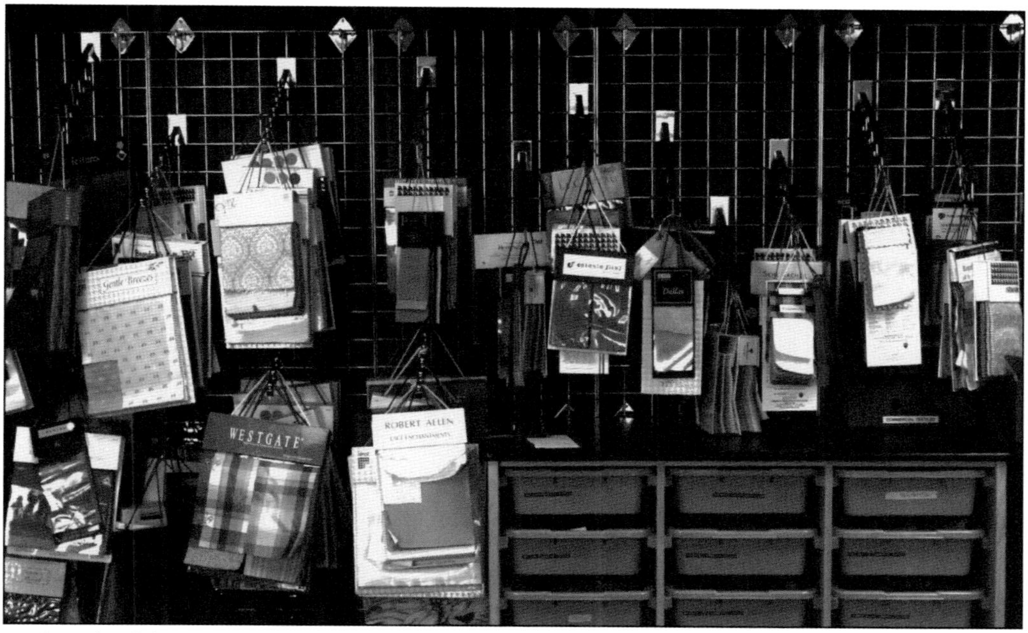

Today the fabric room is called the Nancy F. Ruttner Interior Design Resource Room. Located within the library on the third floor of the Boulevard of the Allies building, the new room has computers with the latest software in addition to the ever-present samples hung from the wall and organized in bins and cabinets. (Photograph by Abby Parker.)

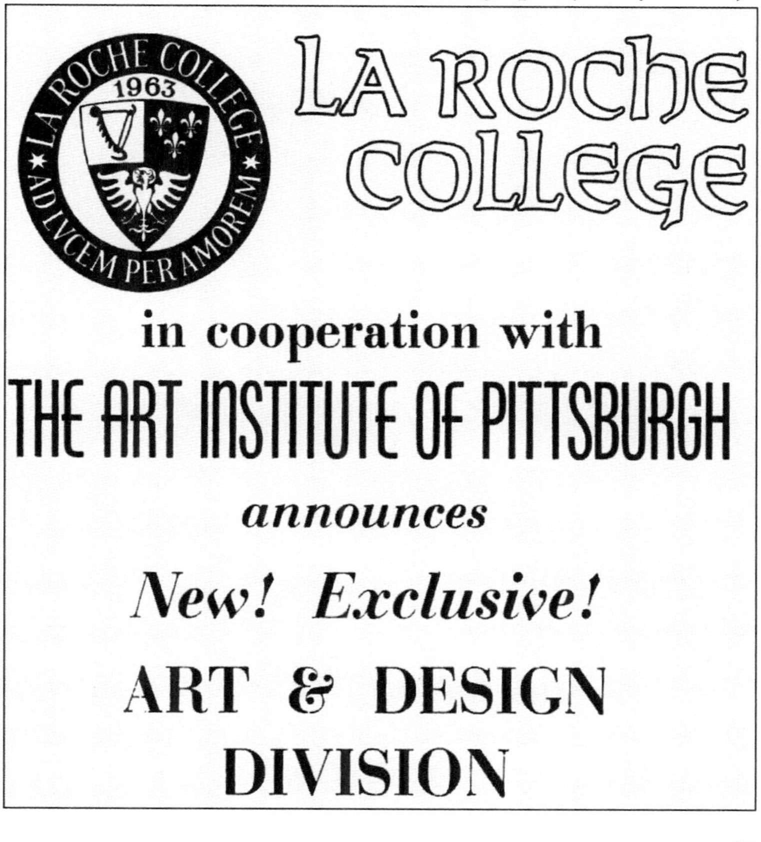

During its early years, the school offered two-year associate's degrees. During the 1970s, the school partnered with LaRoche College to provide four-year degrees in commercial art, fashion illustration, and interior design. The Art Institute of Pittsburgh began offering bachelor's degrees in 2000.

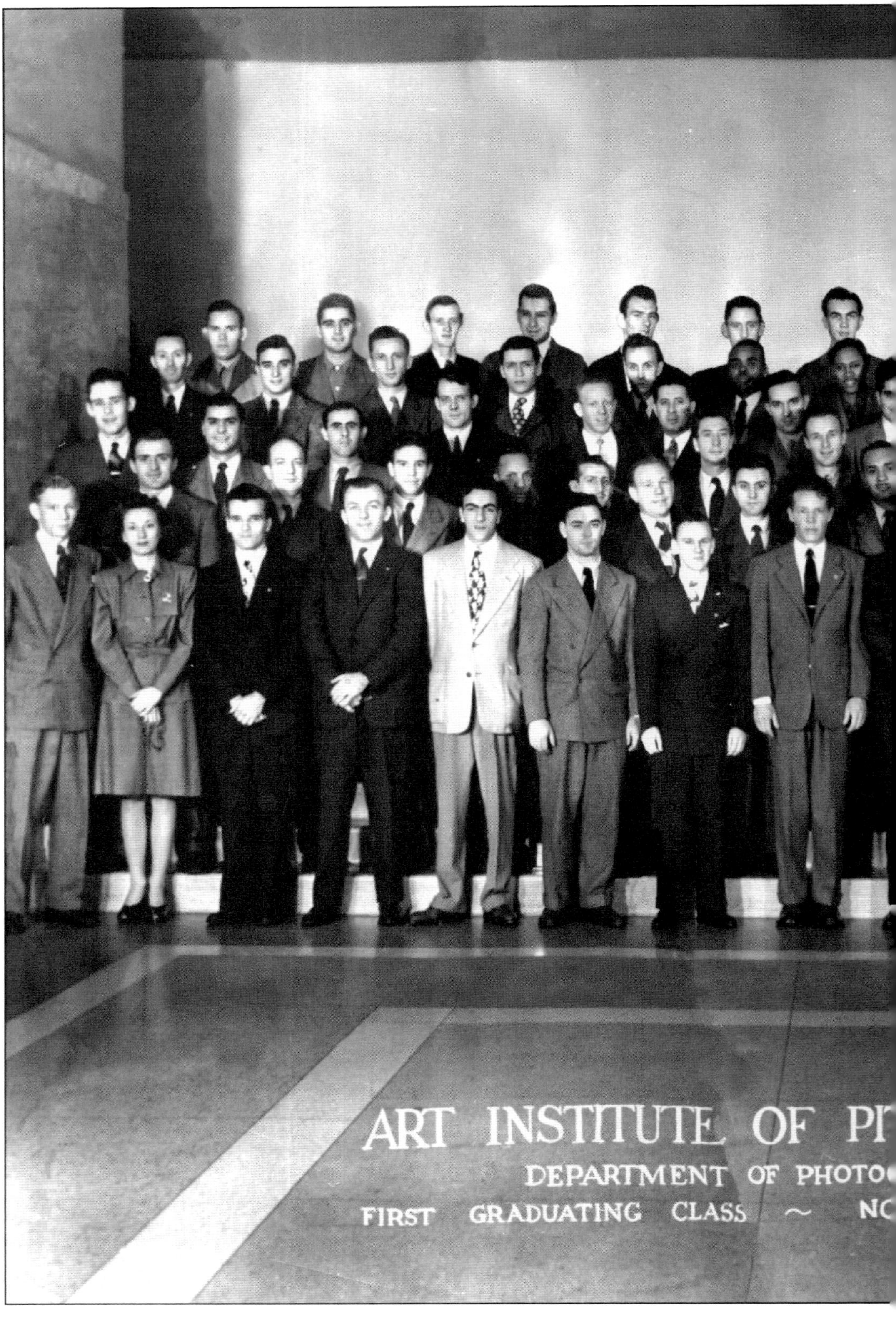
ART INSTITUTE OF PI
DEPARTMENT OF PHOTO
FIRST GRADUATING CLASS ~ NO

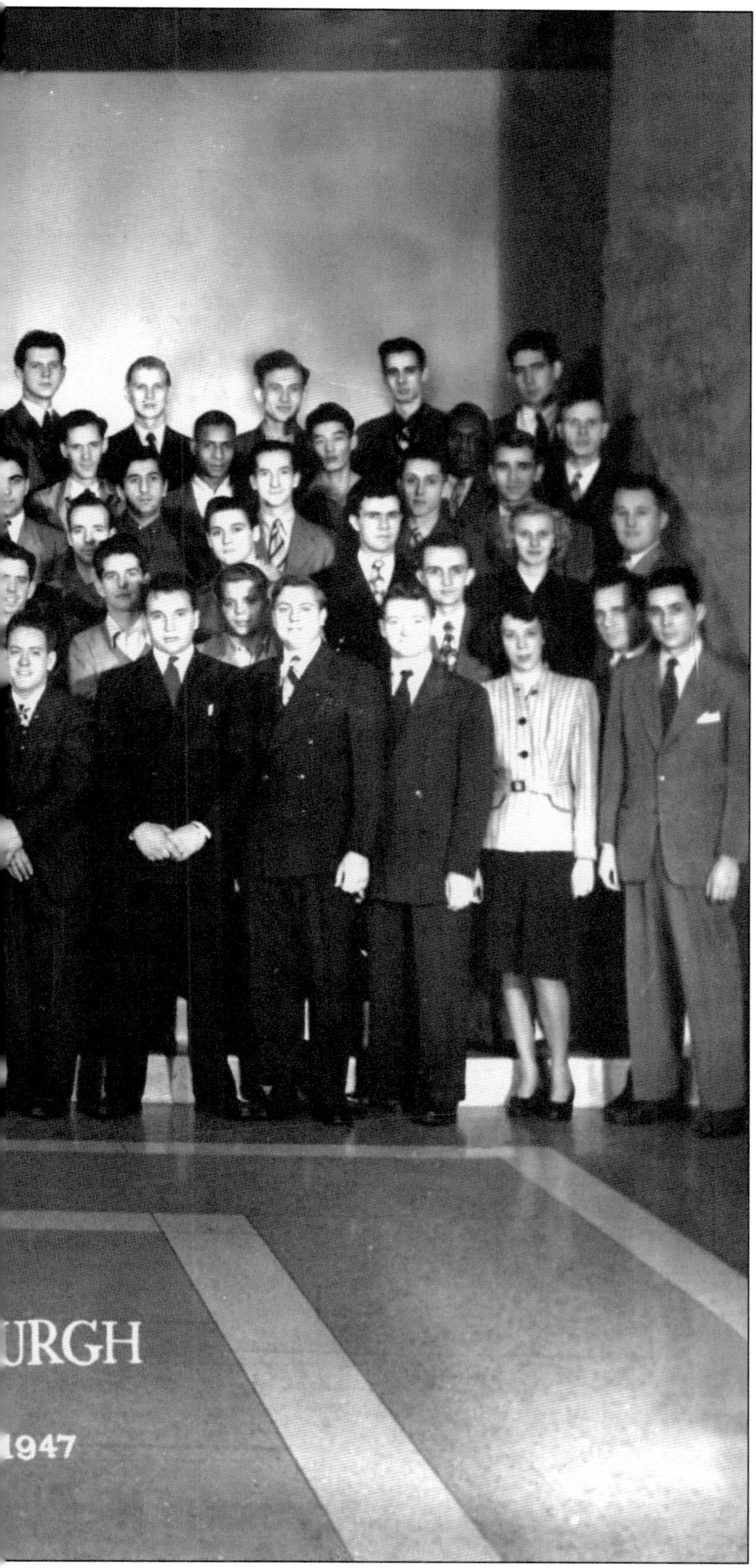

A photography course made its first appearance in the years following World War II. A school catalog describes the nine-month course to "prepare beginners for successful careers in studios, advertising agencies, newspapers, magazines, or their own businesses." Students were quickly immersed in the techniques required to set up the perfect shot and the delicate process of developing those shots. In 1947, the school's first class in photography graduated.

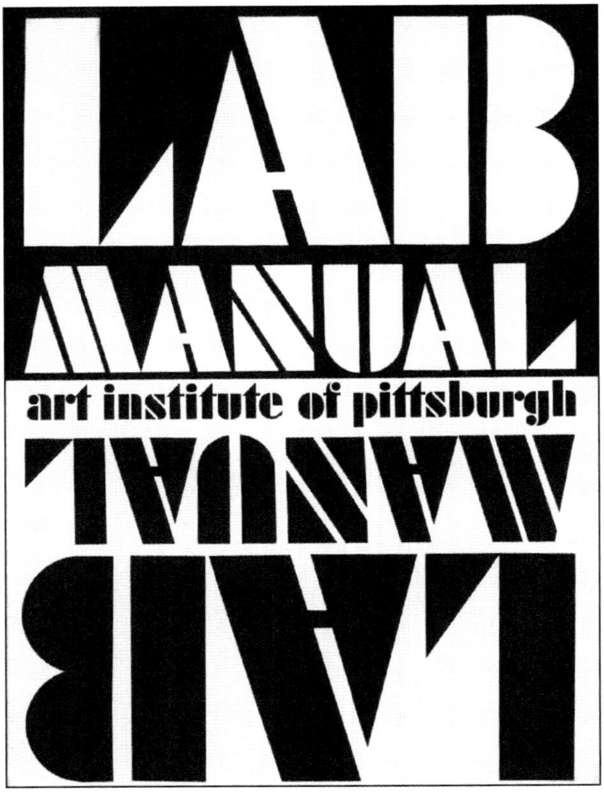

Despite its initial popularity, the photography program was discontinued in the 1950s. Photography returned to the school in 1972 as a nine-month certificate program. It later grew into a two-year associate's degree program. Barry Lavery wrote the lab manual in the late 1970s to help students get the best results from the darkrooms and film-processing equipment.

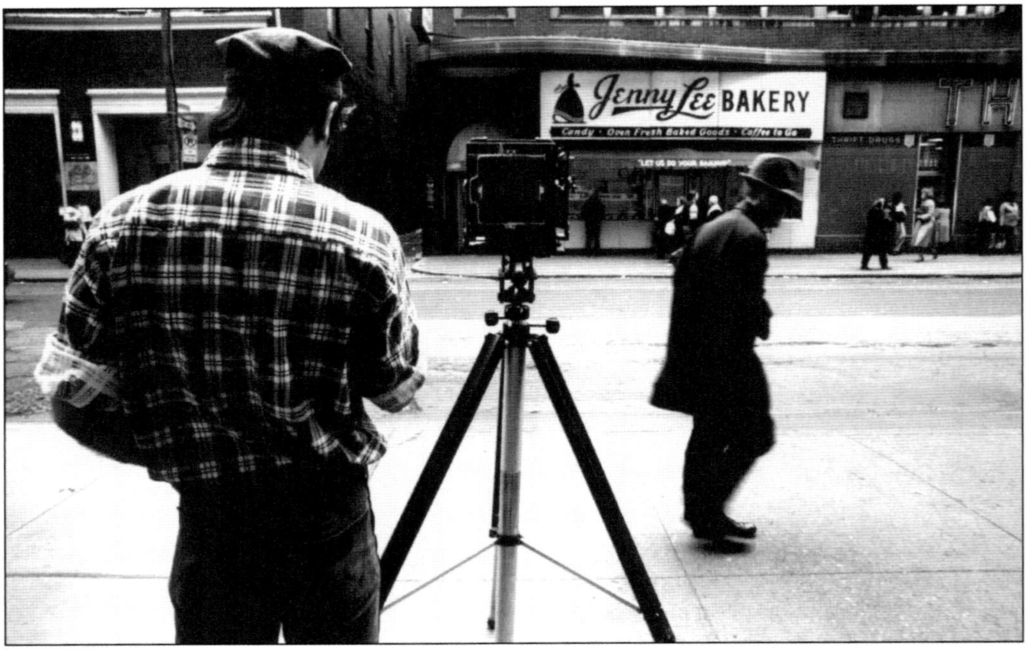

Photography is now offered as both a two-year associate's and a four-year bachelor's program. Students learn both the traditional photographic processes as well as the exciting new world of digital photography. Tripods and cameras can often be found on the streets of downtown, as students practice their art.

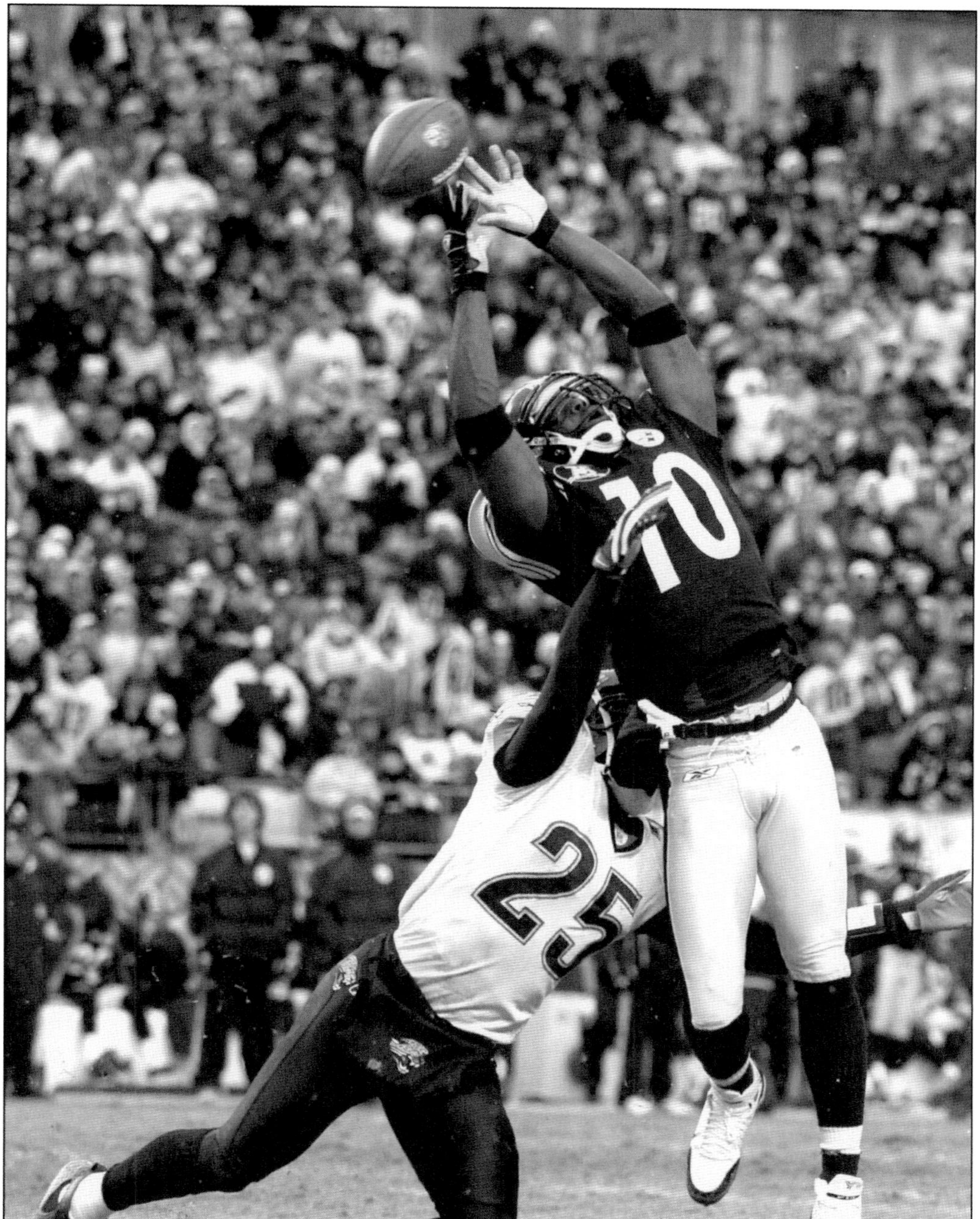

Many photography students do freelance work outside of school, polishing their skills in the industry. Students often sell their photographs, take photographs for news agencies, and do portrait and wedding photography for clients. A small group of lucky photography students work each year with the Pittsburgh Steelers. The team of photographers visit home games and photograph the fans in the stands and tailgating, which are then posted online for purchase. Students have at times been permitted onto the sidelines for special shots of the players. Jared Wickerham took this great shot of 2009 Super Bowl MVP Santonio Holmes. (Photograph by Jared Wickerham.)

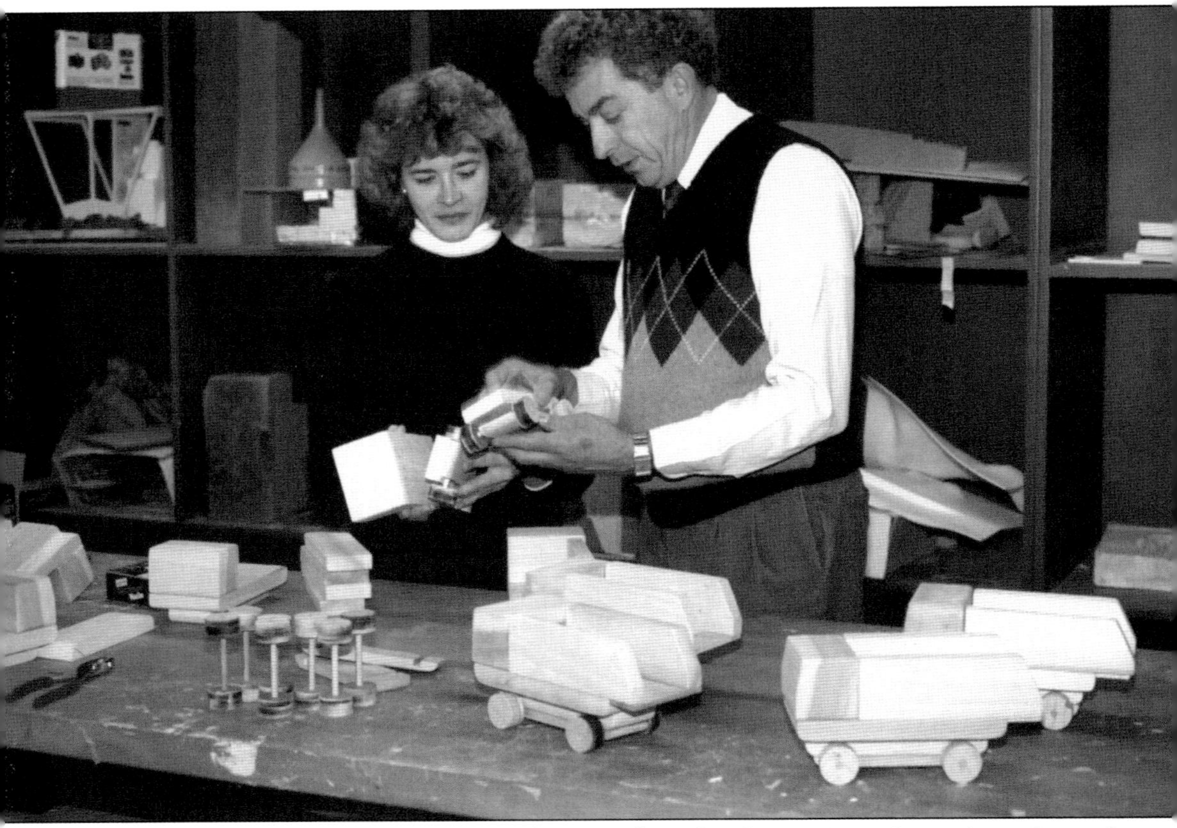

The industrial design program has been at the school at various times since the early years. In the 1940s, the focus was on store displays. Since the 1980s, the department offers students training in all aspects of design in three dimensions. As described in the 1988–1989 catalog, "Industrial Design Technology is designing toys, creating prehistoric monsters or creatures from outer space for television and motion pictures, designing new products, displays, and exhibits for trade shows." Industrial design students are often called upon to create games, toys, and life-size models for businesses and charities all over the city. Allan Agamedi and Janice Kuzminsky put the finishing touches on toys created for the Salvation Army's Angel Tree Christmas program in 1988.

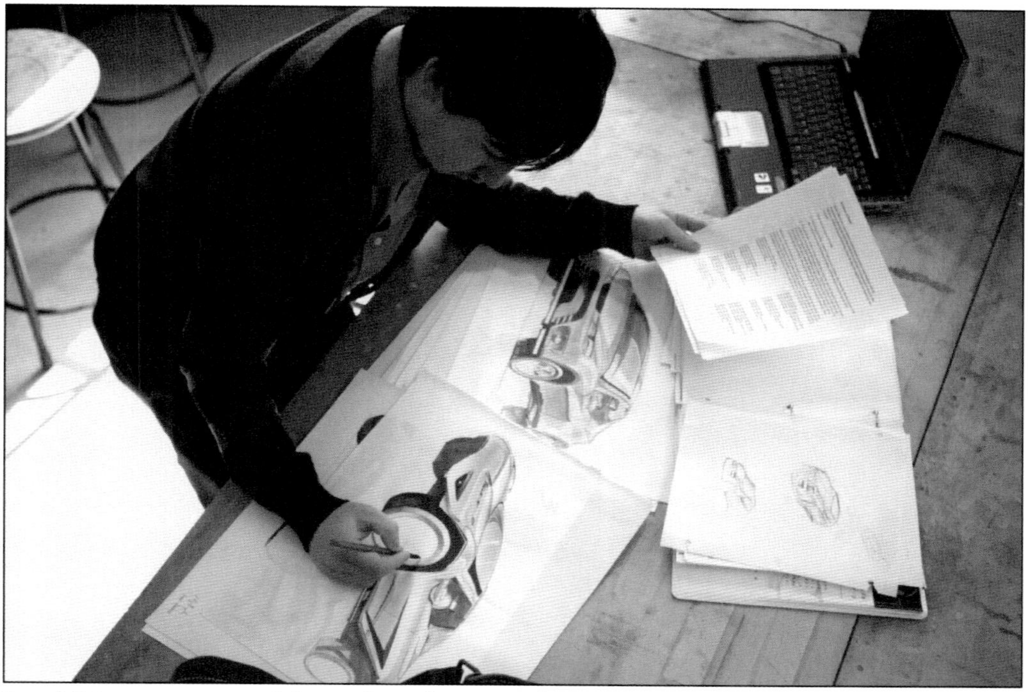

In addition to toys, models, and products, students in the industrial design program can also study automotive design. This recent graduate works on his design for a new car.

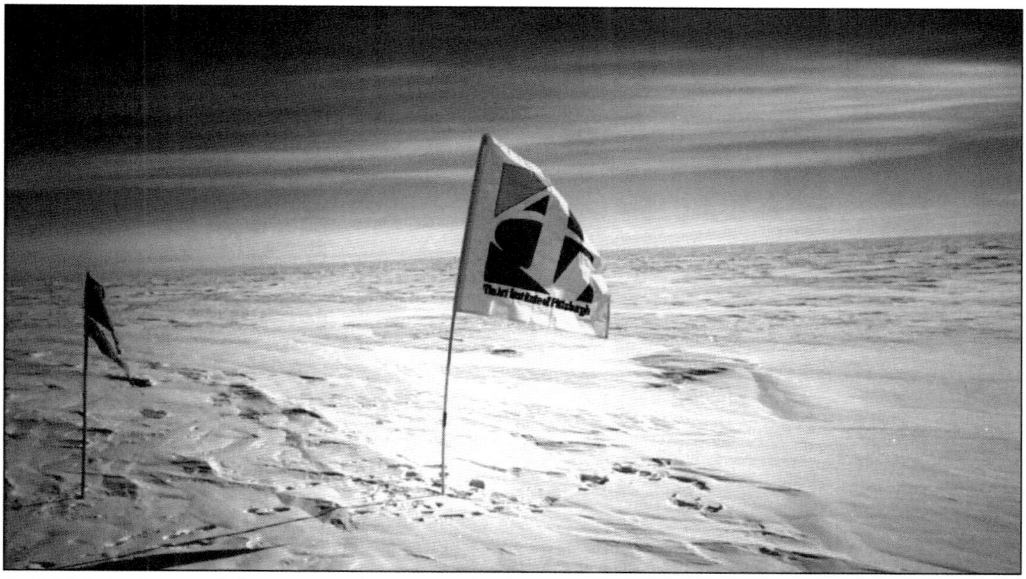

In 2000, industrial design students worked with the Center for Astrophysical Research in Antarctica to create the Ice Prowler, a bicycle designed and built for extreme weather conditions. Stephen Butler, now associate dean of academic affairs, traveled to the desolate location so that scientists could test the cycle. While there, he left this flag in the tundra.

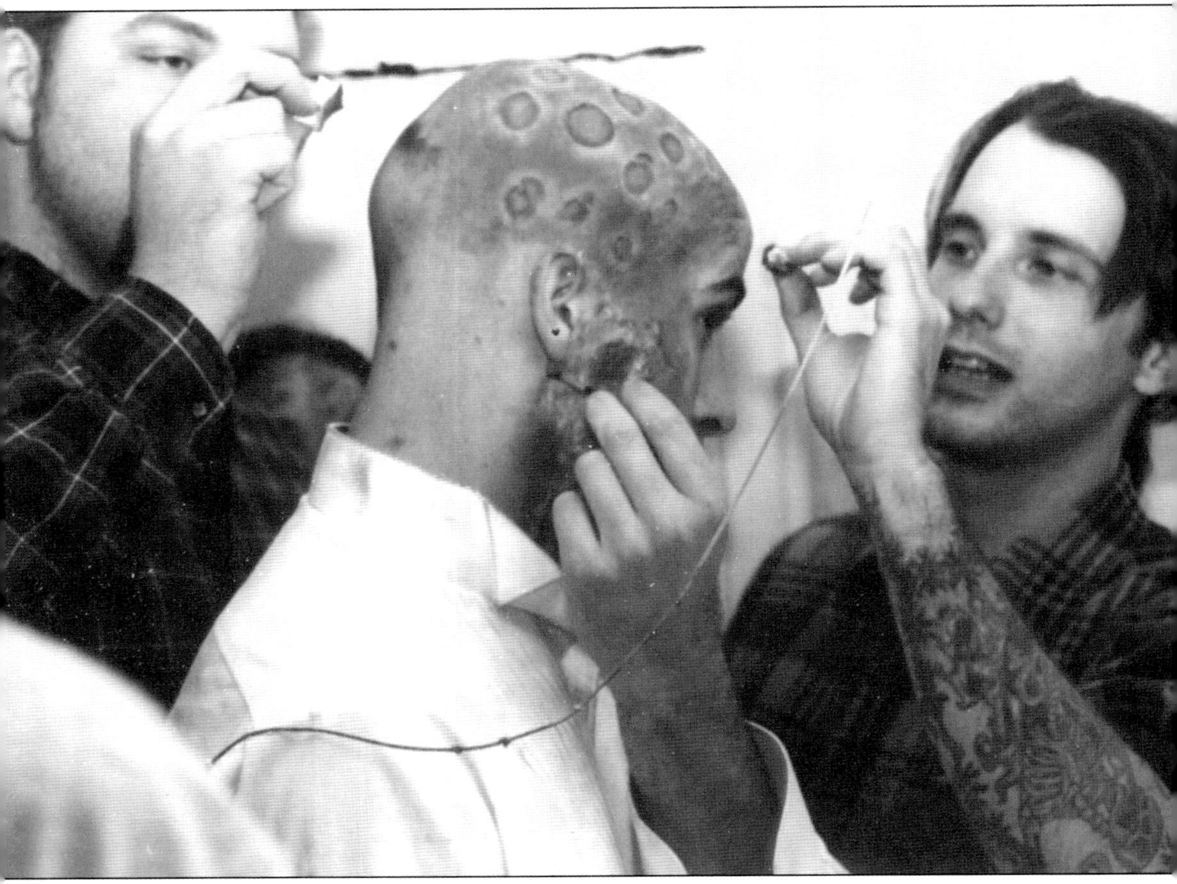

Every day is Halloween when students are mastering special effects. The program began as part of the industrial design department and has grown into a specialized program, entertainment design. Students learn the techniques and theories needed to make the impossible become possible by utilizing makeup, appliances, and animatronic systems; it is not uncommon to ride the elevator with a possessed doll, to sit at a table in the library with Sweeney Todd, or to pass a zombie in the hall. Visiting the eighth-floor industrial design shop can be a terrifying experience for the faint of heart. In this photograph, students use airbrushing and traditional sponge applications to give their fellow student a makeover.

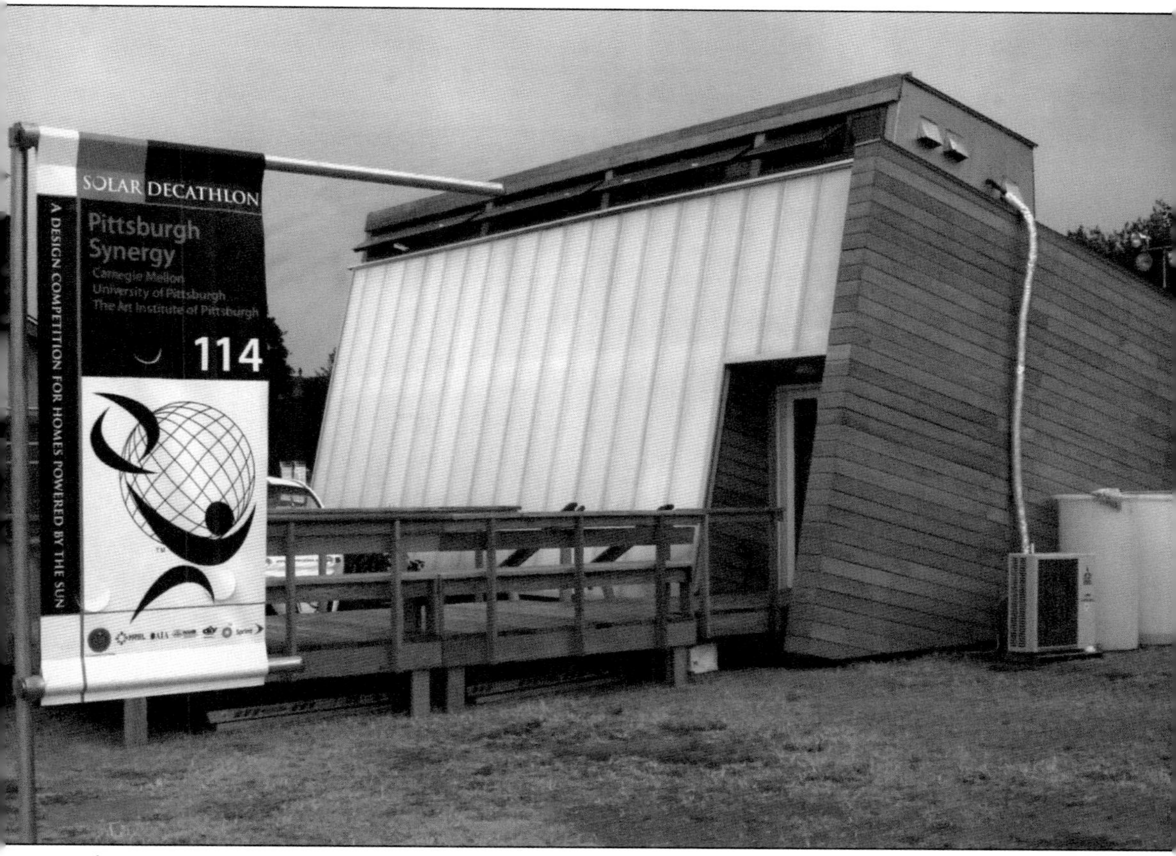

Students and faculty from different programs often work together on special projects. Interior design and industrial design students worked together with students from Carnegie Mellon University's School of Architecture to compete in the 2007 Solar Decathlon in Washington, D.C., sponsored by the U.S. Department of Energy, Office of Energy Efficiency and Renewable Energy. The national competition comprised of 20 teams asked students to create an attractive, livable home powered only by the sun. The team was led by William Farrell, industrial design faculty, with Lori Claus and Lisa Whitney, interior design faculty. Student participants included Lauren Smith, Heather Fuller, Brian Redmond, Amber King, LaCie Moore, Garrick Tai-Lee, Jack Peterson, Dan Oman, Lee Perry, and Kyle Mickiewicz.

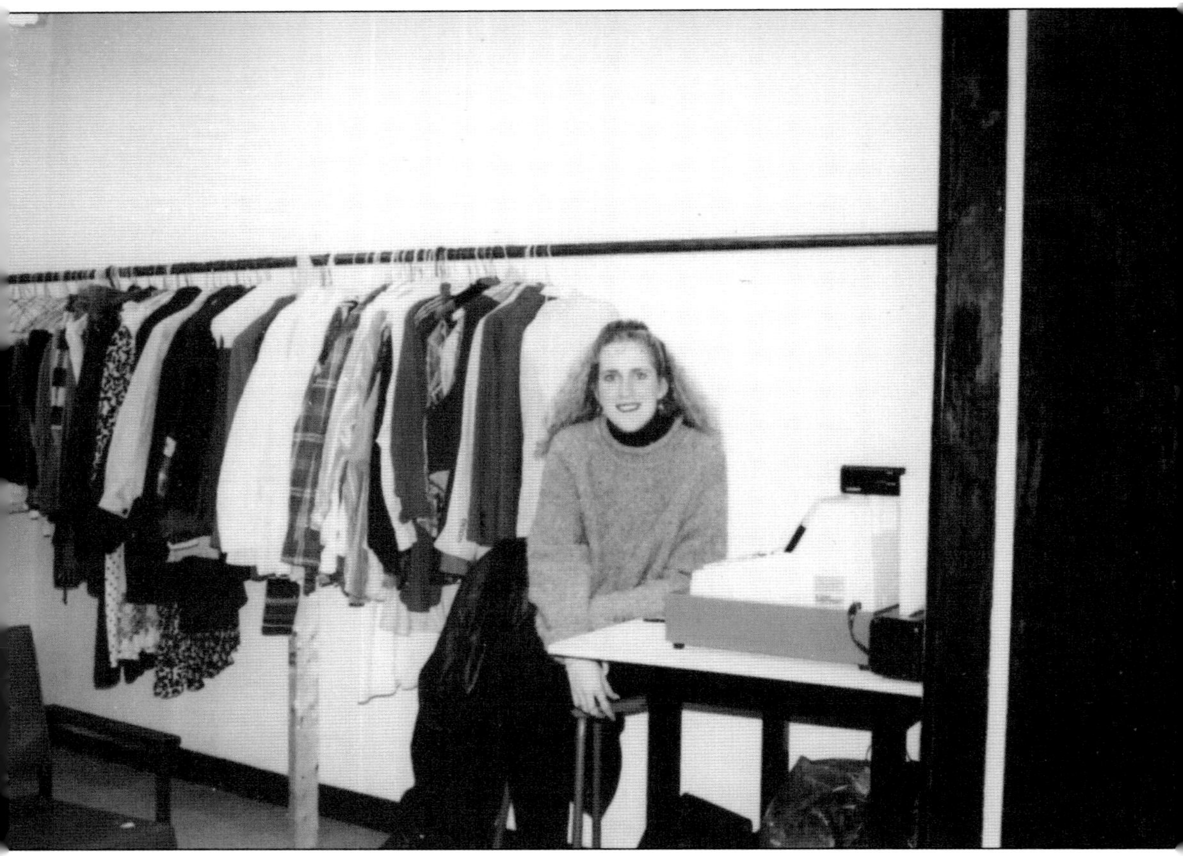

In addition to design, students have also studied the business side of the fashion industry. Fashion merchandising started in the fall quarter of 1982 and prepared students for busy careers in retail as buyers, visual merchandisers, and fashion coordinators. Students conducted fashion shows, prepared displays, and throughout the 1990s, operated Neat and Cheap, a small resale shop on the ninth floor of the Penn Avenue building. Staff and faculty donated items to the store, which fashion merchandising students then inventoried, priced, and sold to their peers. In 2006, the school started the fashion and retail management bachelor's program, which focuses on product lifecycles, trending, buying, retail planning, and marketing. (Courtesy of Alberta Certo.)

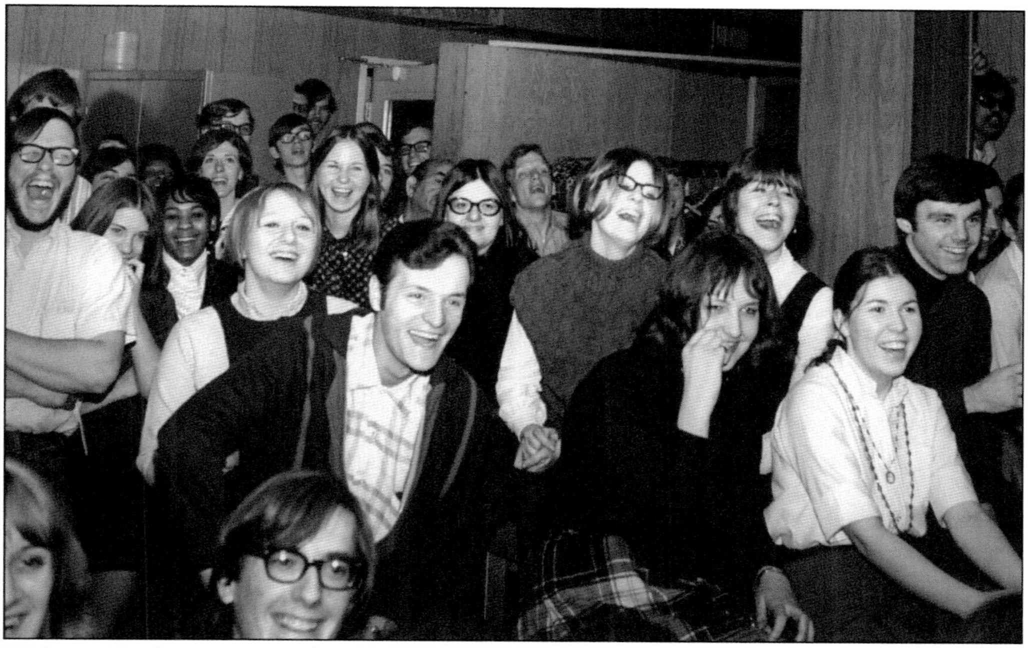

With rapid advances in technology came new programs. Many of the new programs had their origin in earlier experiments. The animation program, now called media arts and animation, was first formally offered as a degree program in 1996, but as early as 1969, Fran Ford produced the school's first animated film. From this photograph, it is clear that the students enjoyed the results.

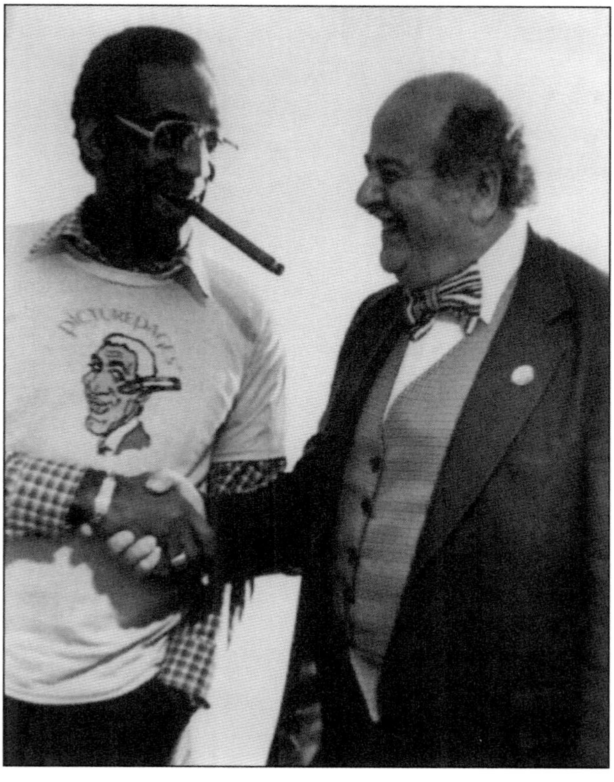

Students were learning the quick-draw exaggerated style often used in animation long before animation was offered as a program. John Johns, president from 1970 to 1982, was known as one of the country's best caricature artists and worked for a wide variety of clients. In the early 1970s, he did caricatures for *TV Graphic*, including one of Bill Cosby.

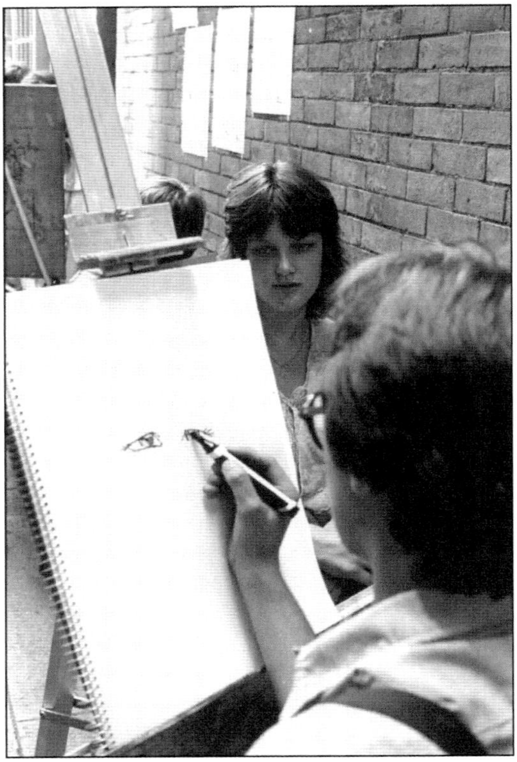

John Johns taught his students a 10-step method for caricature. Once they mastered the technique, students could earn money by drawing caricatures at school events and all over the city. This was a part-time job for many students, and the money helped them pay their school expenses.

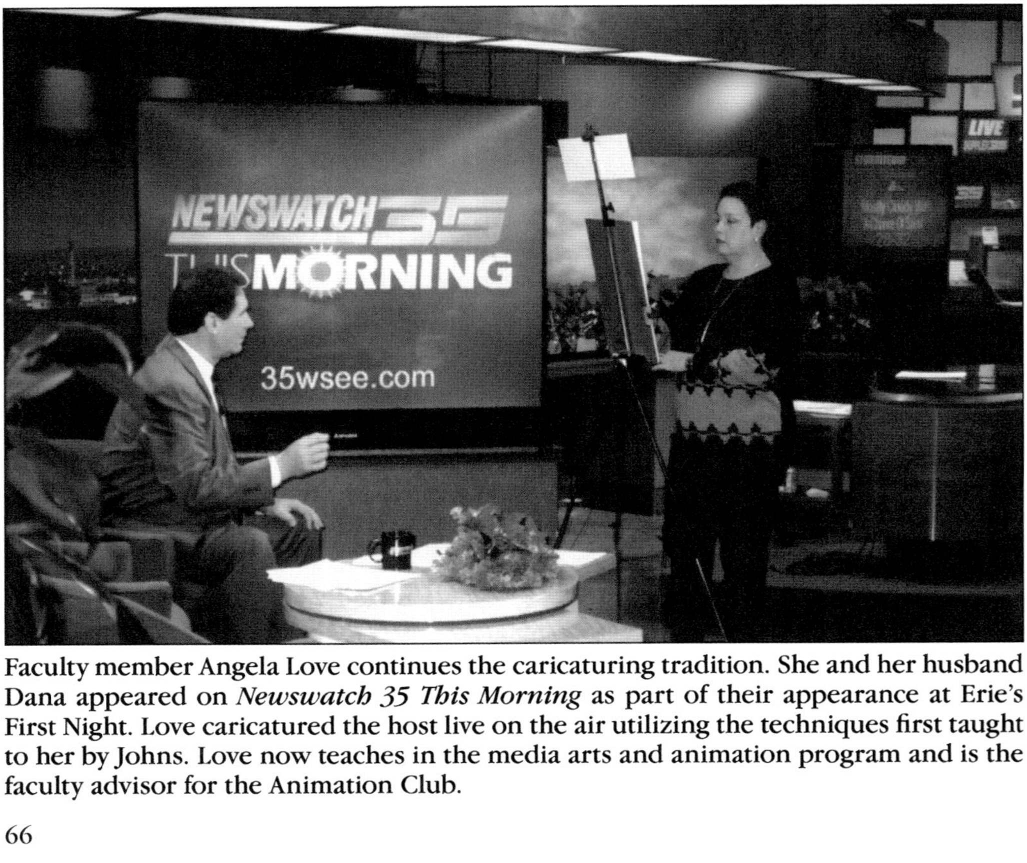

Faculty member Angela Love continues the caricaturing tradition. She and her husband Dana appeared on *Newswatch 35 This Morning* as part of their appearance at Erie's First Night. Love caricatured the host live on the air utilizing the techniques first taught to her by Johns. Love now teaches in the media arts and animation program and is the faculty advisor for the Animation Club.

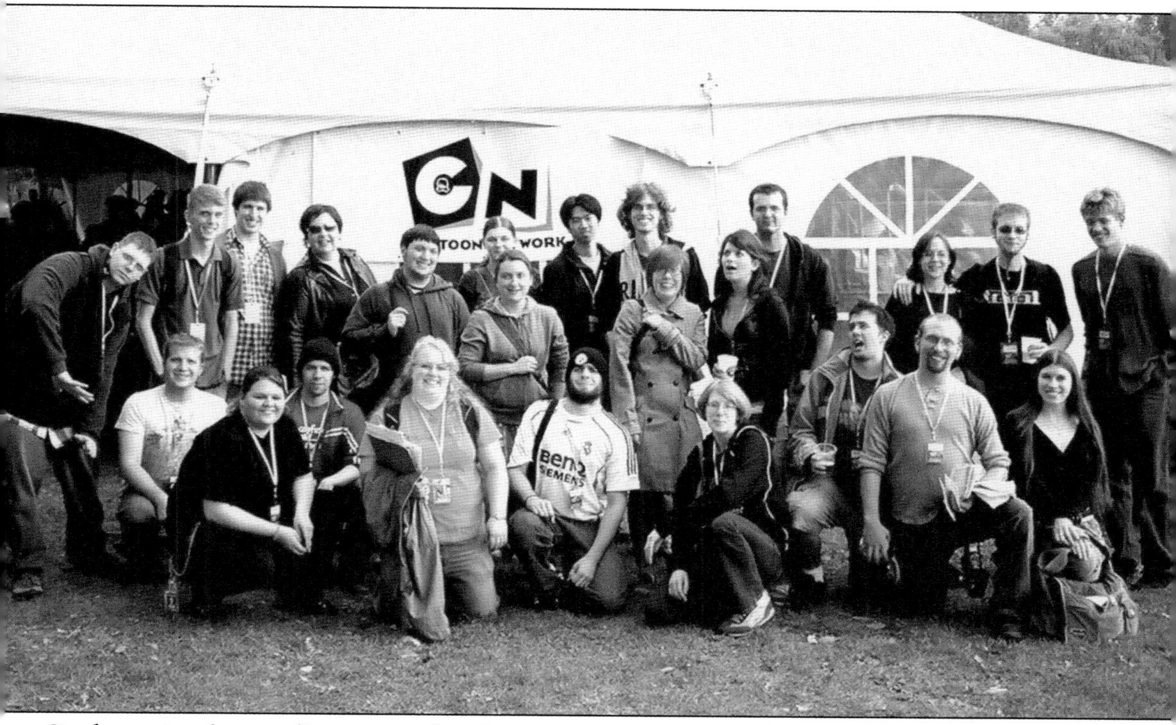

Students in the media arts and animation program spend long hours developing characters, storyboards, and backgrounds. Those working with two-dimensional animations must illustrate the numerous cells that make up a single second of a film, while students working in three-dimensional formats manipulate the computer programs that bring their visions to life. Every year students get the chance to meet their peers at the annual picnic, sponsored by the Cartoon Network in Ottawa, Canada. A feature of the event is the pumpkin carving competition. As Angela Love writes, "Since Ottawa's an International animation festival, many cultures are mystified and horrified by the vegetable carnage." This group from 2007 thought that it had the competition won, only to lose to another team.

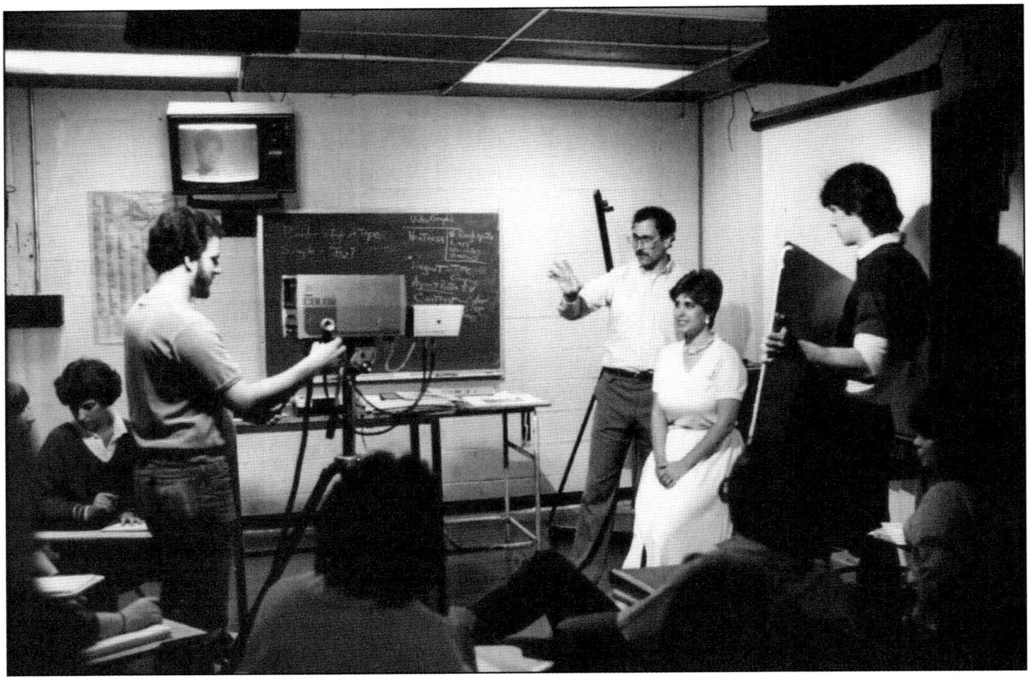

Before video was offered as a degree program, the photography program began teaching and exposing students to the requirements of this technology. Leon Salvayon instructs students on lighting techniques using this color video camera.

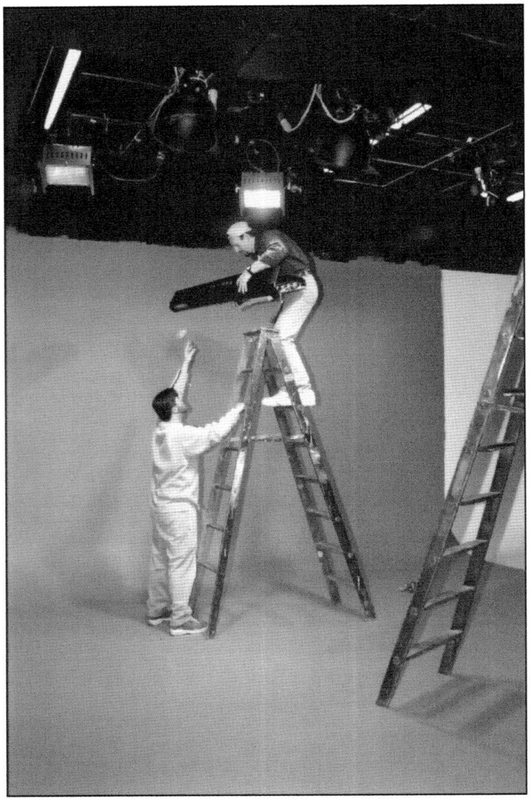

Music and video production was offered as a degree program in the late 1980s. Since then, it has evolved and grown into the digital filmmaking and video production program and the visual effects and motion graphics program. Students are trained on the technical and theoretical aspects of film and special effects graphics.

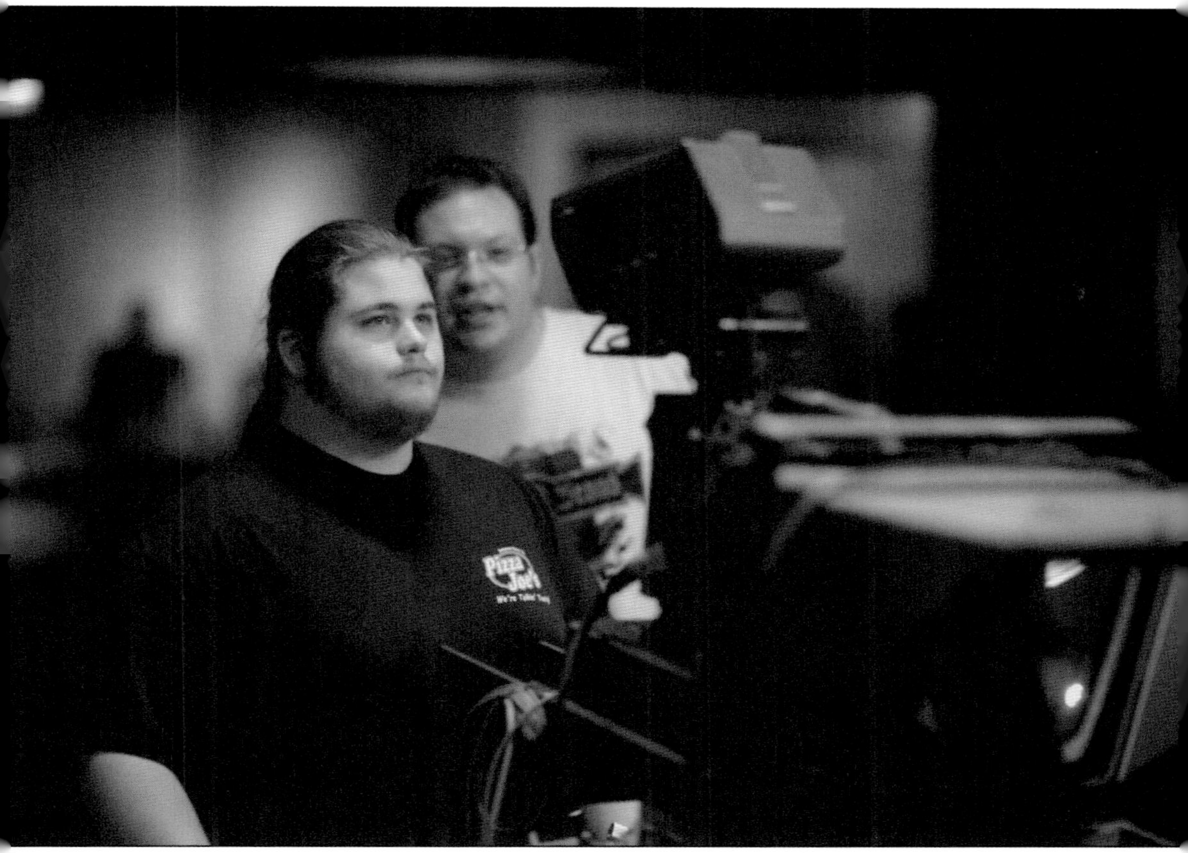

Students Jordan Neff (left) and John Christopoulos use state-of-the-art cameras, high-definition studios, and computer editing software to immerse themselves in the production environment. The video center, known as the "cage cave," is available for students to check out equipment for use on location. Video students can often be found in the halls of the building and on the streets of the city shooting scenes for independent and school projects.

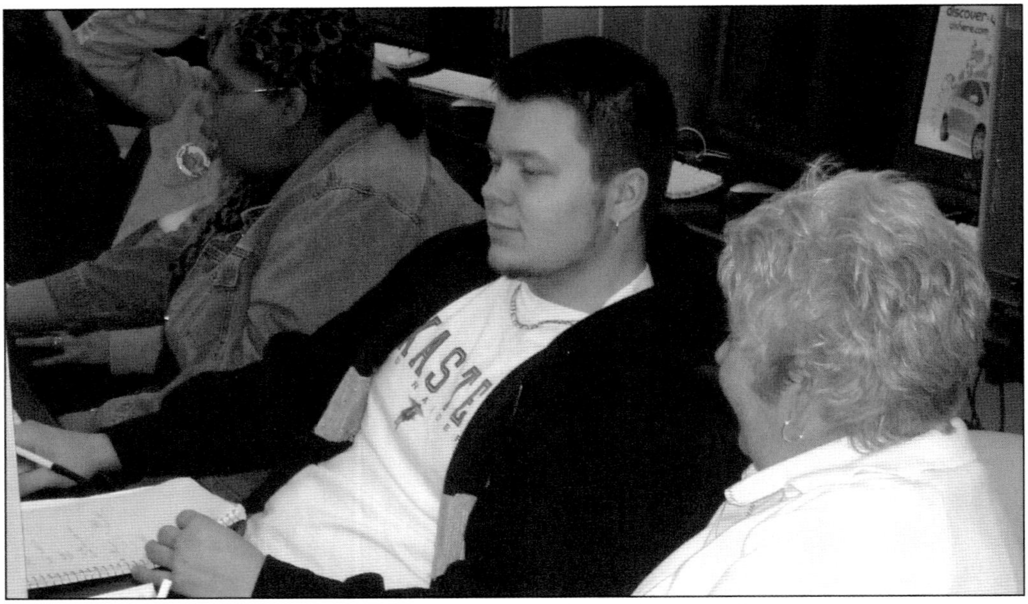

Web site administration, Web design, and multimedia have been degree programs, with various names, since 1997. The program focuses on creating Web sites and the applications that enliven the digital world. In 2006, the department worked with the Allegheny Country Library Association to create new Web sites for district libraries. Conceived as a modern version of the barn raising, faculty member David Barton formed a team of students that conducted interviews, site visits, and then built the Web site. Pictured here is student Zack Taylor with Nicole Eleby and Jo Ellen Kenney.

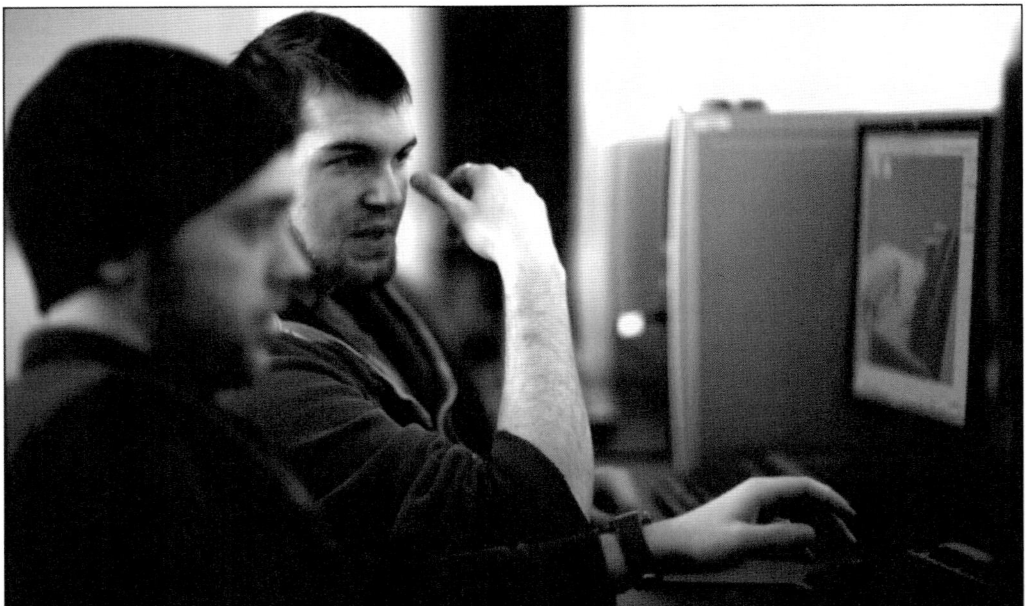

Game art and design students Ryan Smith and Robert Kreps use Photoshop and 3ds Max to render a game background. Game art and design students rely on technical expertise to create realistic scenes, characters, and environments where impossible things can happen. The school has offered the program since 2002.

Students in the marketing-oriented advertising program learn both business and creative arts skills that will take them into business careers. This advertising campaign, created for their client, 2007 culinary graduate Craig Jones, was a project conceived by students who worked together from Jackie Felix Fisher's marketing course and Shawn O'Mara's design studio course. Jones developed his own brand of espresso-flavored barbecue sauce and drew on the creative strengths of these students for research, branding, and packaging ideas to bring his product to market. Craig Jones landed his first career position after graduation at the Wolfgang Puck Grille in Detroit.

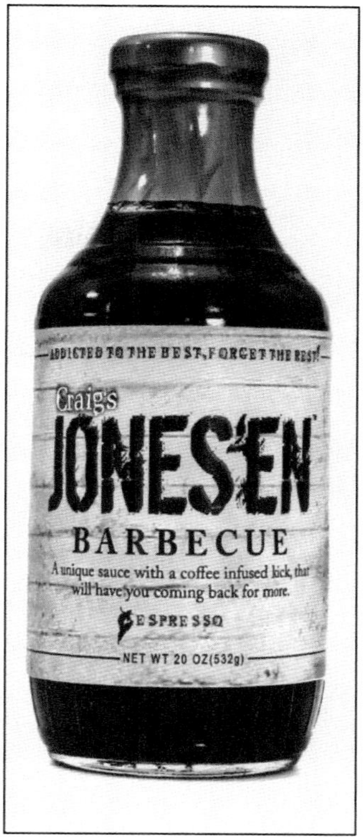

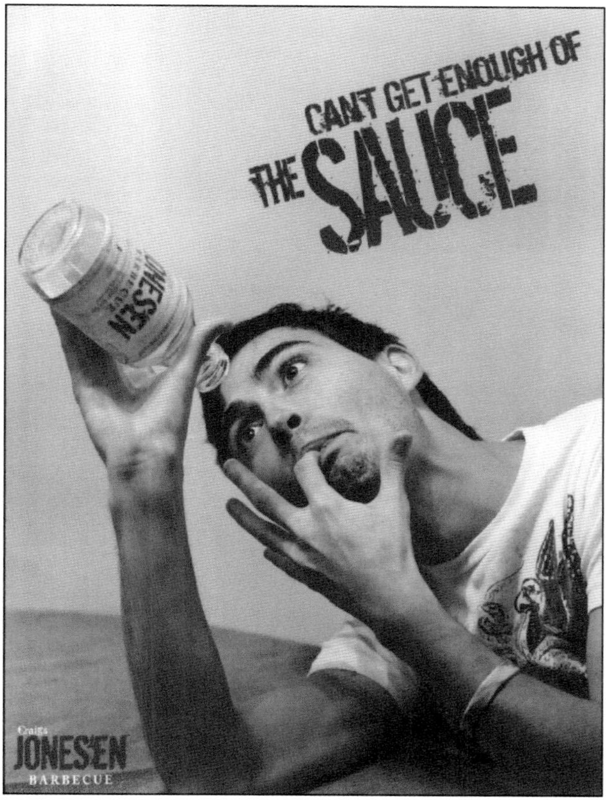

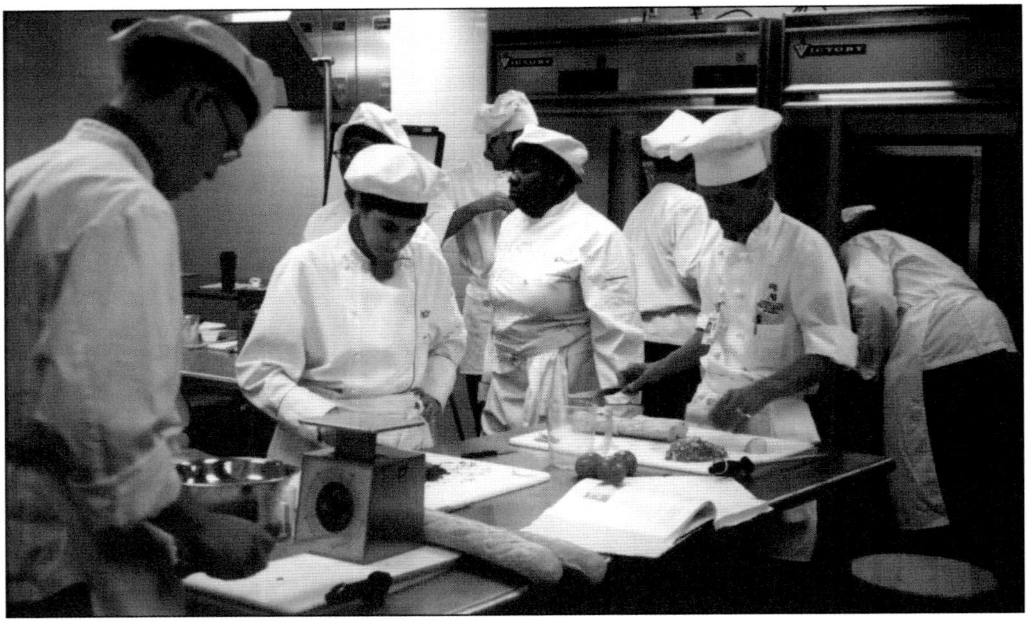

During the fall quarter of 2002, the Art Institute of Pittsburgh launched the culinary program. The school converted storage space on the ninth floor of the present building into three teaching kitchens. The kitchens include professional appliances, stainless steel work tables, and the latest equipment, where students are trained as chefs and hotel and restaurant managers.

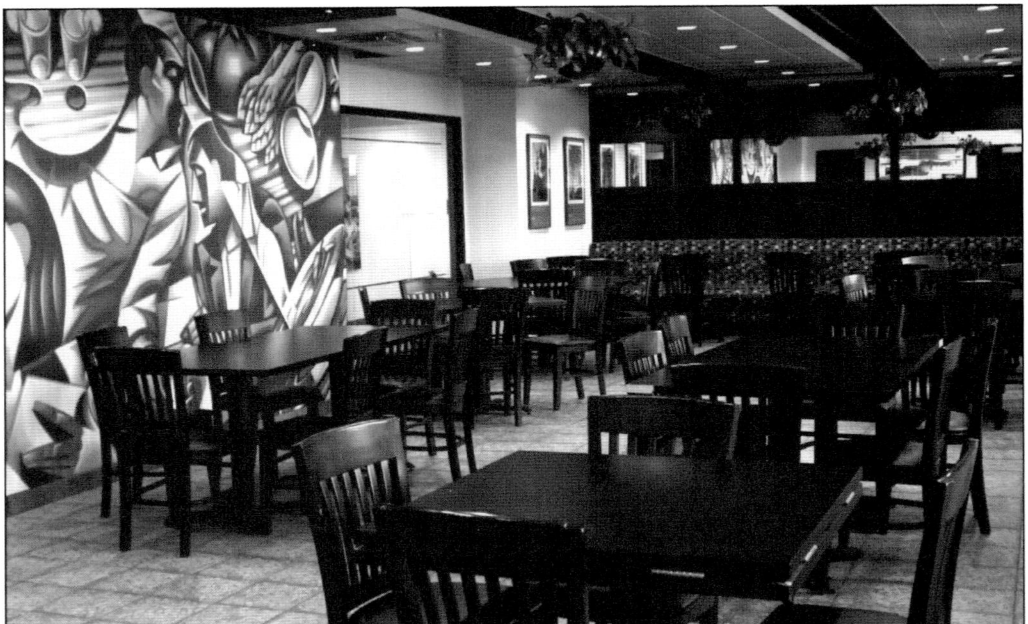

A popular feature of the ninth floor is the program's 50-seat teaching restaurant, Taste of Art. Students in the a la carte course rotate through the many positions, both serving and cooking, making this a popular lunchtime restaurant. Open to the public, the eclectic menu features European culinary classics as well as Asian-inspired flavors. (Photograph by Abby Parker.)

Three

An Environment of Creativity

The Art Institute of Pittsburgh has had eight homes during its history. In the first 25 years, the school called five different downtown buildings home. The move in 1946 to 635 Smithfield Street proved to be its longest lasting. The school did not move again until 1971, when continued growth created the need for a move to the new facility on Penn Avenue. In 2000, rapid changes in technology required the Art Institute of Pittsburgh to make significant upgrades and hence the move to the present Boulevard of the Allies building.

But it is not enough just to mention the buildings that have housed the Art Institute of Pittsburgh. The city itself has served as a vibrant, ever-changing classroom for the students. The students have lived, worked, and visited every neighborhood and pocket of Pittsburgh. The city's museums, buildings, bridges, and sports teams have provided a rich assortment of artistic subjects. Students have been involved in numerous projects and events that keep the city alive. The entire city of Pittsburgh has served as the students' campus and canvas.

For some students of the Art Institute of Pittsburgh, the physical locations of the school are irrelevant. In 2000, new technology allowed the school to bring education to people all over the world as the Art Institute of Pittsburgh–Online Division was launched. The school has transcended mere bricks and mortar and now reaches students internationally. In this chapter are photographs inside and outside classrooms, in and around the city of Pittsburgh—the places where creativity has been nurtured.

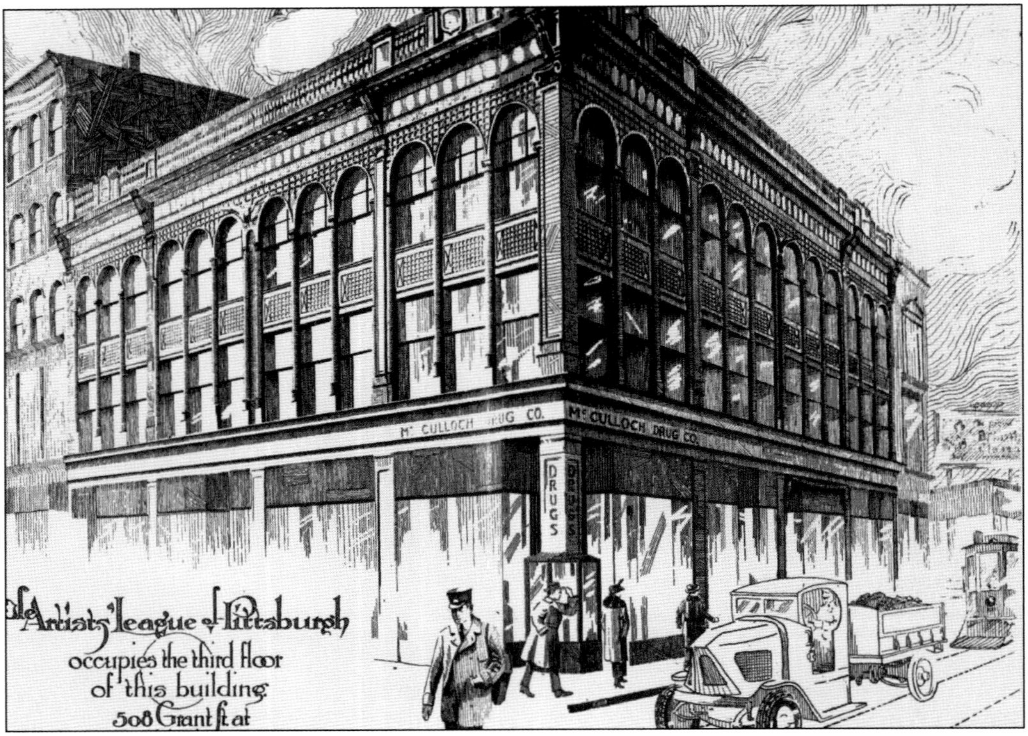

The Art Institute of Pittsburgh started in one room in the Fulton Building on Sixth Street in downtown Pittsburgh, now home to the Renaissance Pittsburgh Hotel. The 500-square-foot room included a classroom, locker room, art store, dressing room, and office. As the school grew, so did its space requirements, and the Artists League of Pittsburgh moved to the corner of Grant Street and Fifth Avenue, across from the courthouse. The pen rendering (above) made by student Anthony Aiello in 1923 depicts that building, which no longer exists. Later the school moved to the Stanwix Shops Building on Stanwix Street across the street from Horne's Department Store. The pen drawing (below) of the Stanwix Shops Building was done by student Charles McCurday in the 1930s.

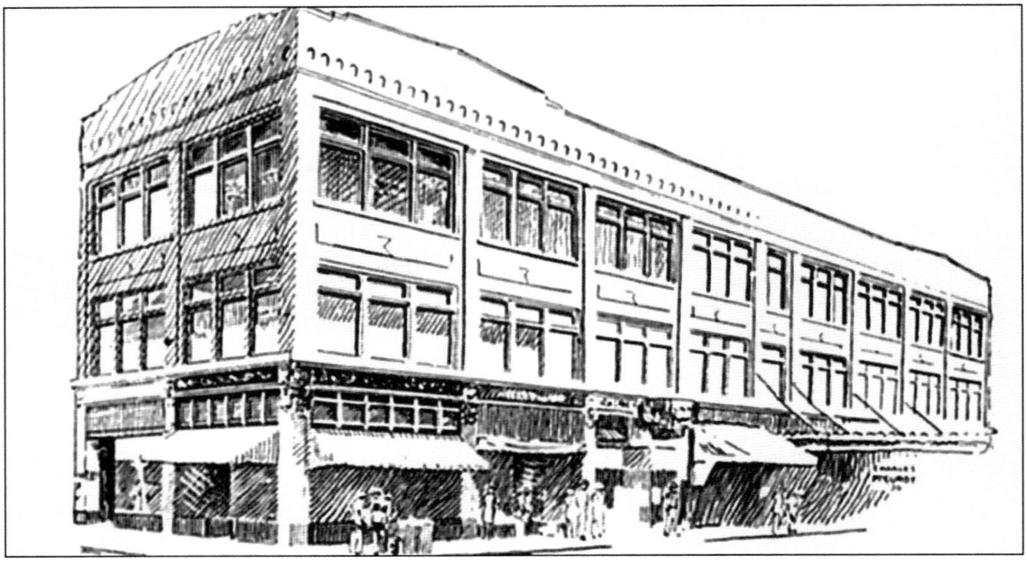

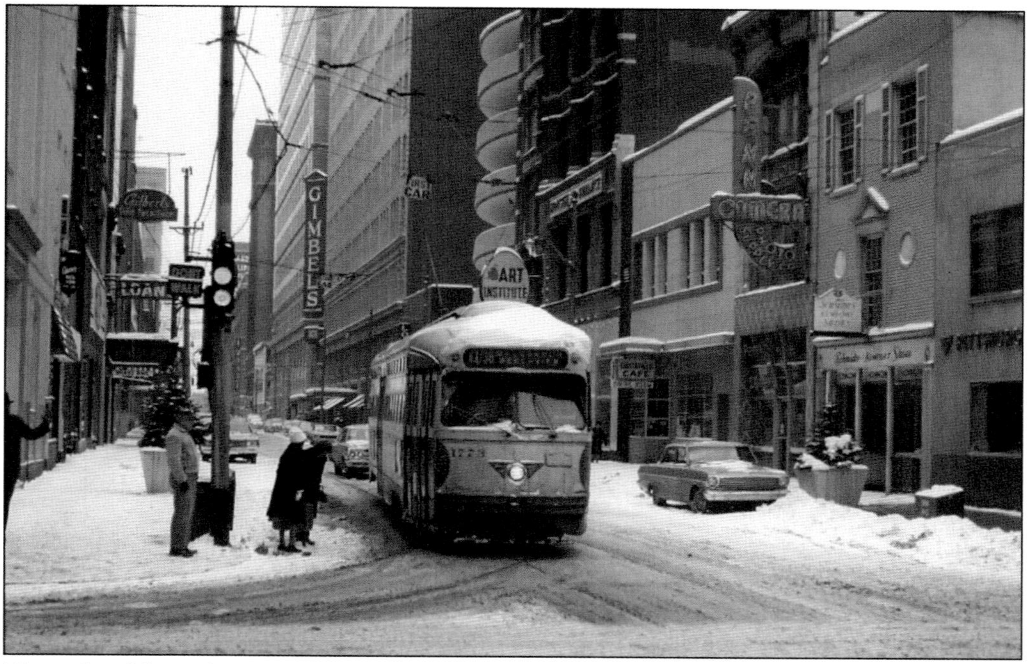

The school has always remained in downtown Pittsburgh. In 1946, the school moved to the building known as 635–637 Smithfield Street. This location between Gimbel's department store and Seventh Avenue was easily accessible by train, bus, and the mass transit of the day, streetcars. (Courtesy of Andrew Sujdak.)

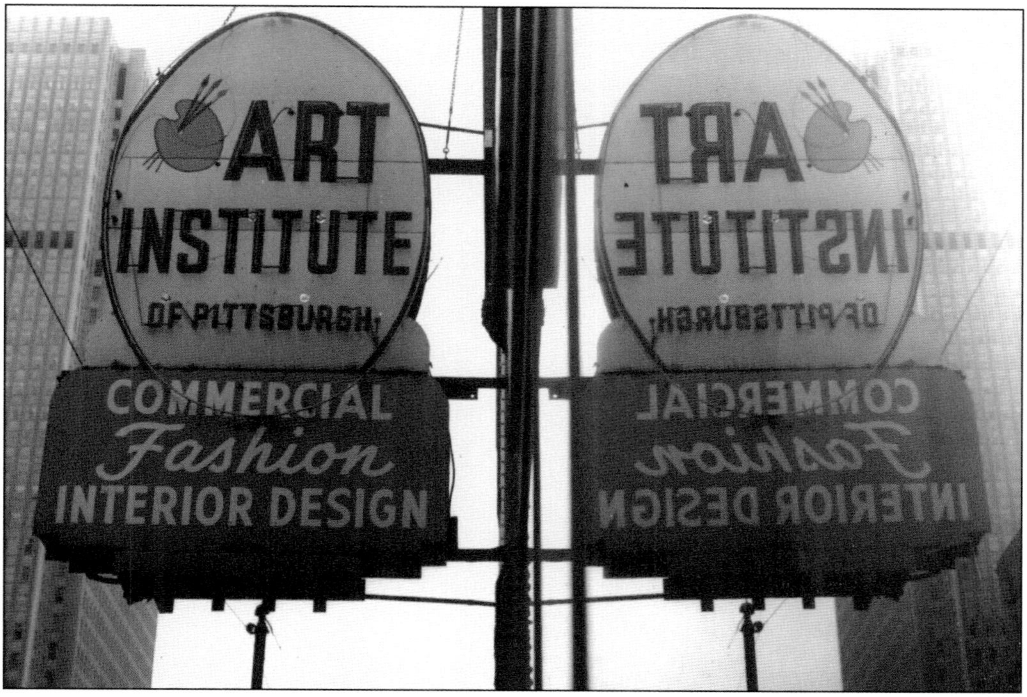

This sign and its reflection could be seen the length of Smithfield Street. It proudly advertised the school's three main programs: commercial art, fashion, and interior design.

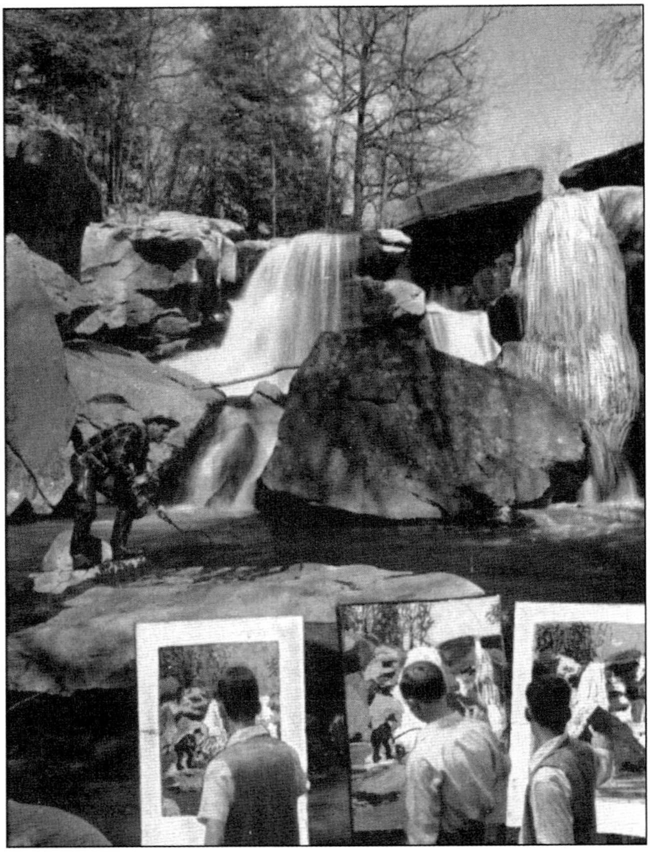

In the 1950s, Willis and Elizabeth Shook purchased Muddy Creek Falls and adjacent land near Portersville in Lawrence County, where they built their home. They invited students, instructors, alumni, and friends to use the grounds for recreation and artistic inspiration. Visitors could hike the grounds and bring their sketch pads, pencils, oil boxes, watercolors, and cameras to capture the scenic views. Art Institute students are shown here, sketching at the bottom of the waterfalls and enjoying a picnic on the terrace.

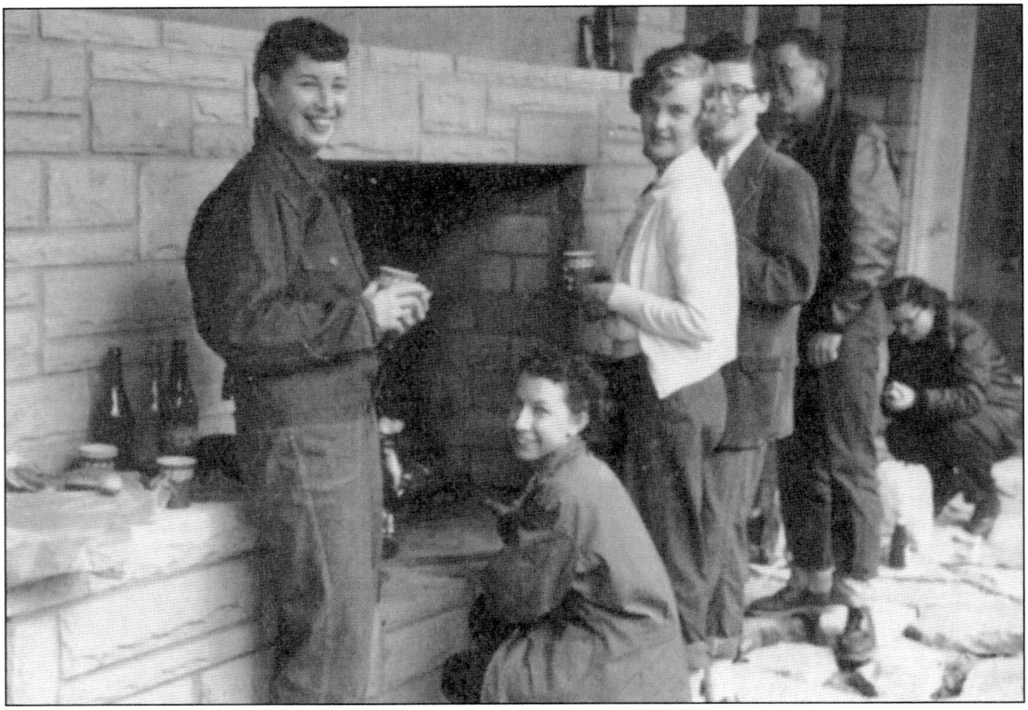

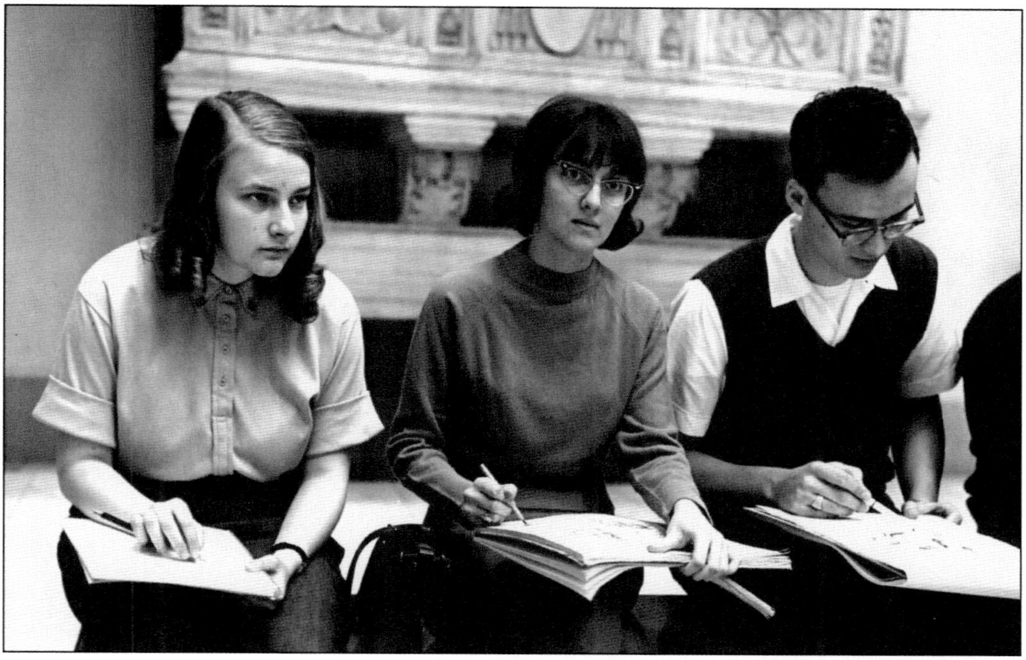

Willis Shook encouraged students to visit the many resources offered by the city, including Buhl Planetarium, the Carnegie Museum of Art, and the Pittsburgh Zoo. As Shook wrote in the 1940s, in *Your Home in Pittsburgh,* "Pittsburgh, as one expects of a city of three-quarters of a million people, offers many attractions in the way of parks, museums, and other recreational facilities." Students took his advice, visiting the Carnegie Museum of Art during class and on their own time to sketch the museum's collection. The Hall of Architecture, with its collection of over 140 plaster casts of architectural details and facades, was a popular location for students practicing their drawing skills. In the photograph above, students Caroline Mahoy, Janice Spewock, and Richard Shaulis concentrate on copying facade details. At right, students experiment with capturing the beautiful drapery of these stone figures.

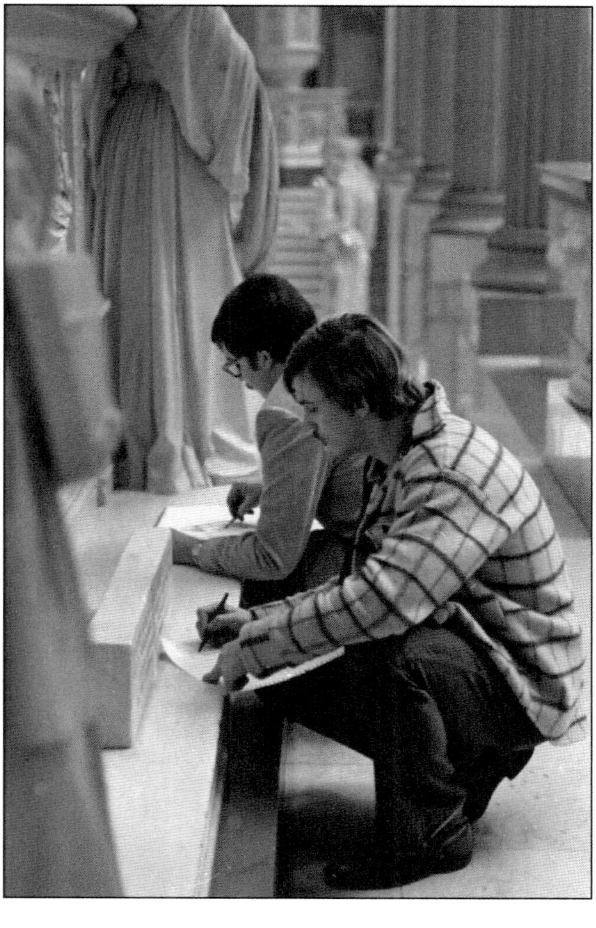

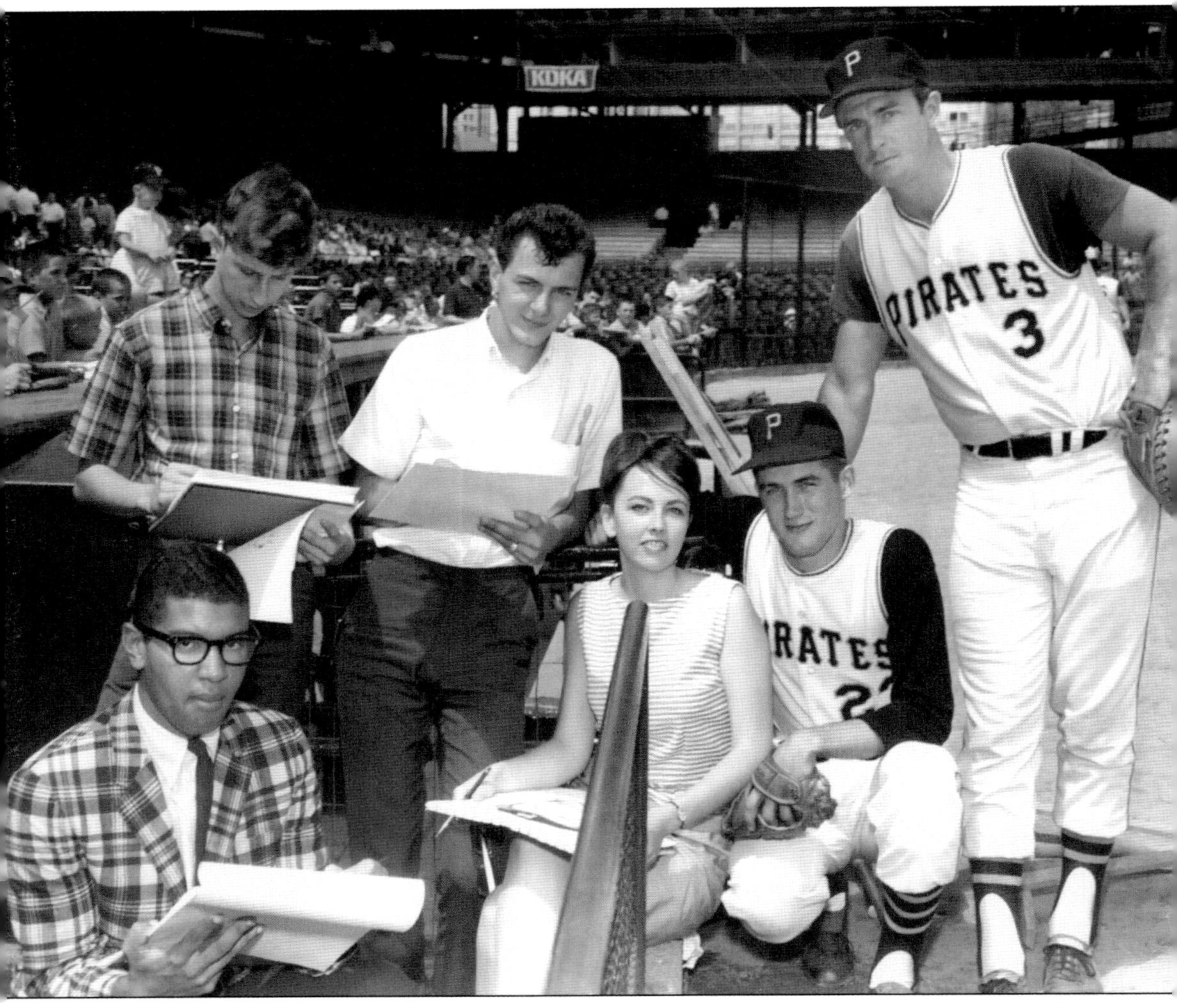

Pittsburgh loves its sports teams, and Art Institute students have always joined in the fun. Students traveled to Oakland to cheer on the Pittsburgh Pirates and practice their drawing skills. The players were a popular subject for the students, but so was the beautiful old ballpark. Forbes Field opened on June 29, 1909. At the time, it was regarded as a marvel for its technical innovations like elevators and its immense size. But by the time this photograph was taken, plans were under way to move the Pirates to a new stadium. The Pirates moved out of Forbes Field in 1970, and it was demolished in 1971. These students had the opportunity to visit the Forbes Field and meet Pittsburgh Pirates Jim Pagliaroni, No. 3, and Steve Blass, No. 23. (Photograph by A. Church.)

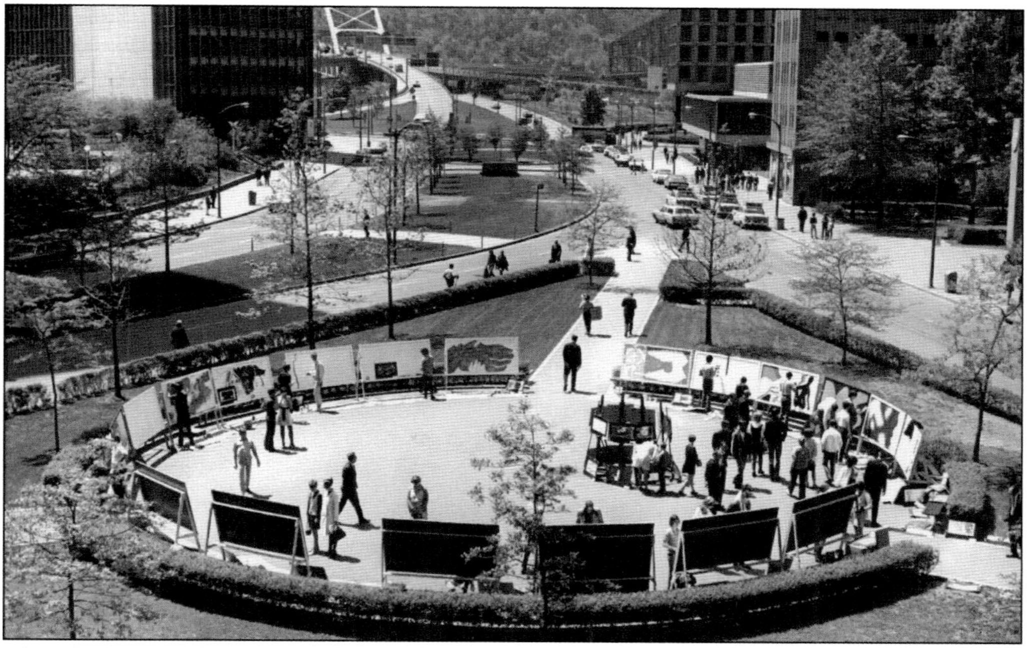

The Three Rivers Arts Festival is one of the city's signature events. Known as "Arts Fest" by Pittsburghers, it began in 1959, taking place downtown during the first two weeks of June. Students often visit the outdoor stands throughout the Point to listen to live music, enjoy the work of the visiting artists, and eat the lip-smacking food. Throughout the 1960s and 1970s, students also did painting demonstrations during the two-week event. In these photographs, curious onlookers enjoy a beautiful day and the work of students as they meander around the display in Gateway Center. It is likely these students were working during the second week of Arts Fest, because as Pittsburghers know, one can always depend on rain during the first week.

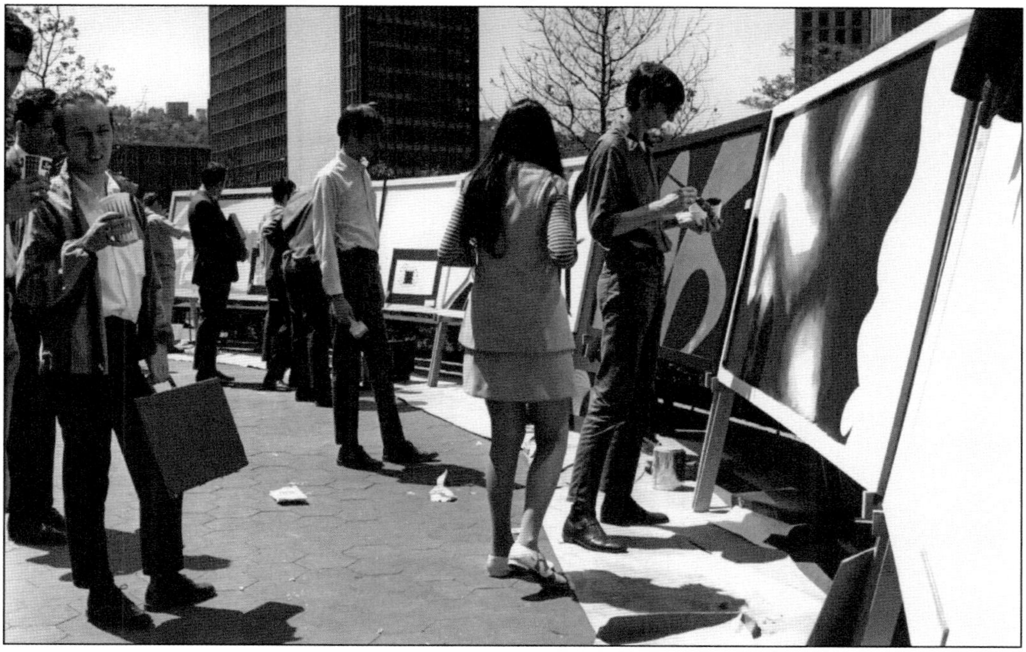

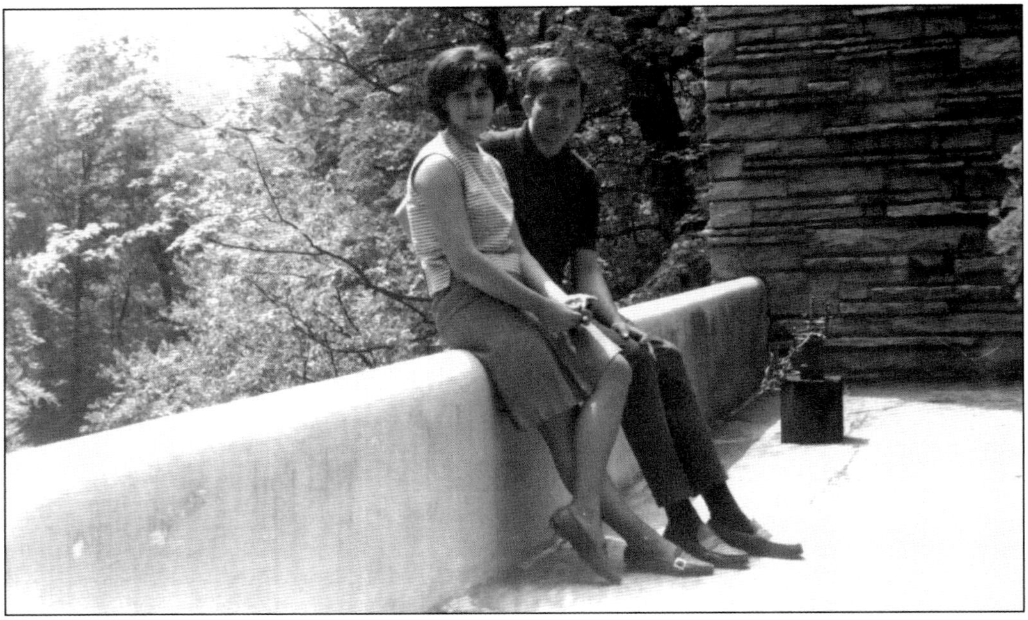

Students often expand their horizons by visiting the many art, design, and cultural attractions near Pittsburgh. Mary Jean Stabile and her friend toured the famous Fallingwater shortly after it opened to the public in the 1960s. Considered by many to be architect Frank Lloyd Wright's most spectacular creation, it was built as a weekend home for Edgar J. Kaufmann. (Courtesy of Mary Jean Stabile.)

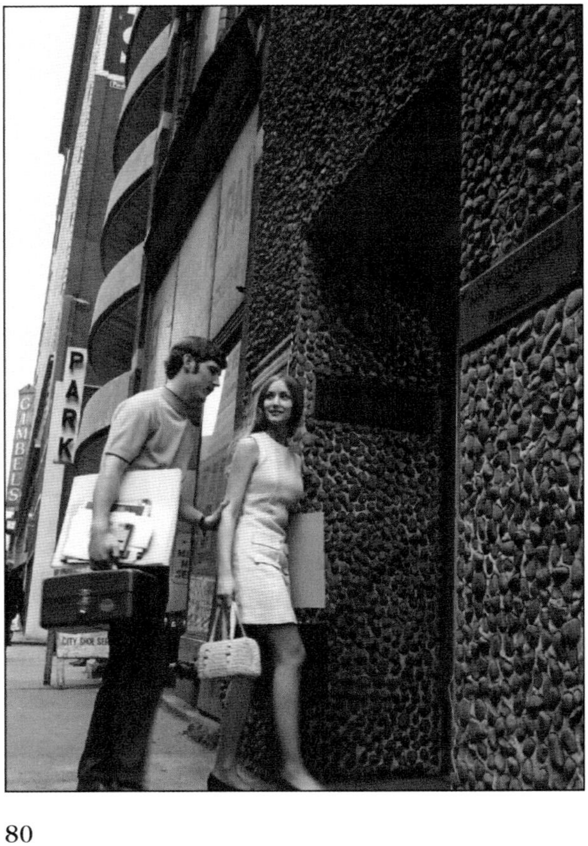

By the time this photograph was taken in the late 1960s, many dramatic changes had taken place at the school. Willis Shook had retired, the streetcars had been replaced by buses, and the building's facade had received a face-lift. The school was rapidly growing out of its home on Smithfield Street.

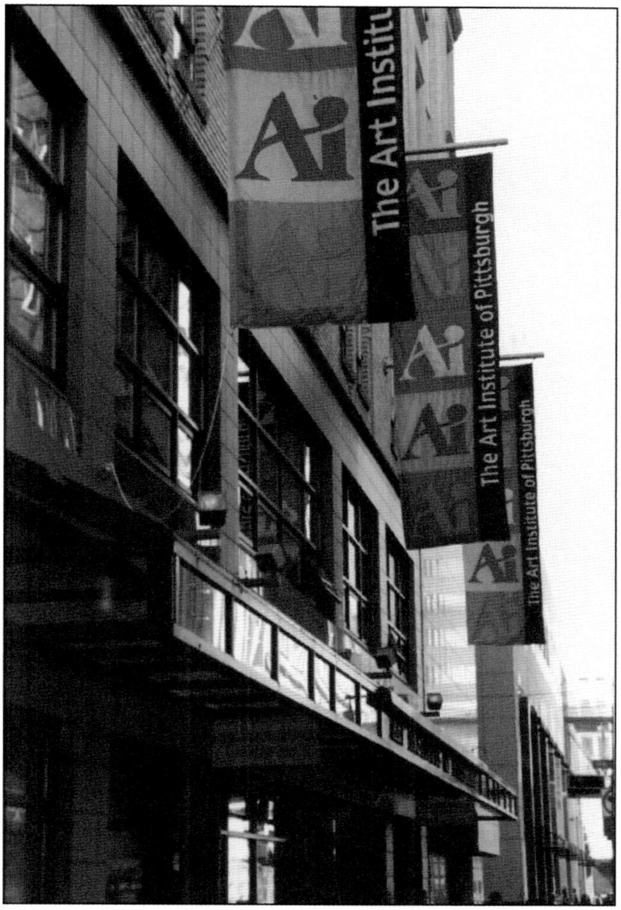

In 1971, the school moved to the Jackman Building on Penn Avenue. This nine-story building in the middle of the Pittsburgh Cultural District provided ample space for the school's offices and four departments: visual communications, fashion illustration, interior design, and photography. The unique ribbon-cutting ceremony featured a 10-story-tall environmental sculpture designed by instructor Angelo Ciotti, as an attempt to show how the foreign material in the air stifles all growing things. Ciotti explained that by having people walk through and around the forms, they become a part of the work, making it a true environmental sculpture. Pictured from left to right are founder Willis Shook, "Miss Art Institute of Pittsburgh" Pat Smith, and school president John Johns.

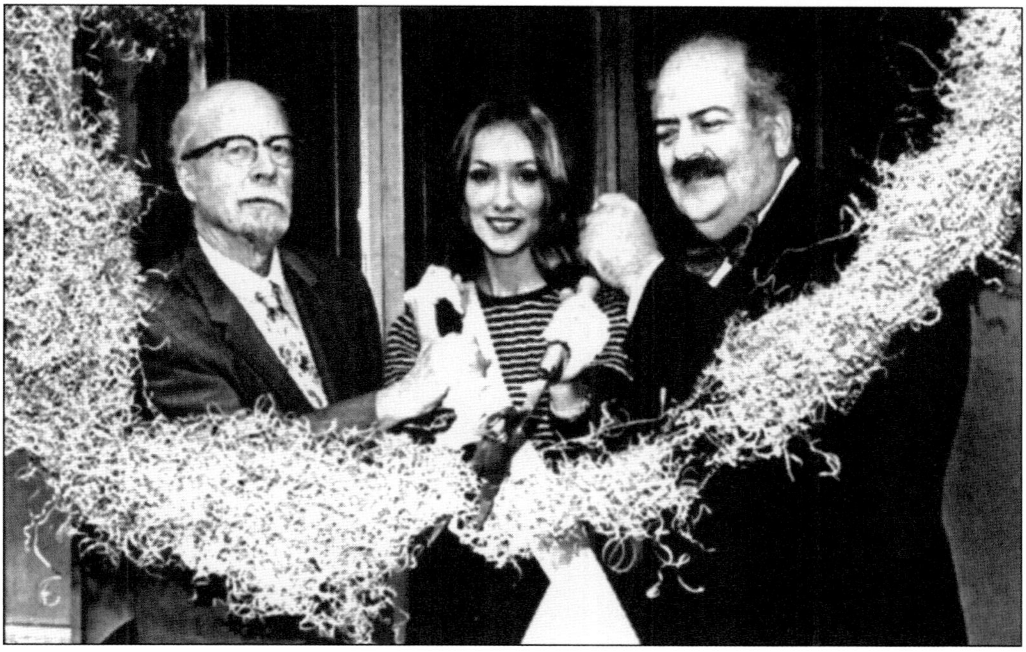

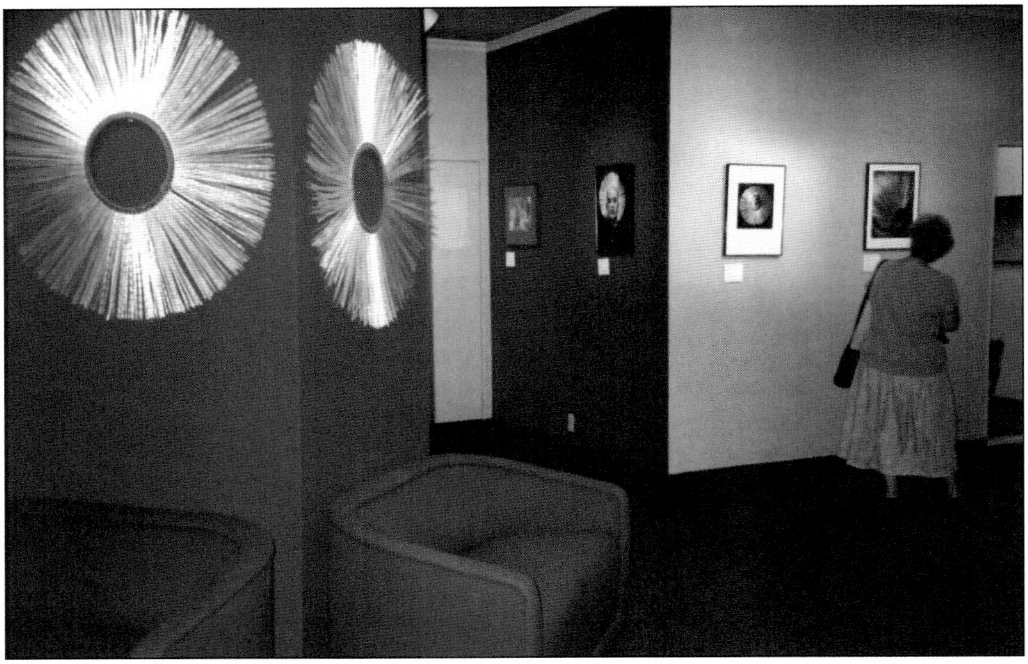

A new feature at the Penn Avenue facility was the addition of the John T. Barclay Gallery in 1972. In addition to student work, the gallery space also hosted an annual faculty show as well as shows by local and nationally known artists.

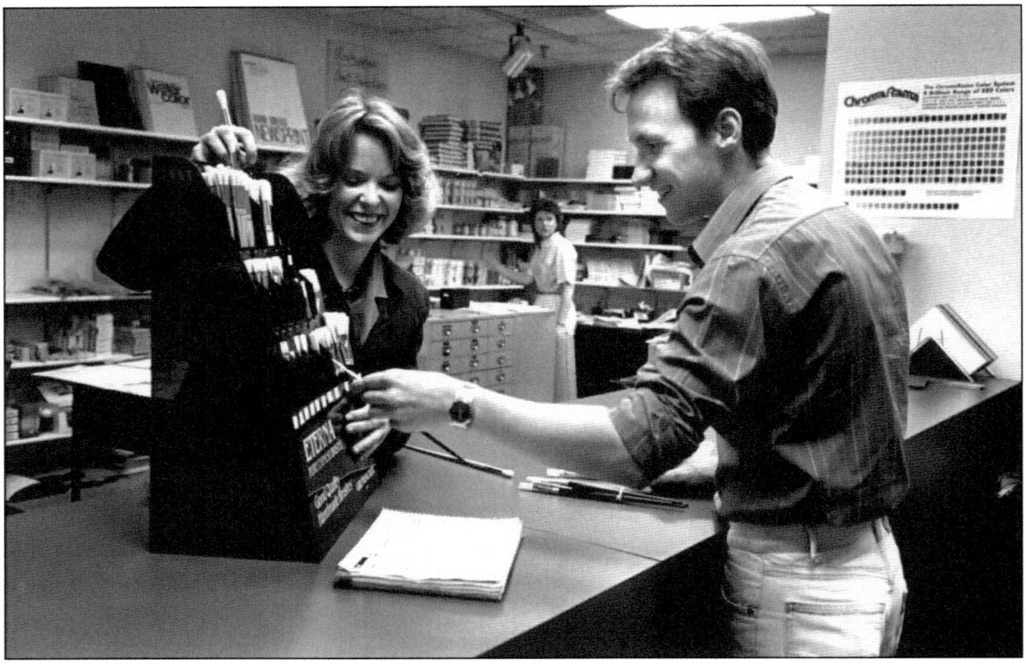

The Penn Avenue building offered an expanded store, the Art Photo Supply Store, featuring tools of the trades and Art Institute of Pittsburgh merchandise. Penn Avenue was also a convenient location for other reasons. Students became quite familiar with Barkus Bakery across the street and especially the kindness of the ladies who worked there, always saving their goodies at the end of the day for the students.

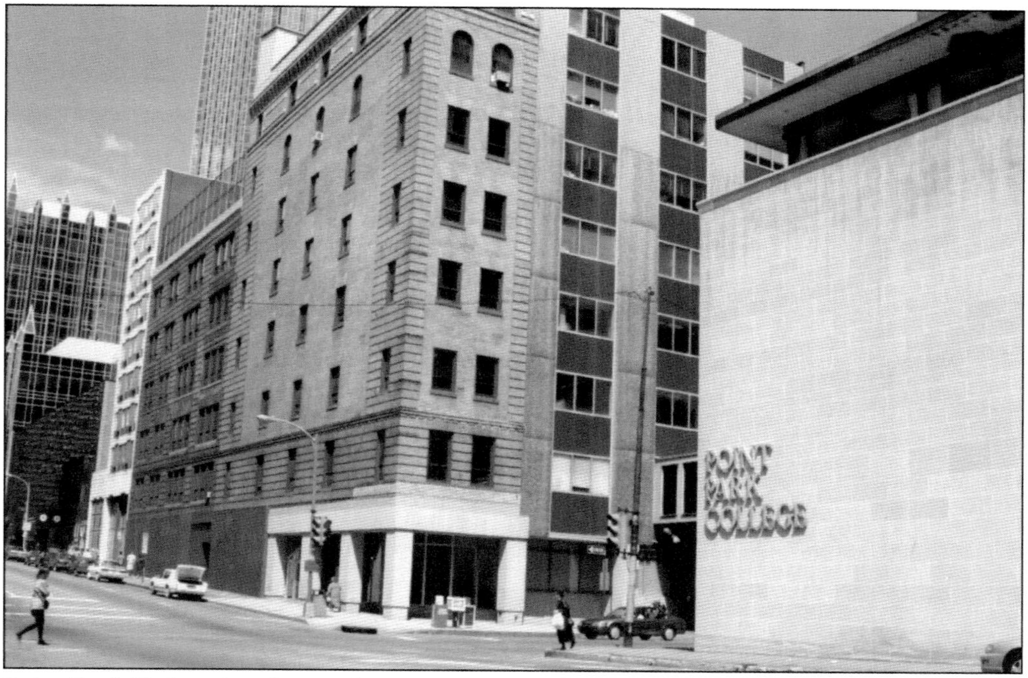

Point Park University shares the Art Institute of Pittsburgh's downtown street address. The school, known as Point Park College until 2004, was a resident of Wood Street and just a short walk away from the Penn Avenue building. Today the school has buildings throughout the Boulevard of the Allies corridor only a couple blocks from the Art Institute's current home. Since the Art Institute of Pittsburgh did not always offer sponsored housing, some students lived in the Point Park dormitories. Point Park generously opened its doors to students throughout the 1980s and 1990s. This student seems to be enjoying his accommodations, even though he is a Michigan fan.

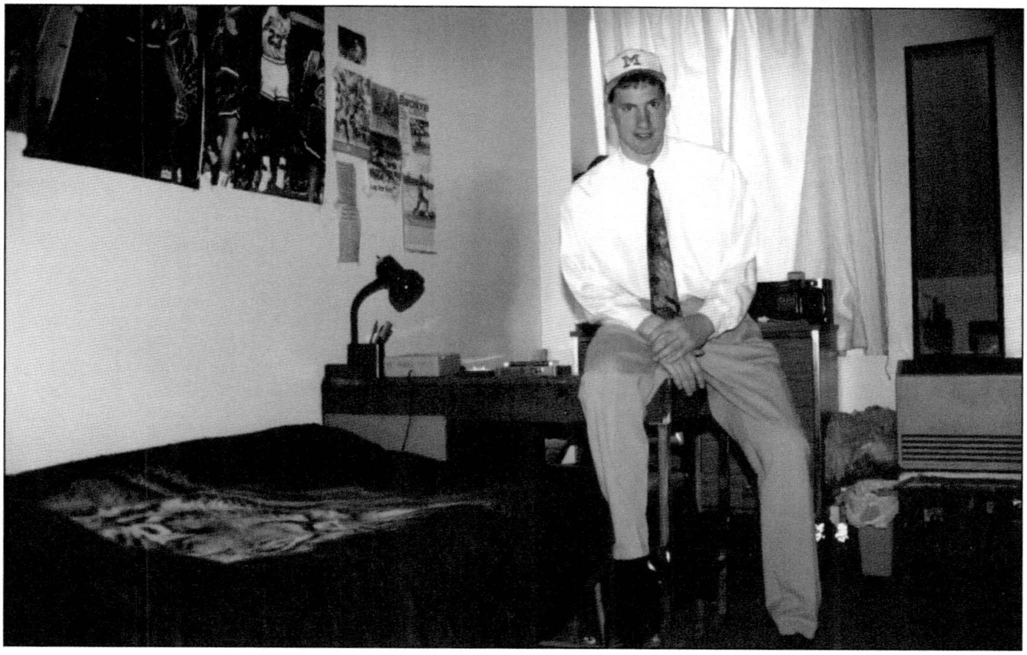

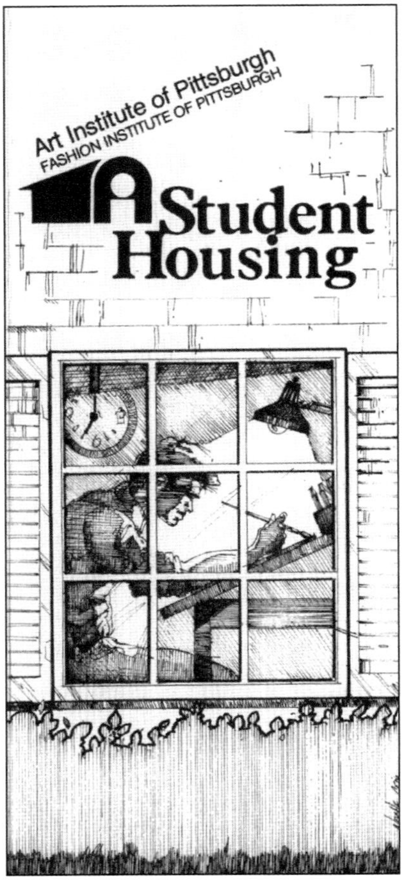

In the 1980s, students also lived on the campus of Duquesne University. Located on the bluff just above downtown Pittsburgh, students could easily walk from the Duquesne campus to the Art Institute Penn Avenue building. Students lived in St. Martin's dormitory along with Duquesne students. This small group of students inevitably grew close. Students living in the Duquesne dormitories clown around in the photograph below from 1981. Lynda Emmerich, director of housing, is seen at the far left.

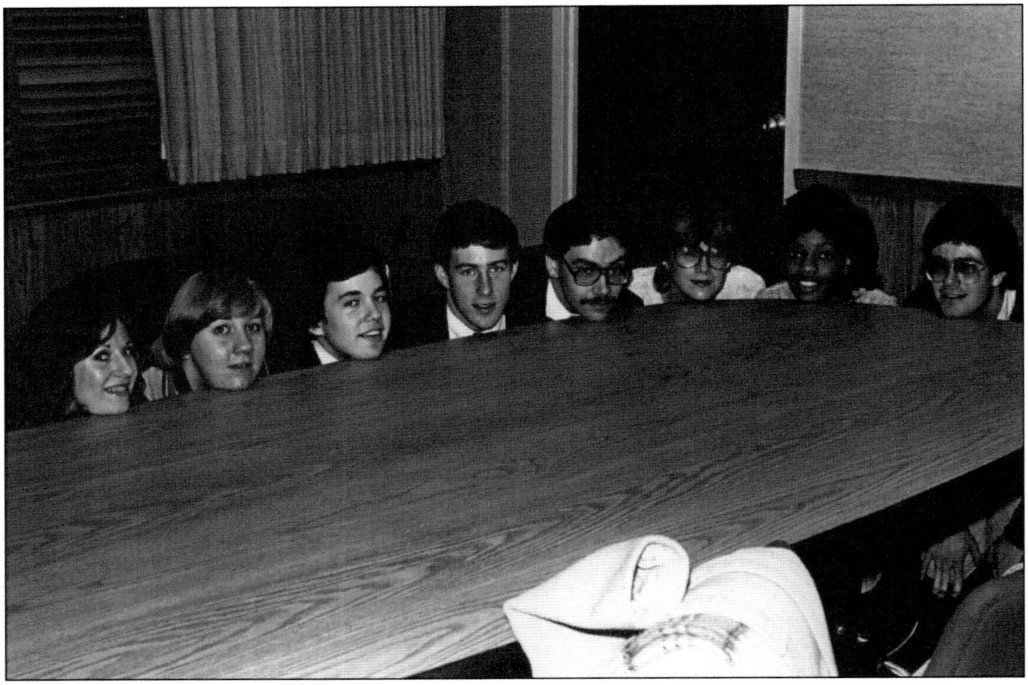

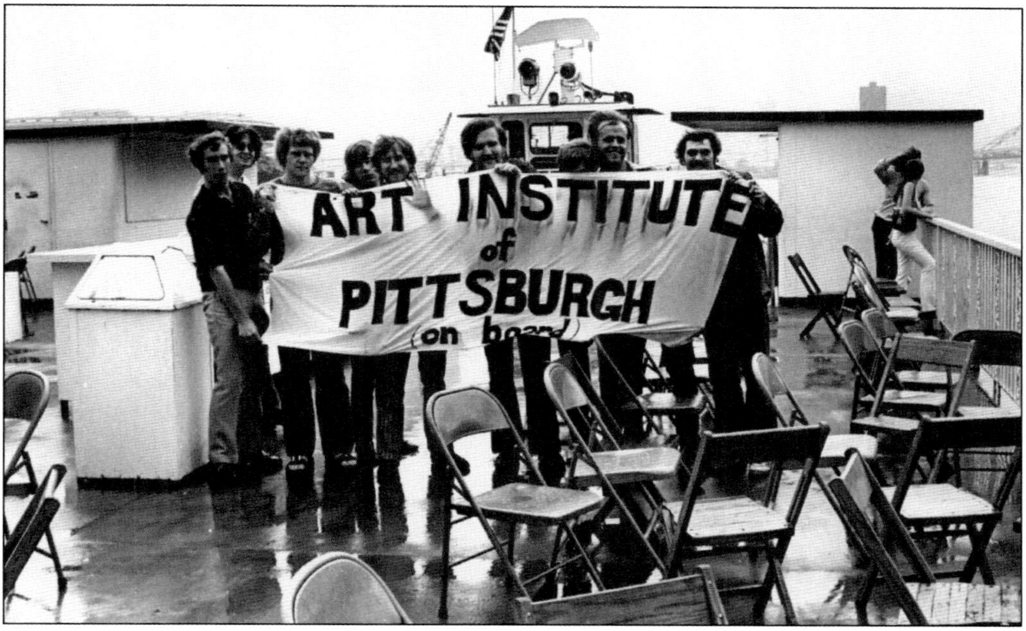

Regardless of where students lived, life in the city would not be complete without the rivers. In the early 1970s, orientation for new students included a welcome boat ride on the Gateway Clipper Fleet.

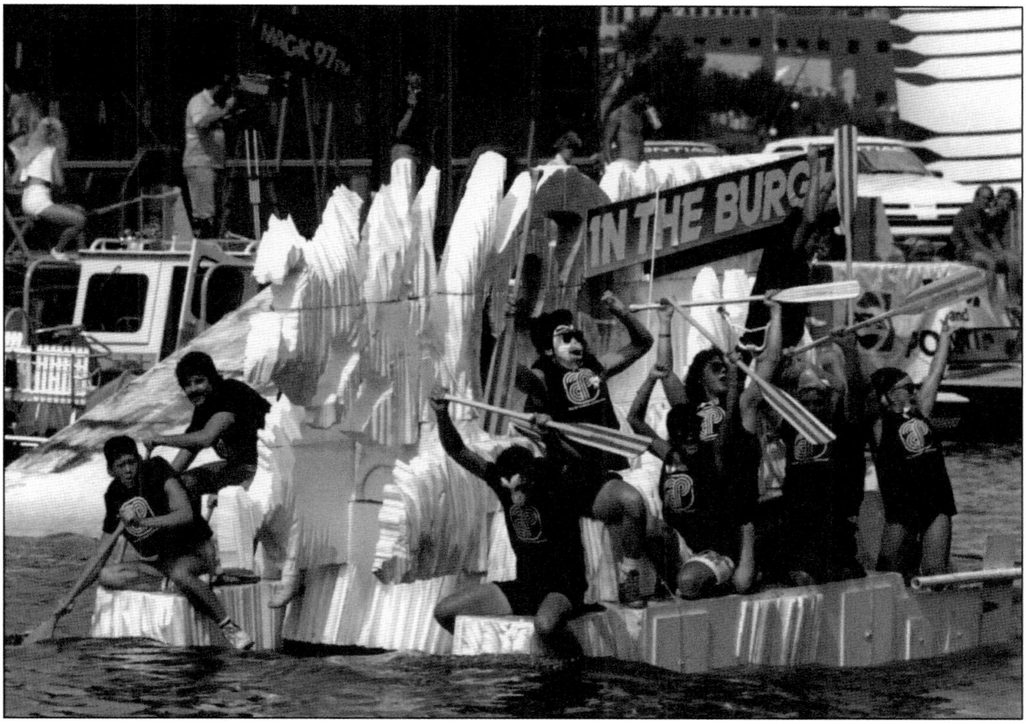

Students in the industrial design department built their own boats. Sponsored by B96 WHTX, students designed, built, and rowed this iceberg as part of the Anything That Floats contest in the 1989 Three Rivers Regatta. They won top honors for Best Corporate Design.

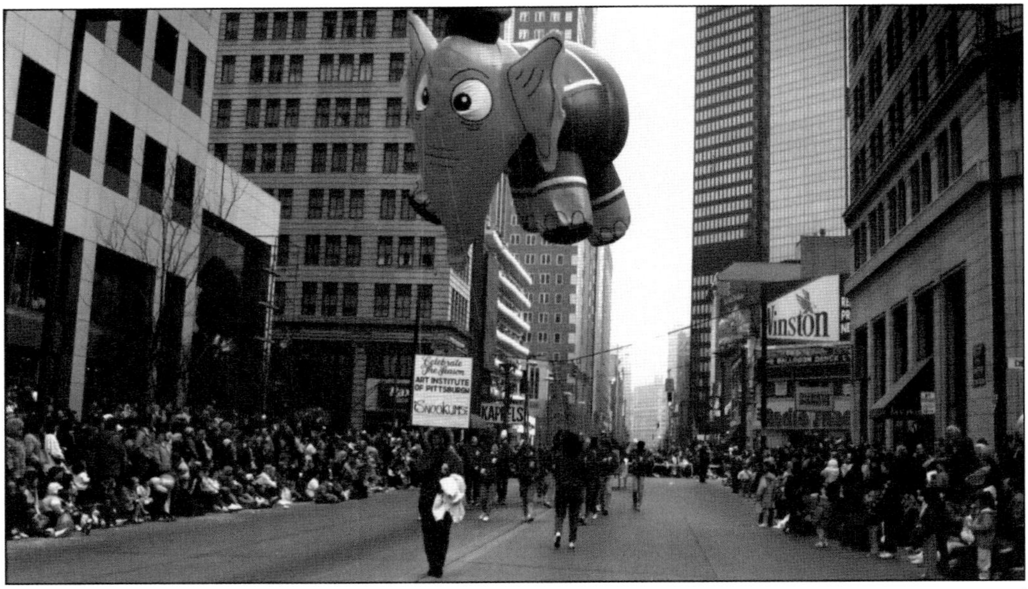

Students were also active on dry land. In 1988, students designed, produced, and corralled Snookums, an impressive parade balloon, as part of the Celebrate the Season parade. The annual parade takes place the Saturday after Thanksgiving and kicks off the holiday season downtown. Students often participated in the parade creating floats and balloons.

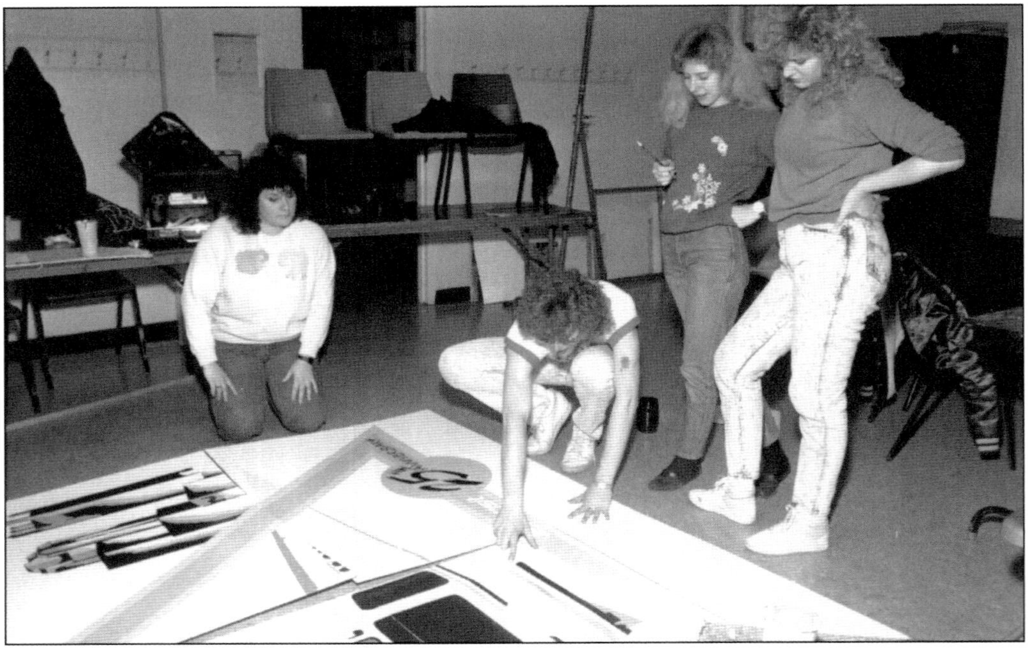

The Port Authority of Allegheny County network gets students all around the city—students take the bus to the east end, ride the T to the south hills, or use the incline to reach the top of Mount Washington. It is fitting then that students created murals to help the organization celebrate its 25th anniversary in 1989. The murals, which appeared at major bus stops and stations all over the city, celebrated the port authority's history, innovations, and staff. In this photograph, students work together refining their design.

Throughout the 1990s, students lived at Allegheny Center on Pittsburgh's north side. This urban redevelopment project featured an urban mall, campus-style outdoor spaces, and apartment buildings. Many students called this building, Seven Allegheny Center, home. Students from other downtown colleges, including the Pennsylvania Culinary Institute, also lived in the building.

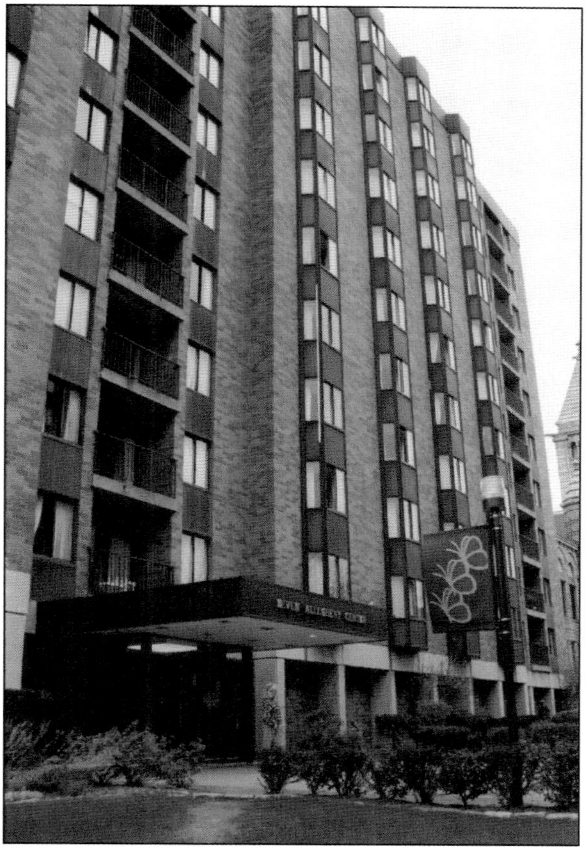

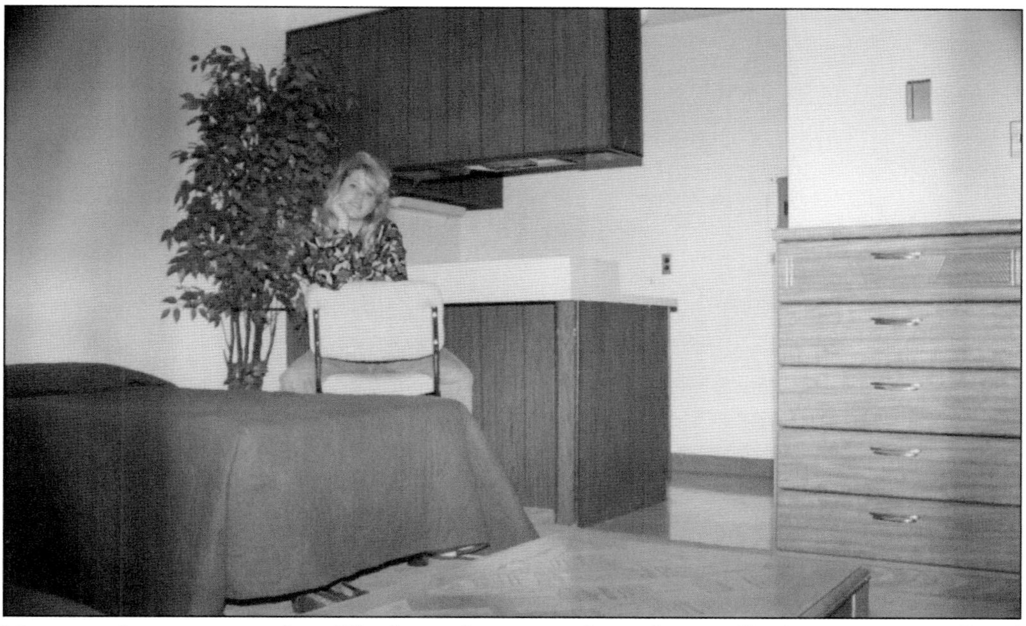

Many graduates remember Allegheny Center as their dorm. Allegheny Center offered furnished studio, one-bedroom, and two-bedroom apartments complete with fully equipped kitchens.

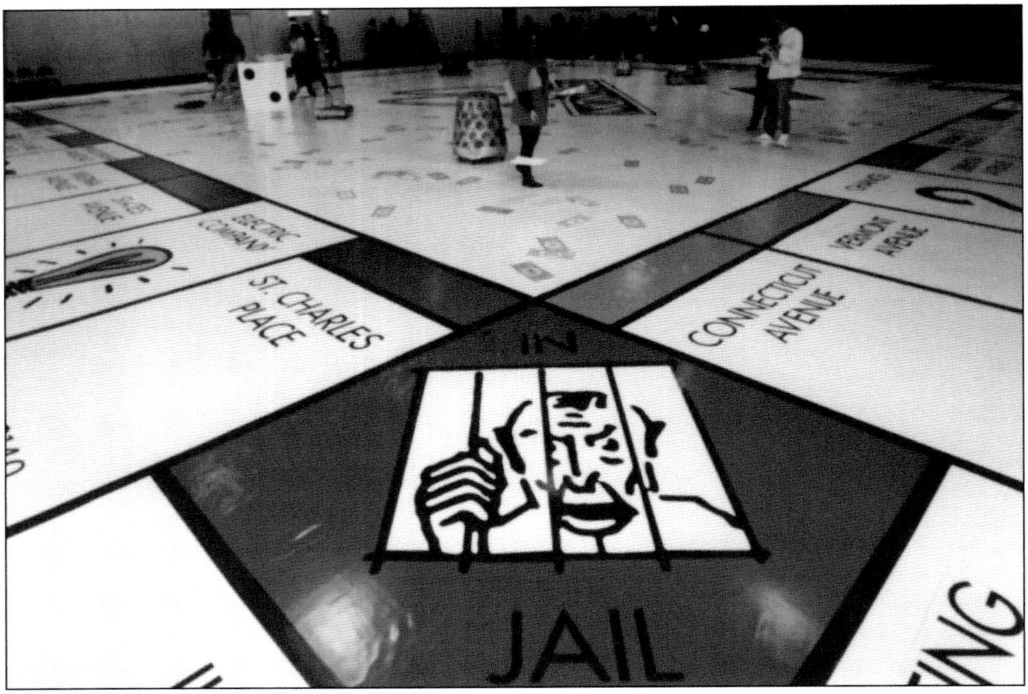

One of the most memorable community projects was the Biggest Monopoly Game You'll Probably Ever See. Local McDonald's owners teamed with Art Institute of Pittsburgh students, who created the board, constructed the giant pieces, and even performed as human motels and hotels. Staff and faculty got in on the action as well. Bill McAnulty, advisor, served as Monopoly's famed policeman and Mick Opalko, graphic design instructor, worked as a hotel. The life-size game of monopoly was played at the David L. Lawrence Convention Center on May 1, 1995. All proceeds benefited the Ronald McDonald Children's Charities of Tri-Ad-Mac.

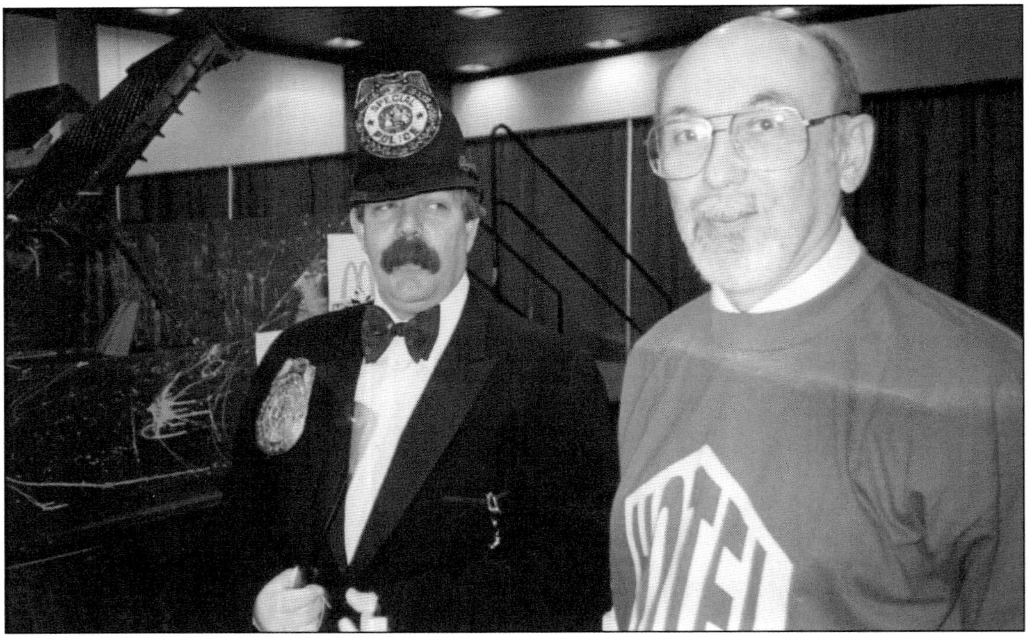

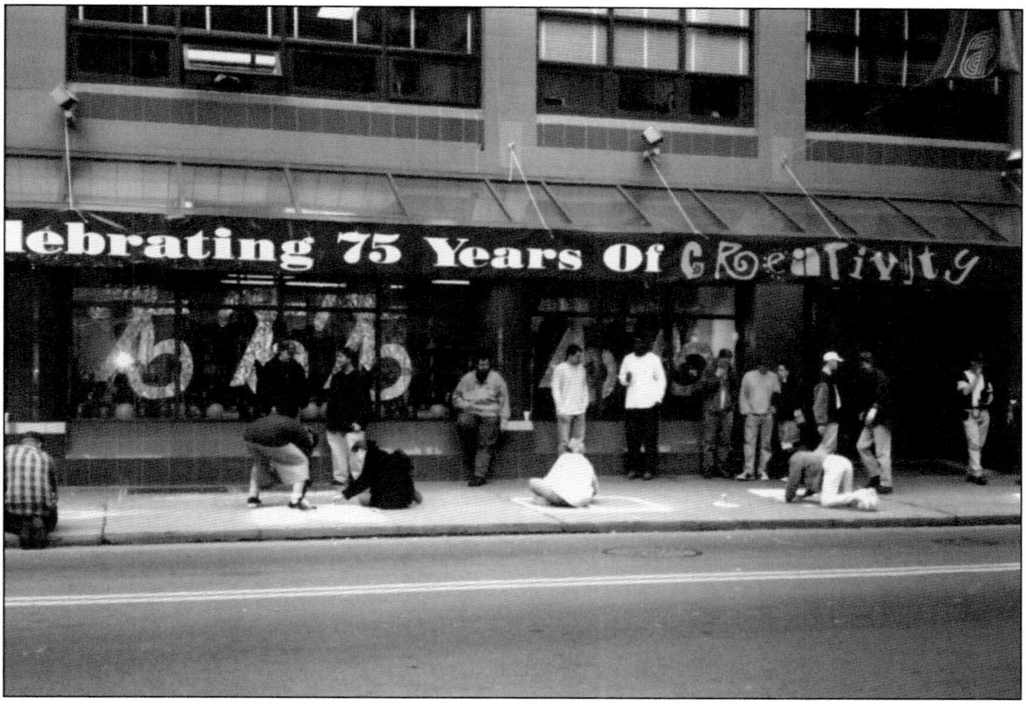

As part of the 75th anniversary, the school proudly decorated the building to share the news with downtown neighbors. Throughout 1996, the school celebrated its 75 years of creativity. The school invited neighbors to share in the festivities by having students create sidewalk art using chalk and ingenuity.

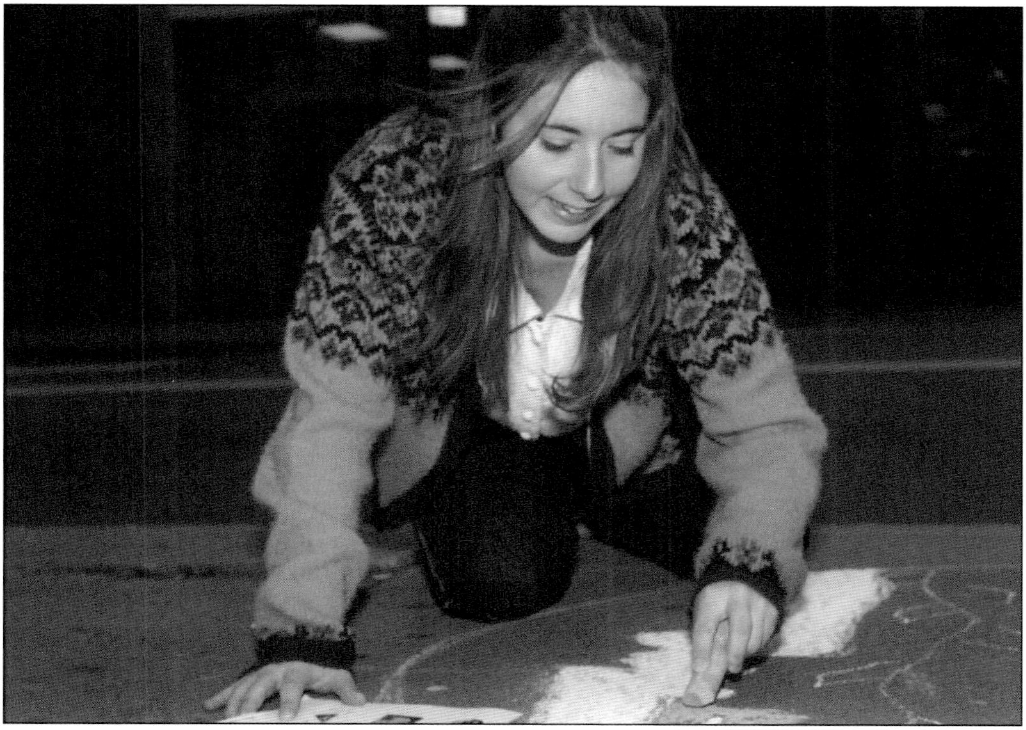

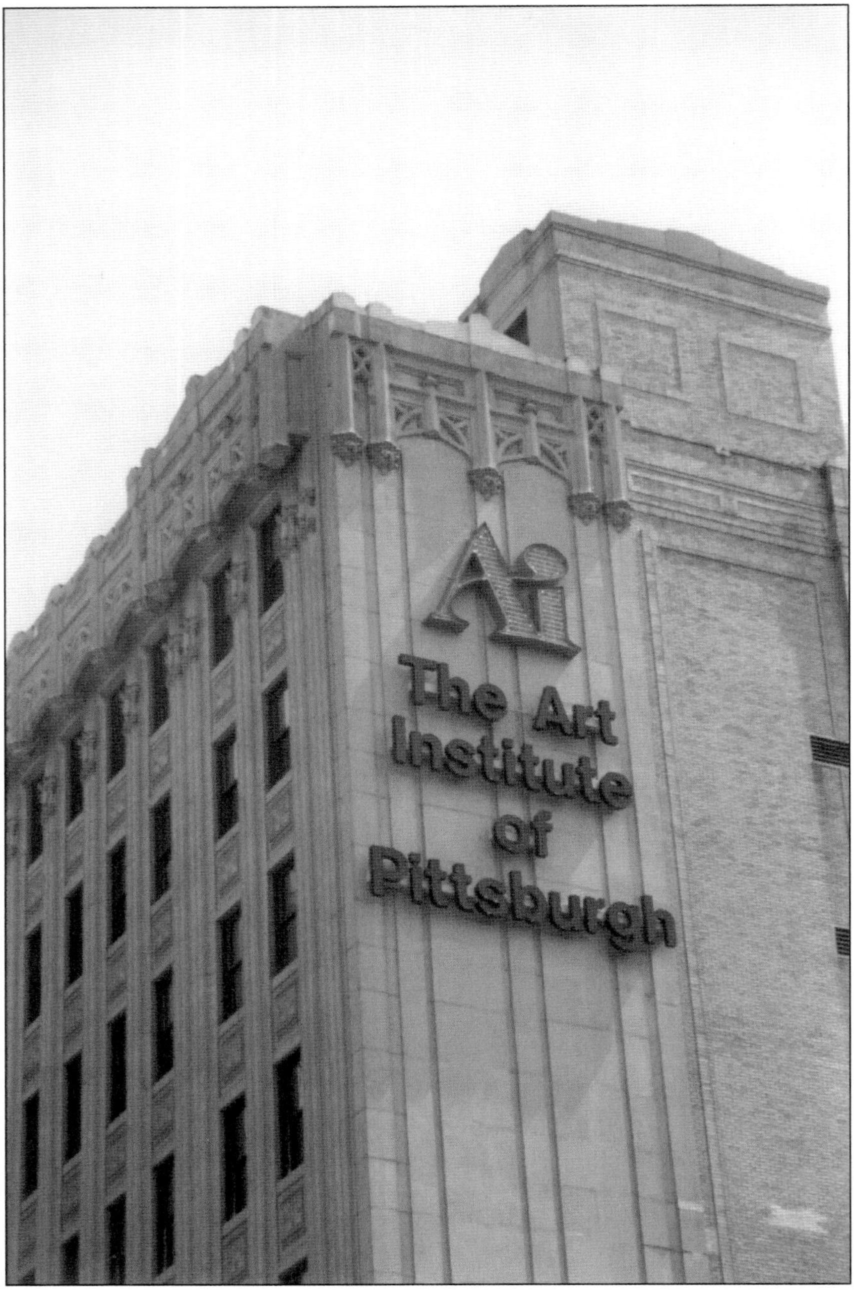

In June 2000, the school moved to its current location at 420 Boulevard of the Allies. Designed by J. F. Kuntz as the home of a pharmaceutical company, this building erected in 1925 is named a historic structure by the Pittsburgh History and Landmarks Foundation. The nine-story building stands just two buildings away from the intersection with Smithfield Street and just a few blocks away from the majestic Smithfield Street Bridge. Thanks to the school's proximity to Carson Street, Station Square, and the Duquesne Incline, south side and Mount Washington have become popular neighborhoods for students seeking to live off campus. The location also places the school into what is quickly becoming known as Pittsburgh's academic corridor.

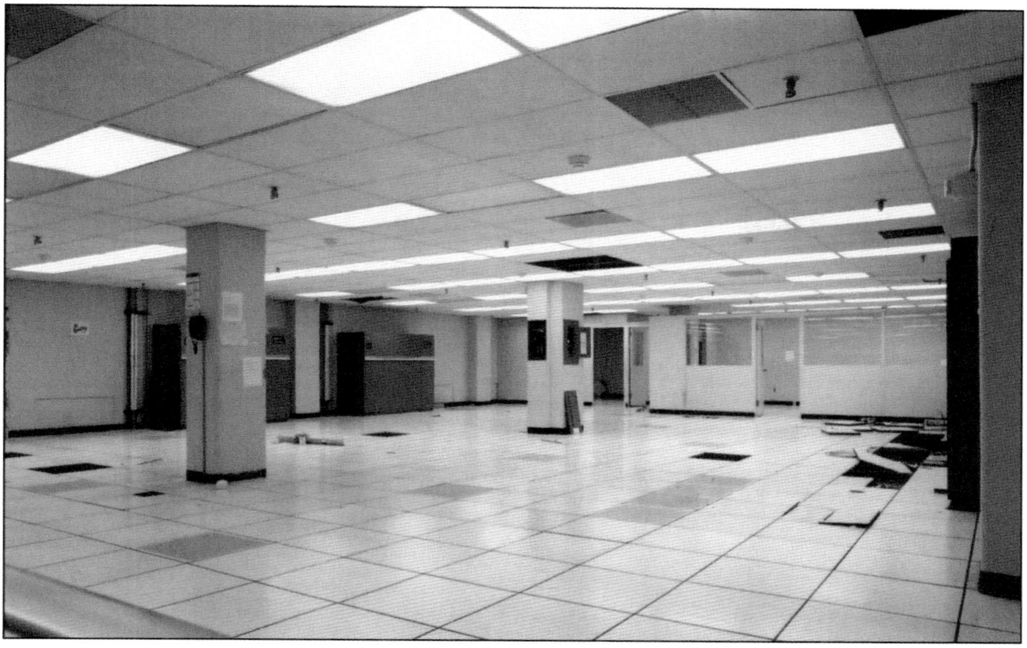

The building was formerly the home of Equitable Gas, and it required a substantial renovation to suit the needs of the school. The project, managed by Design Alliance Architects, cost over $20 million and netted the school an additional 45,000 square feet. It also allowed the school to dive into the 21st century with technical amenities including fiber-optic wiring.

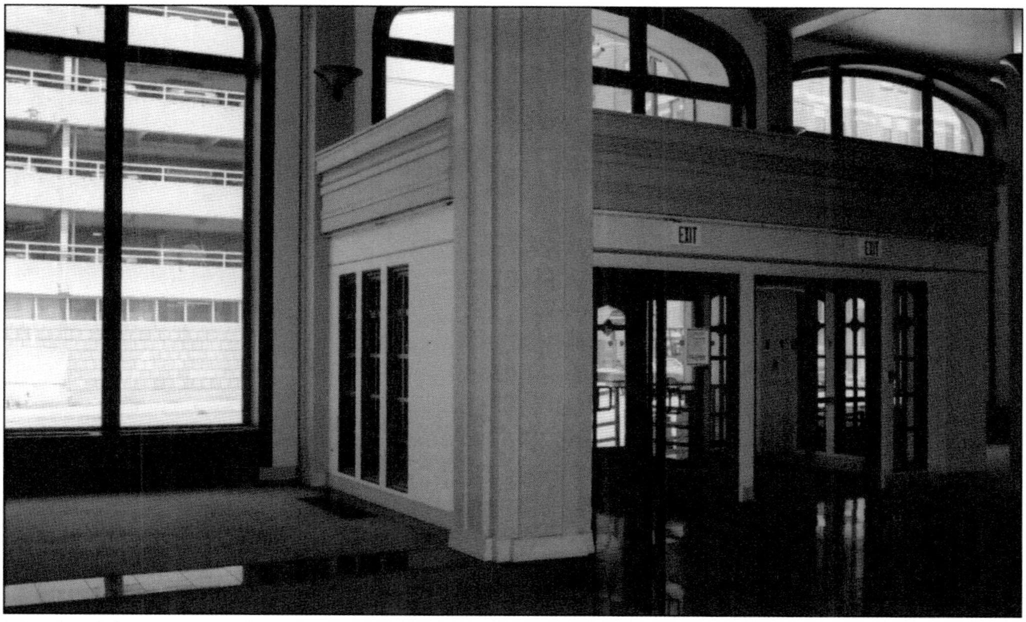

The building's grand two-story lobby was retained. It now houses the school's gallery and is the setting for many special events, including new student orientations, employee awards ceremonies, and retirement parties. Prospective students can gaze down at the artwork below while they wait for an interview, meet their admissions representative, or fill out paperwork.

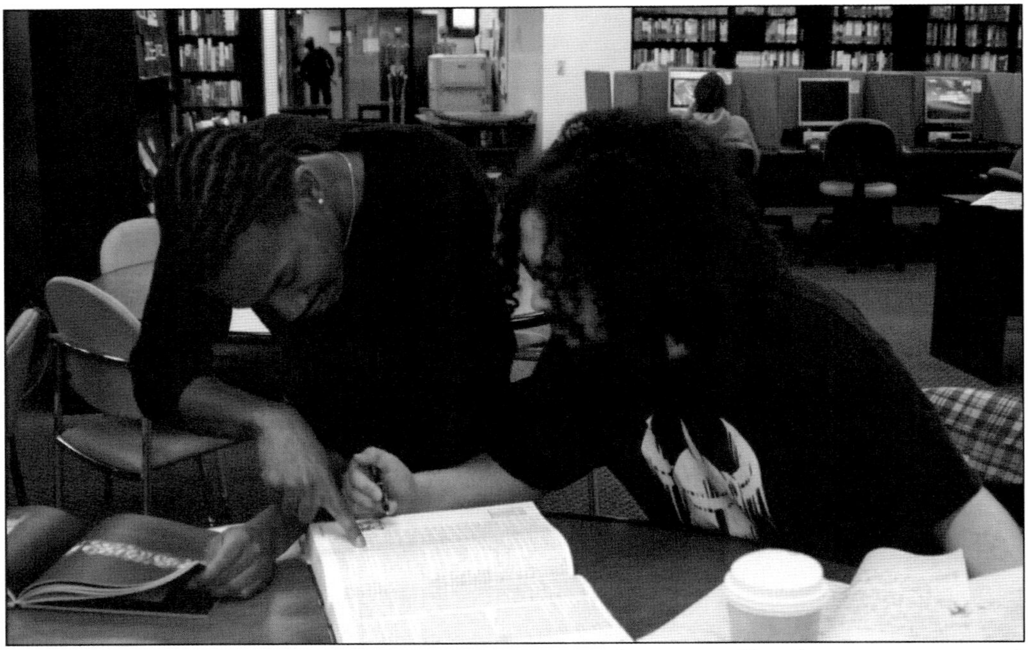

The library is on the third floor and features a wide array of books, magazines, and audiovisual materials for students to check out. Computers allow students to do research and check their e-mail while large tables allow for group meetings or individual study. Maurice Smith and Jaycen Poole take advantage of this space to work together on a research project. (Photography by Abby Parker.)

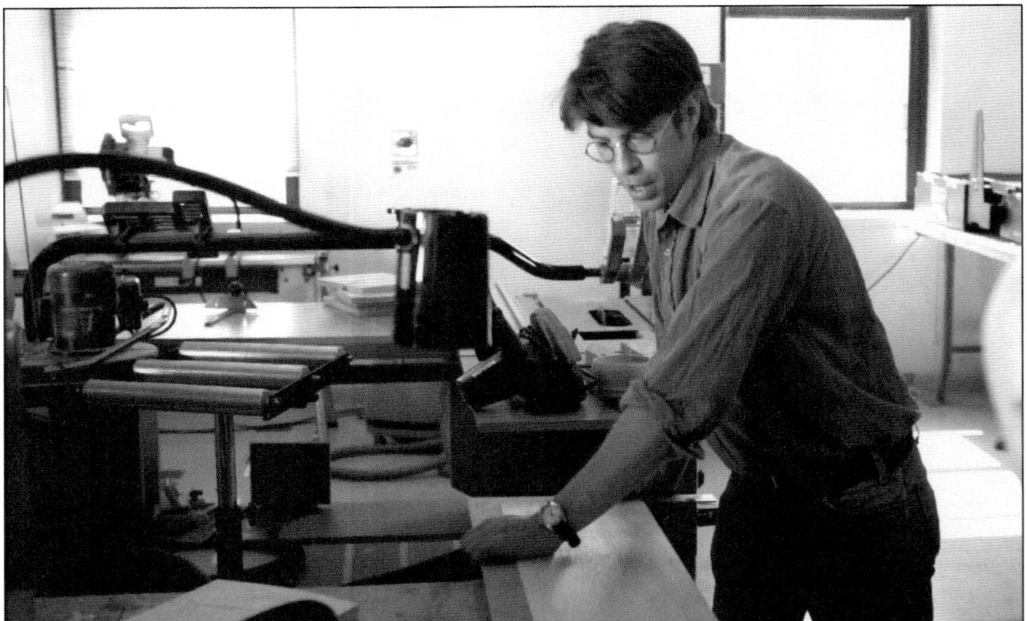

The eighth floor of the building is dedicated to the industrial design department and features an impressive mix of classrooms and work areas that include the design shop, spray room, mold room, makeup classroom, foam mixing room, and the ceramics classroom. In this photograph, faculty member Eric Hahn works on a project.

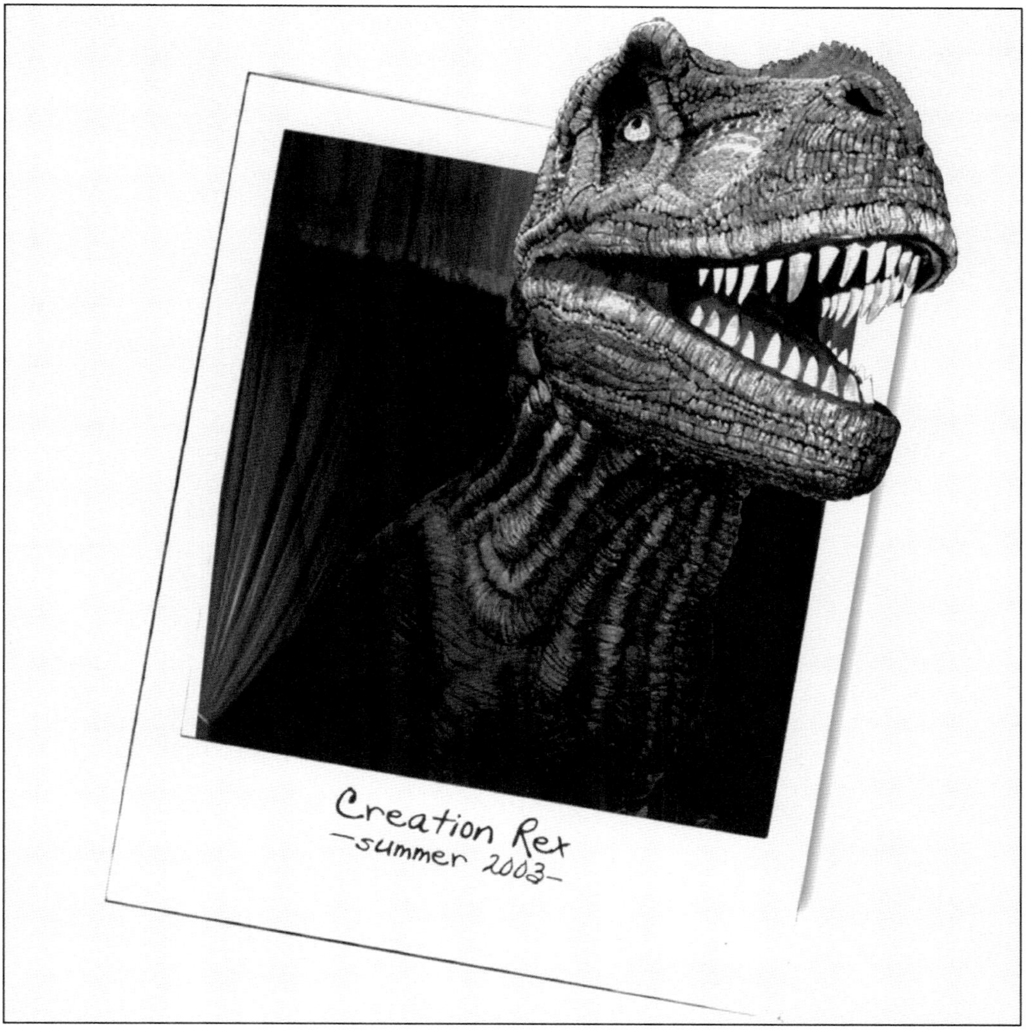

One of the most popular residents of the Boulevard of the Allies building is Creation Rex. This seven-foot-tall *Tyrannosaurus rex* was installed as part of Dinomite Days. One hundred fiberglass dinosaurs were sponsored, decorated, and assembled throughout the city. The Art Institute sponsored three dinosaurs for the event, and prepurchased the *T. rex* as its signature piece. Faculty members Stephen Butler and Bill Farrell and student Phelan McDonald helped bring Creation Rex to life as an exploration of the creative process. While most of the other dinosaurs in the city received a one-time makeover, Creation Rex routinely gets new looks, which he happily discusses in his blog, creationrex.com. He has been known to celebrate the holidays, run in the city's marathon, and even support the local sports team. In 2009, he supported the Steelers in their run to their sixth Super Bowl championship.

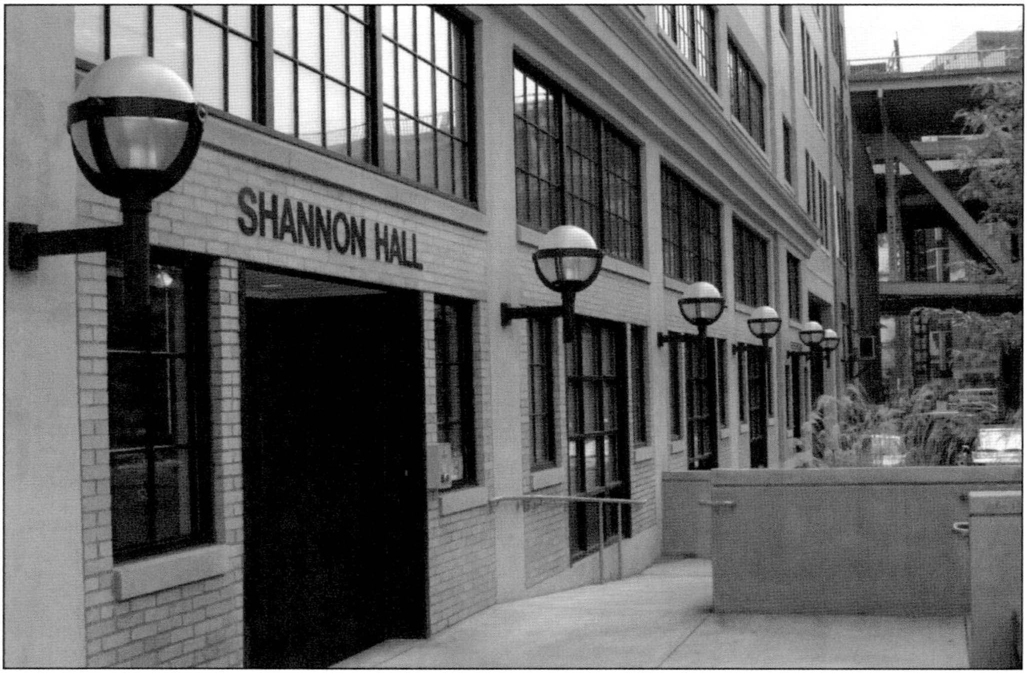

On June 5, 2007, the Art Institute of Pittsburgh opened a residence hall, Shannon Hall. The former warehouse on First Avenue is home to 637 students who share 140 one-, two-, and three-bedroom apartments. Students have a mere five-minute walk to the school passing through the new PNC First Side Center. (Photography by Abby Parker.)

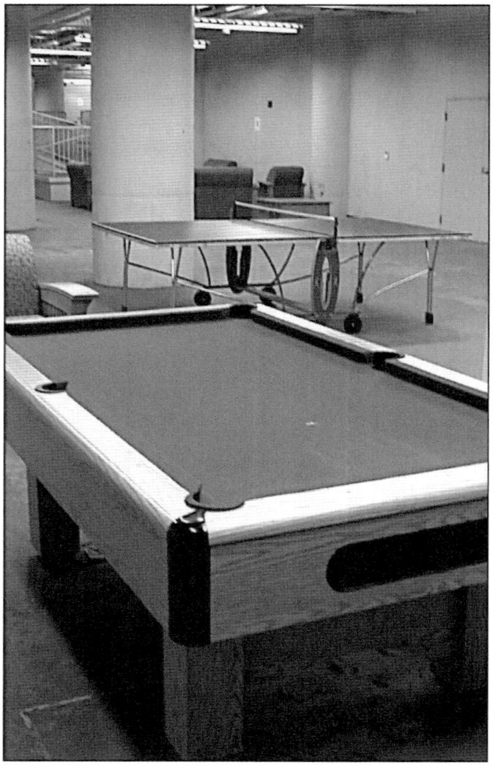

Shannon Hall is also home to an 11,000-square-foot activities center, known as SHAC, equipped with comfortable furniture, televisions, a pool table, and a Ping-Pong table. Upstairs a sport court and recreation space contains weight equipment and a basketball hoop. (Photography by Abby Parker.)

In the fall of 2007, the school added apartments in the Standard Life Building to students' options for housing. The building is situated in the heart of downtown on the corner of Fourth Avenue and Smithfield Street and is home to 147 students. (Photography by Abby Parker.)

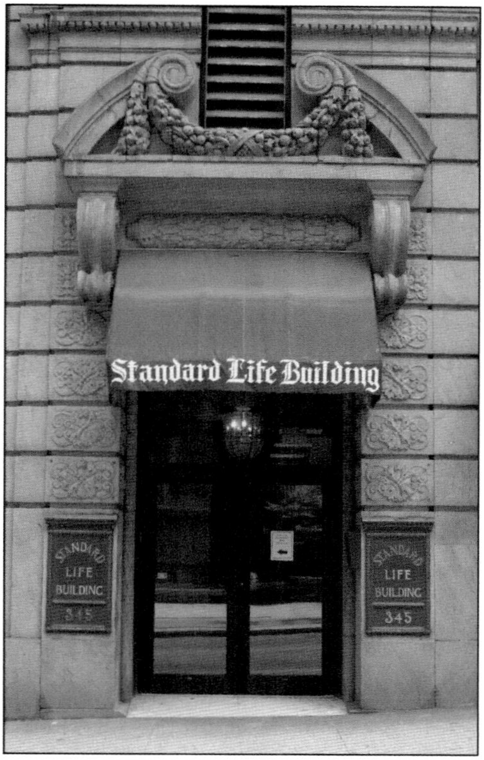

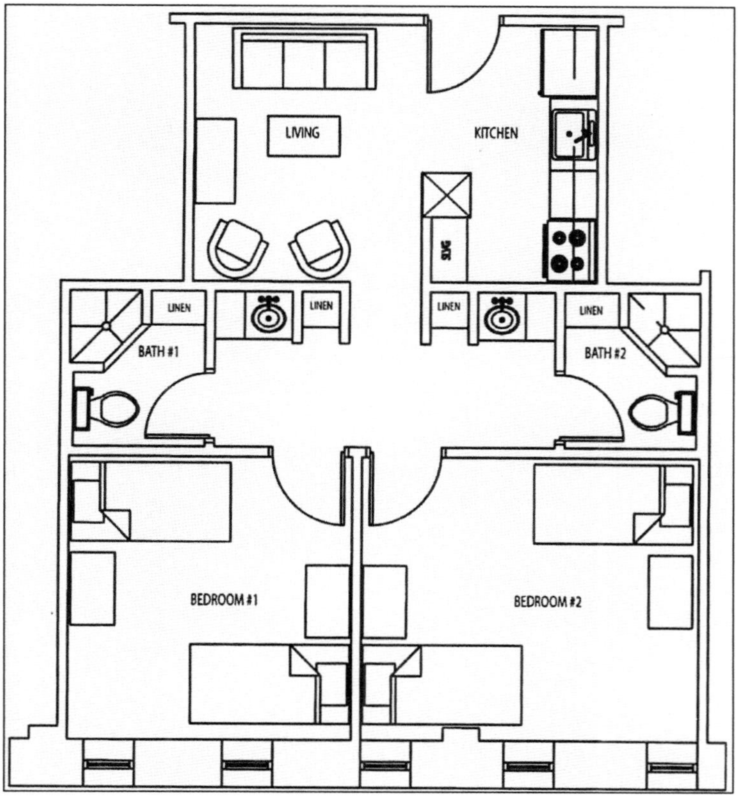

Location is everything. Miller Hall opened in the winter of 2008 and quickly became the most sought after dormitory for students in their later quarters. After all, the apartments are just a parking lot away from the school.

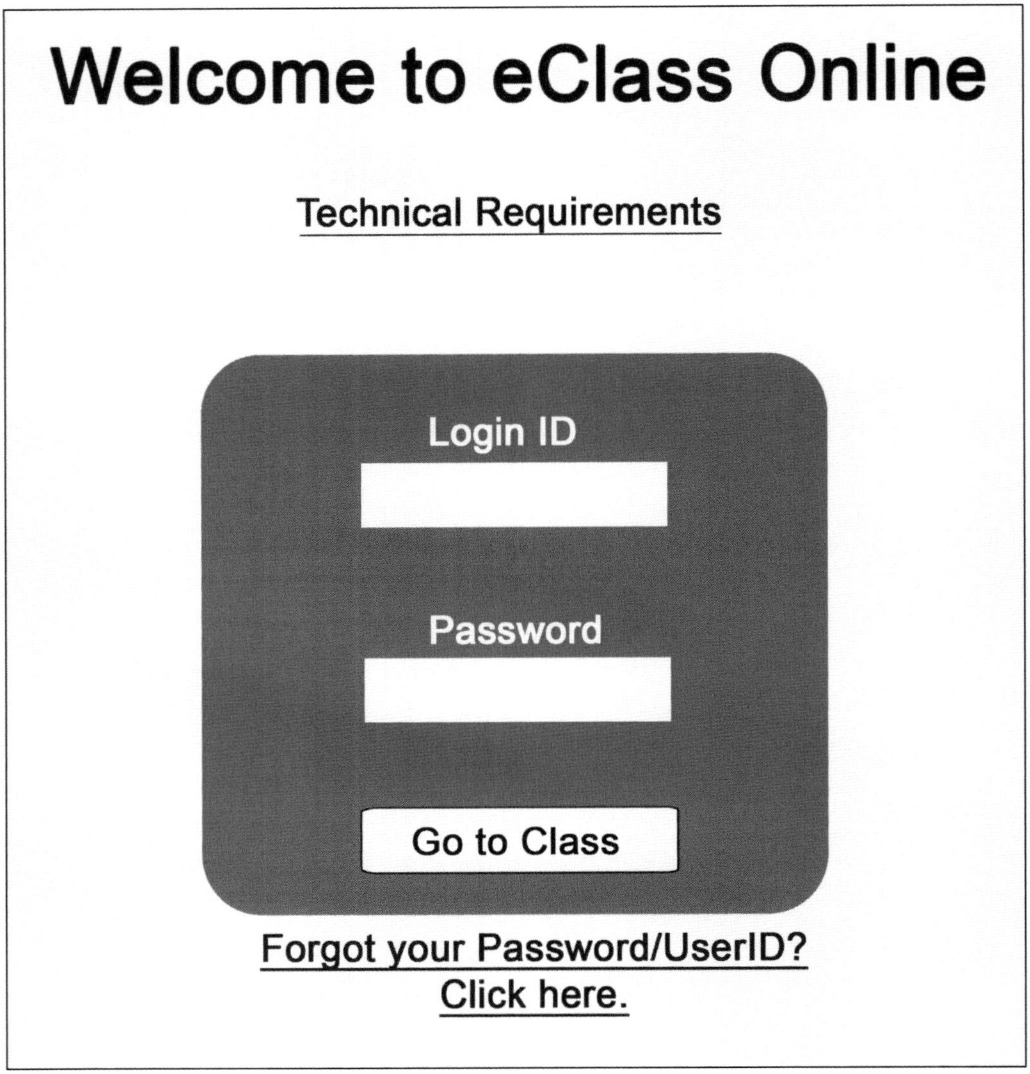

The Art Institute of Pittsburgh–Online Division started in 2000. Students learn in a virtual classroom, an interactive online learning environment where they receive and submit assignments, attend lectures, and chat with peers. Students also receive the benefits of the support services of counseling, career services, and tutoring, all delivered via the Internet. Like the students, the faculty teaches virtually and is geographically located around the globe.

Four

A Dedicated Community of Faculty and Staff

The faculty and staff of the Art Institute of Pittsburgh have enjoyed camaraderie with each other and with the students since the school's inception.

The faculty is made up of professionals who impart their knowledge to the students, while achieving much recognition in their own fields of art and design. Meanwhile, the staff has always played crucial roles in keeping the school progressing; whether it is running the elevator, answering the phones, attending to the rosters, advising, or just being there to lend a helping hand.

Every day these people give of themselves, sharing their knowledge, experience, and personalities with the students to create an atmosphere that nurtures creativity. It is impossible to highlight each of these people in this small space, so in this chapter are just a few of the people who have served students in many capacities throughout the school's history.

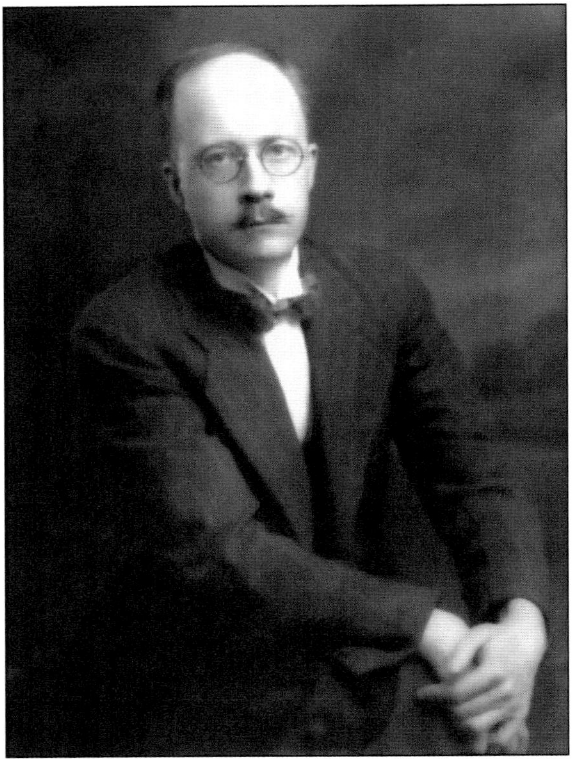

As the founder of the school, Willis Shook was also the first teacher when he started the school in 1921. Throughout his career at the Art Institute of Pittsburgh, Willis Shook, an accomplished artist, traveled on painting trips. The works that he painted include portraits and landscapes of his tours throughout the world in France, Italy, Switzerland, Belgium, Holland, England, West Indies, and the South Seas. During his trips to Tahiti in the 1940s, he visited his friend Edgar Leeteg, the legendary artist known for his black velvet paintings of the women of the South Sea island. (Courtesy of Willis D. Shook III.)

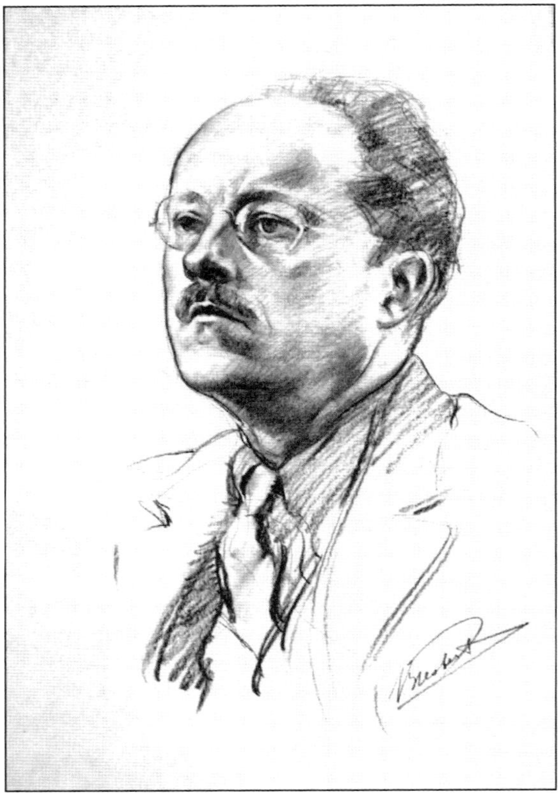

This charcoal drawing of Willis Shook was done by Vincent Nesbert, well-known portraiture artist, member of the faculty, dean of students, and assistant to the director. (Courtesy of Willis D. Shook III.)

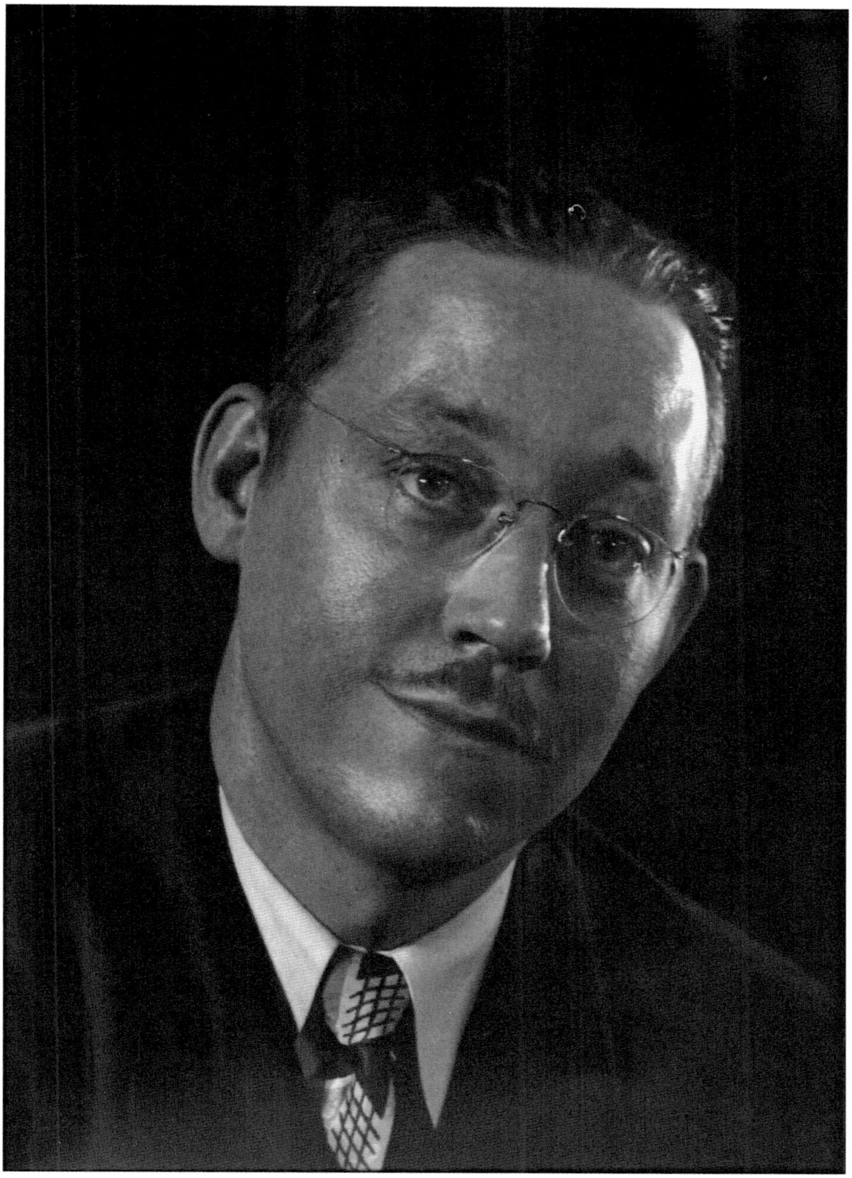

Several members of Willis Shook's family played important roles in the administration and growth of the school. Willis Shook Jr., the son of Willis and Hazel Shook, served as assistant to the director and placement manager from the late 1930s through the 1950s. Shook Jr. often traveled throughout Pennsylvania, West Virginia, and Ohio as a speaker for the Art Institute of Pittsburgh. His work included lectures to civic organizations, where he spoke to parents and students about the school. During the writing of this book, Willis D. Shook III discovered the movie reel, filmed in 1937, that Shook Jr. used as his promotional tool for these lectures. Filmed in the classrooms, there are images of commercial art, fashion illustration, and dress design students as they work at their easels, under the instruction of their acclaimed faculty, including Willis Shook, Vincent Nesbert, Sally Watkins Saeger, and Cholett Parker. Outdoor scenes record Pittsburgh and its skyline as it looked 72 years ago. The movie will now be preserved as part of the school's historic records. (Courtesy of Willis D. Shook III.)

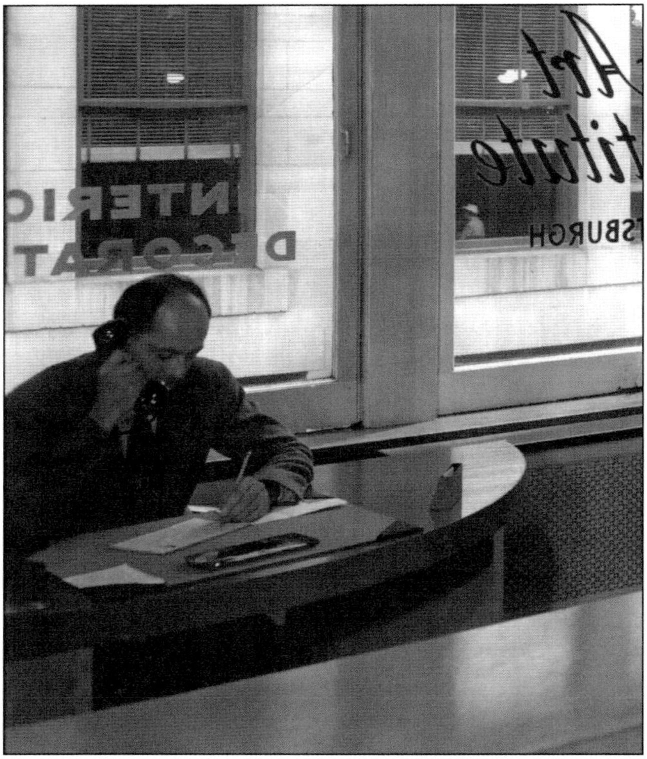

In the late 1930s, the school was located on the third floor of the Stanwix Shops Building at the corner of Penn Avenue and Stanwix Streets. In this photograph, George D. Spahman works in his office, with Joseph Horne's department store across the street through the window. Spahman served as the school's registrar and was a brother-in-law to Willis Shook. (Courtesy of Willis D. Shook III.)

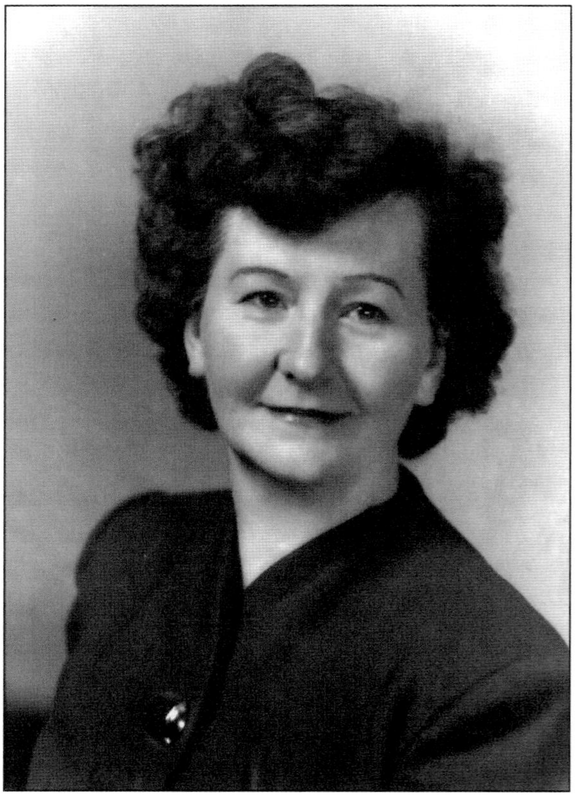

Elizabeth Buckley Shook, herself one of the first graduates of the Art Institute of Pittsburgh, an artist and a teacher, married Willis Shook in 1940. She worked closely with her husband serving in the school's administration as placement manager and counselor until their retirement. (Courtesy of Willis D. Shook III.)

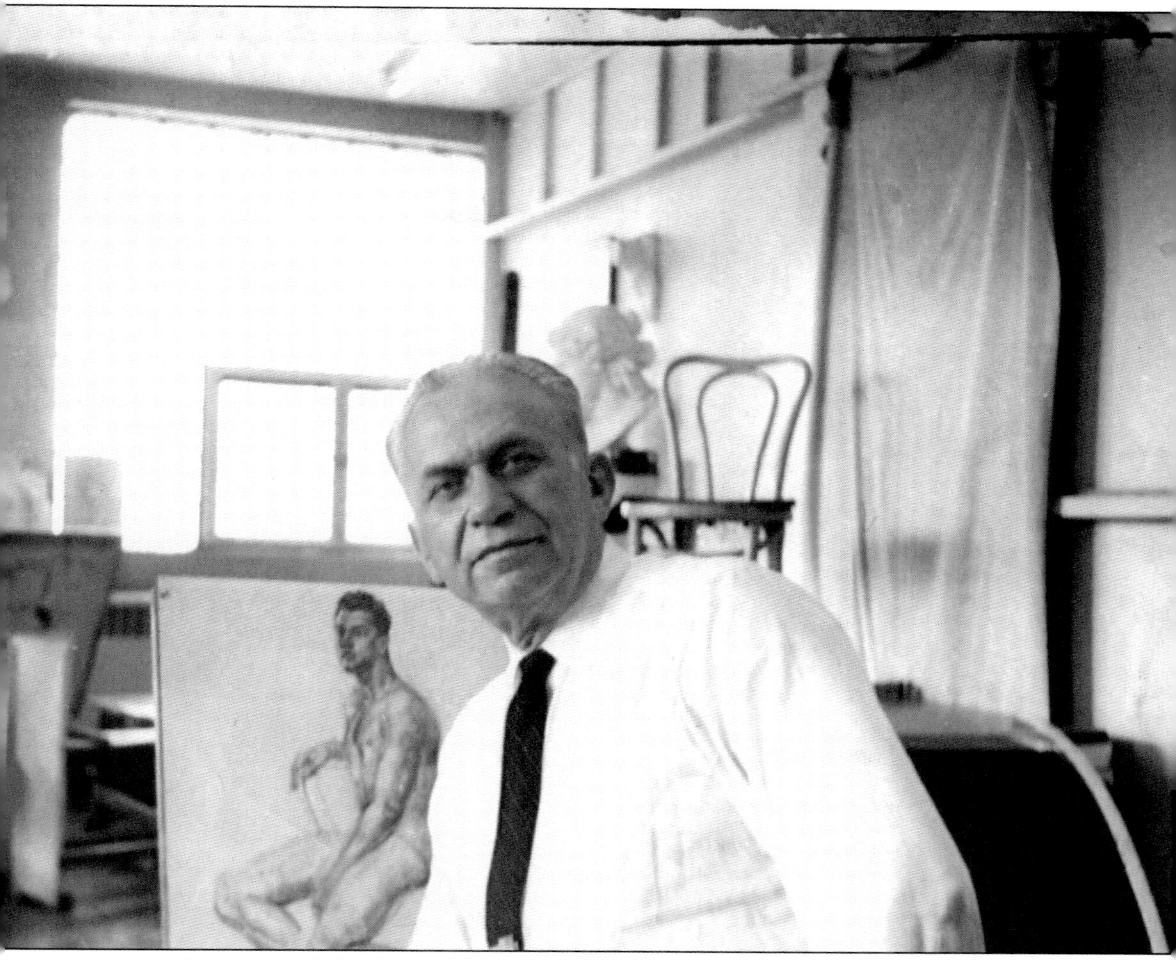

Vincent Nesbert joined the faculty in 1928 and taught for 25 years until his retirement. He served as dean in the 1930s and assistant to the director in the 1960s. He is shown here with a sketch of a model who was well known to Nesbert's life drawing students as Bob. Mary Jean Stabile took this photograph of Nesbert during the time she was a student in the 1960s. Stabile describes Nesbert as a genius, as many would agree. Nesbert came to the United States from Russia, spoke seven languages, and was a magnificent artist. Stabile recalls that in life drawing class, he was a tough professor, and if he thought a student's drawing was not good, in one swift movement he would erase the work and tell the student to start over. It was his passion for art that caused him to push students to always do better. (Courtesy of Mary Jean Stabile.)

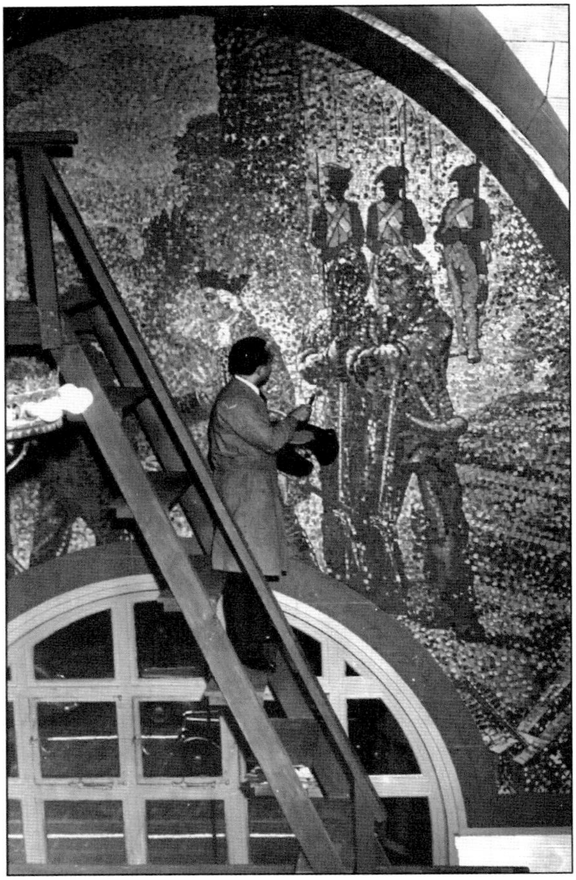

In the 1930s, during his time on the faculty of the Art Institute of Pittsburgh, Vincent Nesbert painted the five impressive murals at the Allegheny County Courthouse titled *Justice*, *Peace*, *Industry*, *The Battle of Grant's Hill*, and *Fort Duquesne*. For the five years they took to complete, Nesbert was a familiar figure on the scaffold, in his green artist smock. The first mural, *Justice*, was initiated in 1931 by the federal art program, which paid him $300 for the design. Dorothy Duke posed as a model for Nesbert as he sketched these now famous murals. It was not until 2000, at 86 years of age, that Duke made the trip to Pittsburgh, seeing the murals for the first time. In the mural *Justice*, her face can be seen as an angel, and in the mural *Peace*, Duke is the young woman carrying flowers and the mother nursing an infant. (Left, courtesy of the Library and Archives Division, Senator John Heinz History Center; below, photograph by Robyn Zaborowski.)

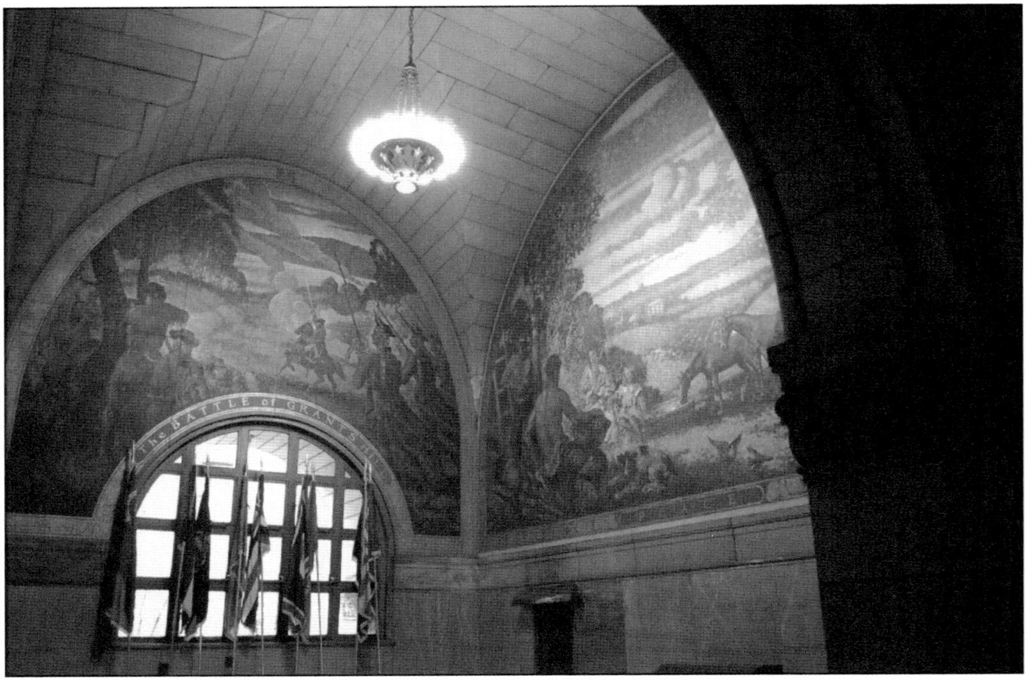

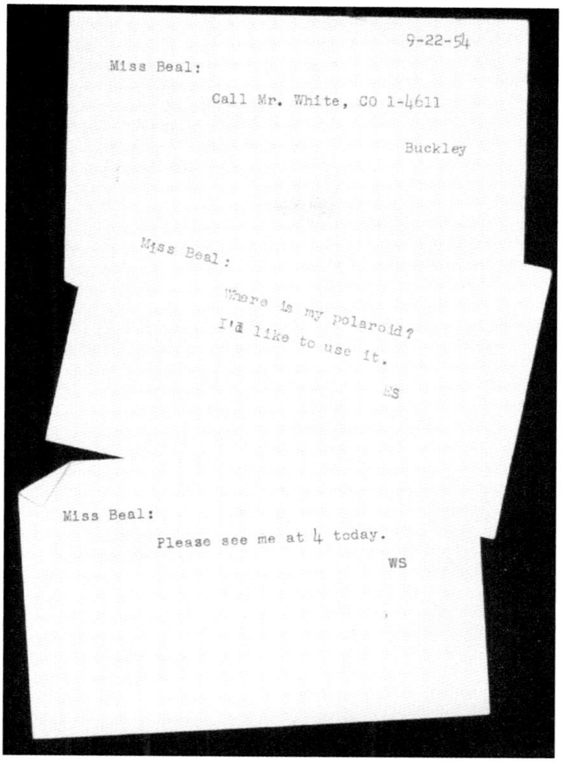
9-22-54

Miss Beal:

Call Mr. White, CO 1-4611

Buckley

Miss Beal:

Where is my polaroid? I'd like to use it.

ES

Miss Beal:

Please see me at 4 today.

WS

Long before e-mail and text messaging, the typewriter was the important means of communications among the school's administration and faculty. In these 1954 notes on small slips of paper, Willis Shook, Elizabeth Shook, and her brother Thomas Buckley, signing their names as WS, ES, and Buckley, sent messages to Miss Beal. Betty Beal was a life drawing instructor. (Courtesy of Willis D. Shook III.)

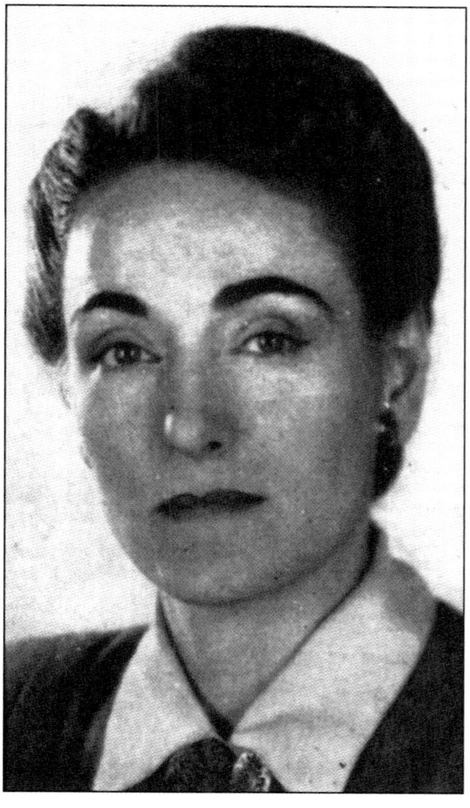

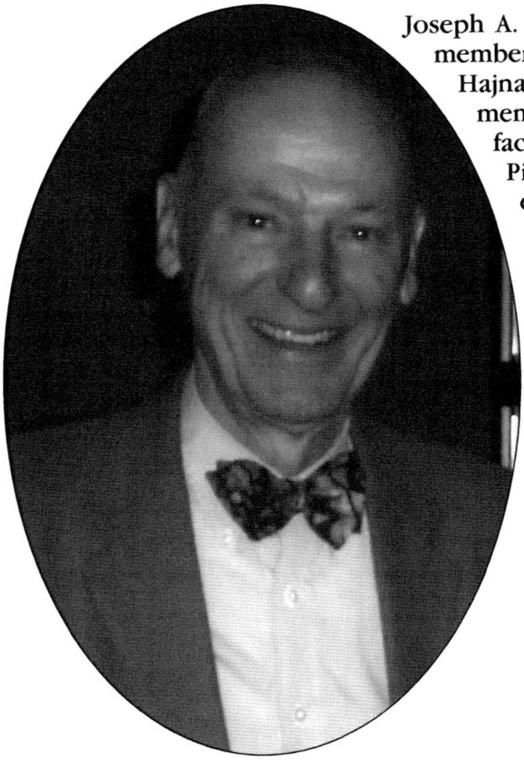

Joseph A. Hajnas was a 1953 graduate and later a member of the faculty. In this current photograph, Hajnas met with the authors to share his memories as a student and a member of the faculty in the 1950s and as an accomplished Pittsburgh artist and landscape architect. He enthusiastically speaks of his time with the Art Institute of Pittsburgh in the foreword to this book.

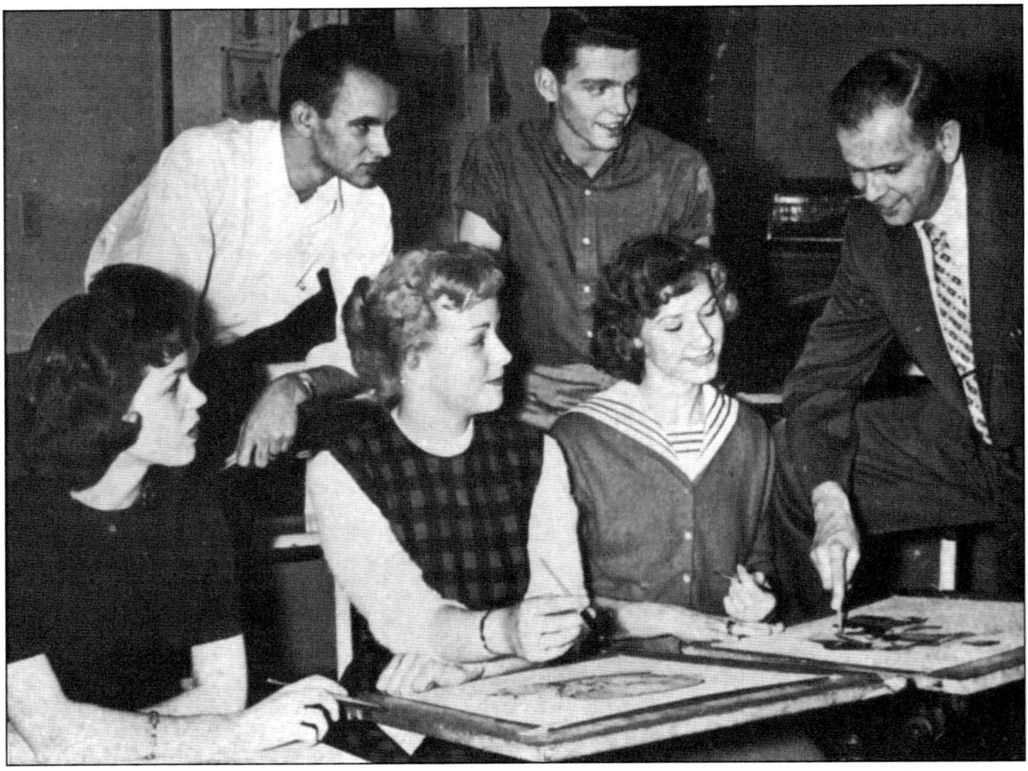

An instructor in a 1953 commercial art class demonstrates to a group of students.

In 1962, Willis Shook sold the school to Earl Wheeler, who was the founder of the Earl Wheeler Finishing School and the Pinkerton Secretarial School.

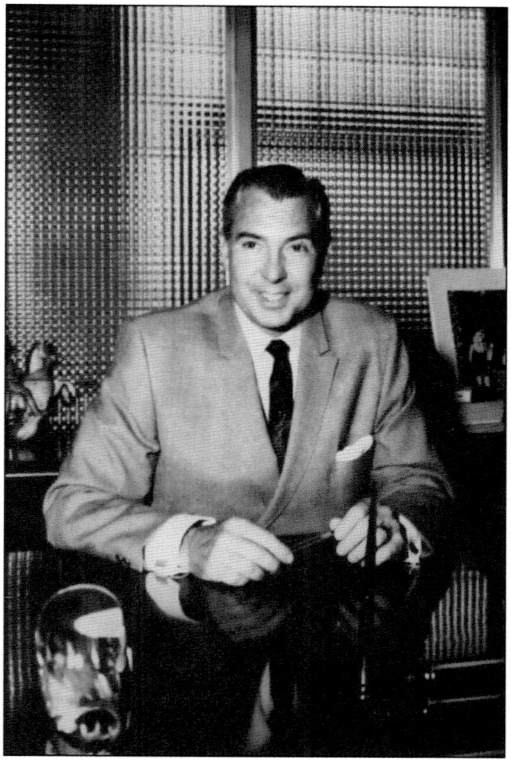

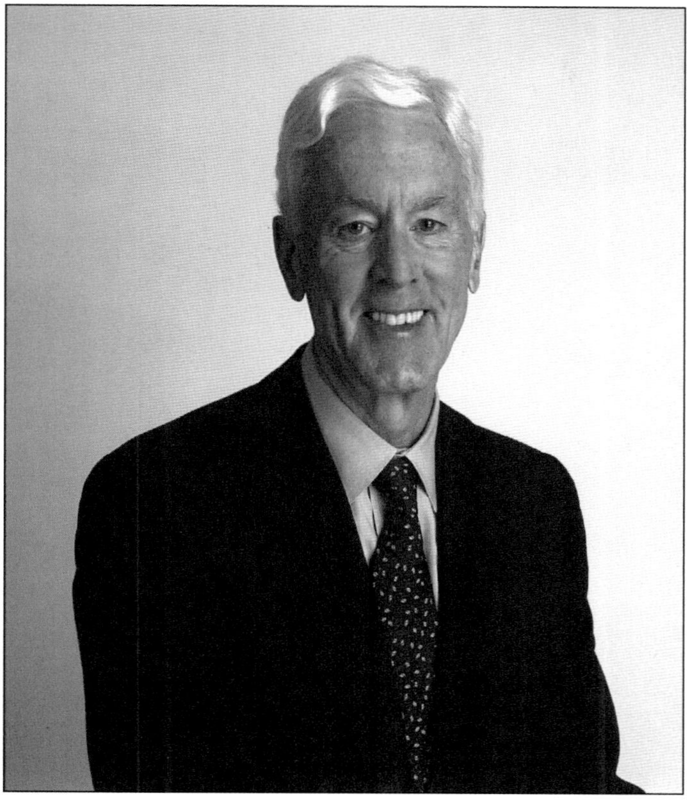

Education Management Corporation (EDMC) acquired the Art institute of Pittsburgh in 1970. Robert B. Knutson, who began working at the company in 1969, played an instrumental role in the acquisition. EDMC named him president in 1971, ushering in a period of growth and transition for the private higher education holding company.

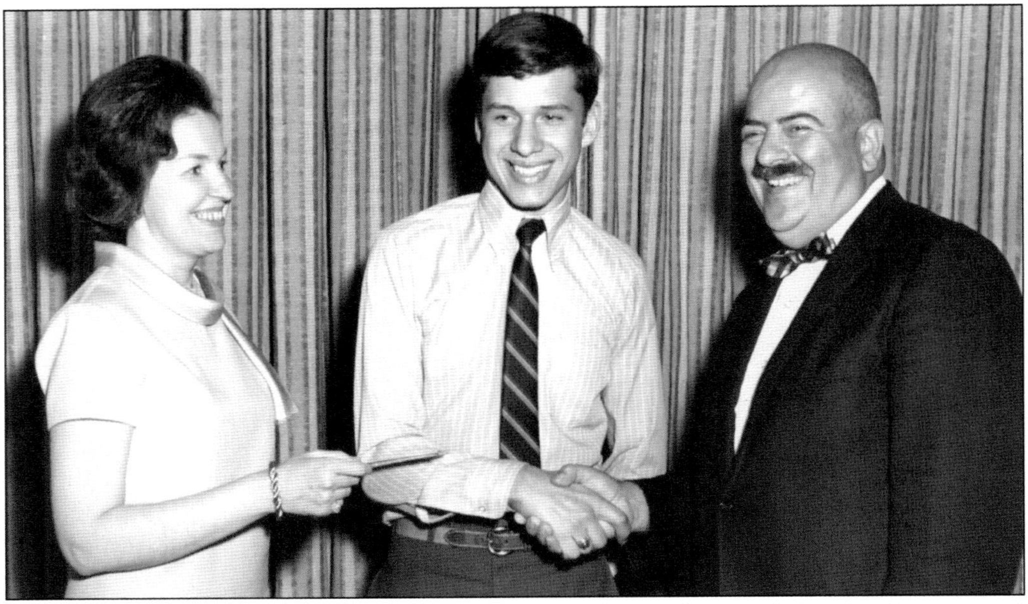

During these transition years, John Johns, a 1940 graduate of the Art Institute of Pittsburgh, became the school's president. Johns worked as an illustrator for the *Pittsburgh Press* before taking this position, which he held from 1970 to 1982. Johns was considered one of America's top caricaturists during this time period, and sharing this gift was a joy for him. He often stopped on the street to demonstrate a technique or help a student. He traveled across the country visiting the other art institutes, teaching even after his retirement. In addition to his talent, Johns is remembered for his snappy dress. His bow ties became his trademark, which he often made from scraps of upholstery fabric sneaked out of the interior design resource room. Johns has been honored by the school with a memorial scholarship. (Courtesy of Bill McAnulty.)

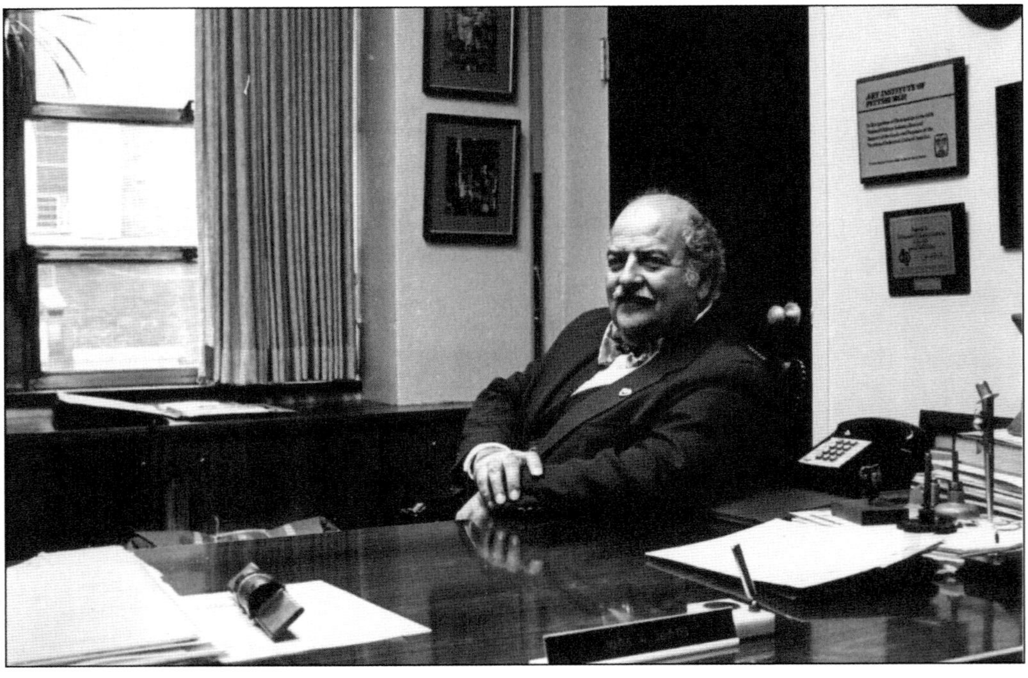

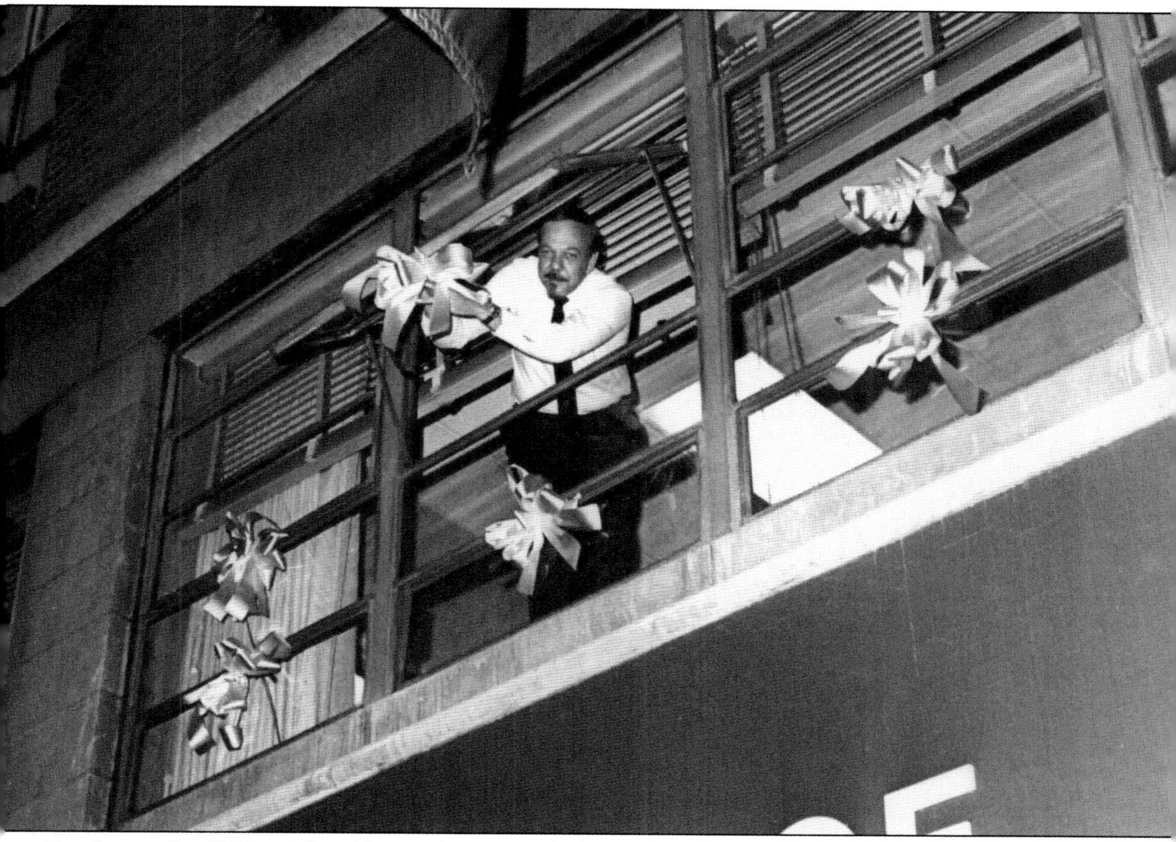

In the early 1970s, John T. Barclay joined the Art Institute of Pittsburgh as dean of students, later becoming administrative vice president and director of admissions. Barclay earned the respect of his staff and faculty. As Bill McAnulty said, "He made you feel that what you did every day was as important as what he and everyone else did. He allowed one to do their job and was always there for support, advice, encouragement and leadership." However, that did not stop the English Barclay from participating in numerous good-natured practical jokes, particularly with his Irish staff. To congratulate the Irish Dan Lafferty on his new position at the Art Institute of Seattle, Barclay sent a completely orange bouquet adorned only with an English flag. The school honored Barclay's memory by naming the gallery at Penn Avenue and a board room in the Boulevard of the Allies building after him. The school also awards a memorial scholarship to students who demonstrate commitment to attendance, outstanding scholarship, and involvement in the community.

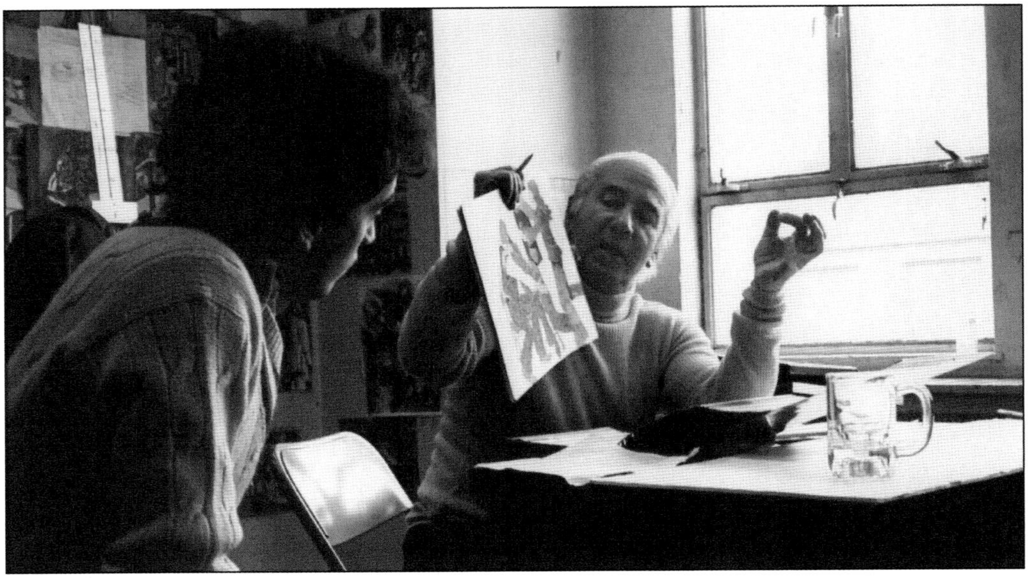

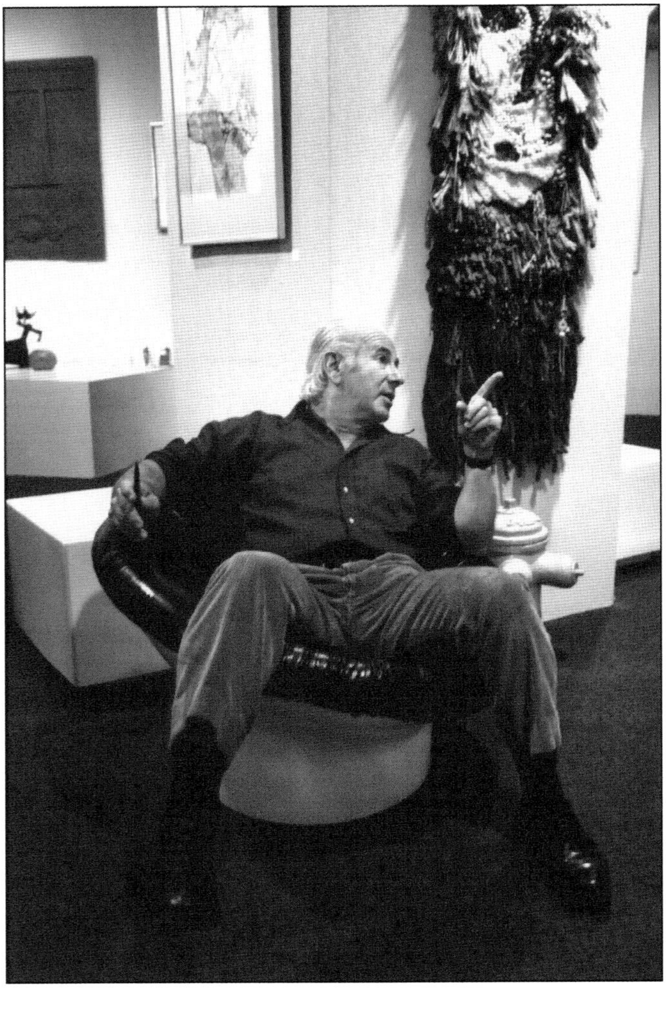

Henry Koerner, a member of the faculty from the 1960s through the 1980s, was one of Pittsburgh's most notable artists. Born in Vienna in 1915, Koerner spent his youth studying art there. In 1938, he moved to the United States, first settling in Brooklyn, New York. Throughout World War II, Koerner designed posters for the Office of War Information and the Office of Strategic Services. In 1952, he relocated to Pittsburgh, where he taught at Chatham College and the Art Institute of Pittsburgh. He is best known for his portraits, which appeared on 50 *Time* magazine covers from 1955 to 1967. During his later years, he dedicated his time to painting, practicing a style called magic realism. Many of his paintings are part of permanent museum collections. (Above, photograph by Richard Breymeier.)

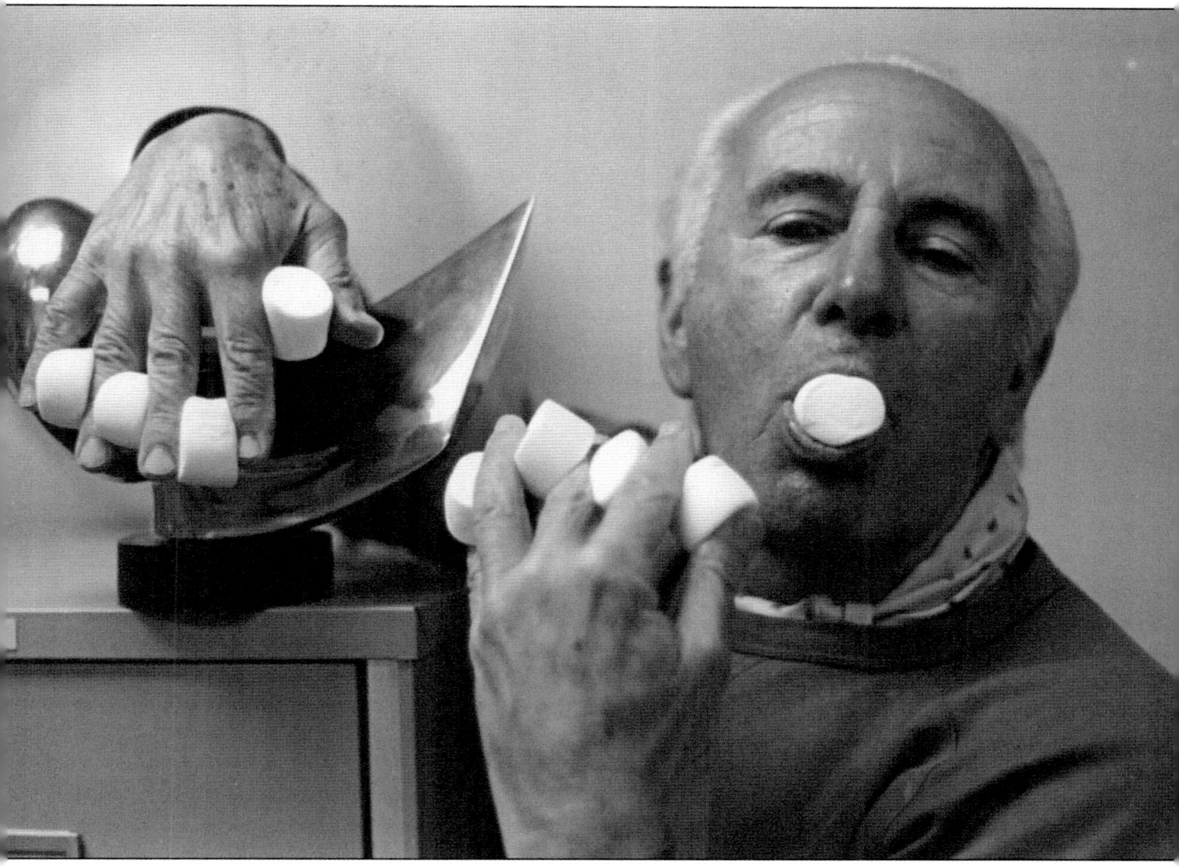

Koerner is remembered by his students and peers for his passionate dedication to art and his dynamic personality. He was on a quest to find the sublime and rarely let anything stop him when he found it. When he did find something that was ideal, he called it "beautiful," in his Austrian accent. He once walked into a glass door, injuring himself, because he could only focus on the beautiful view beyond it. Bill McAnulty recalls seeing Koerner one Saturday morning after playing football with students at Schenley Park. It was a chilly fall day and Koerner had setup with his easel and bicycle in the double lines of the turning lane. When McAnulty asked the artist what he was doing in the middle of the road, he replied that he simply had to paint the beautiful hedges.

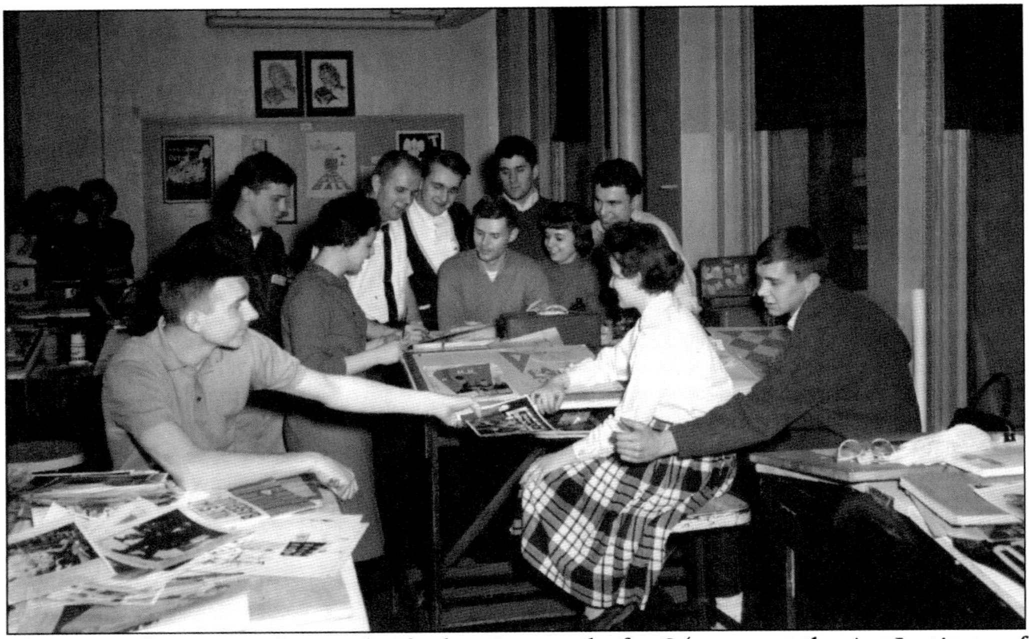

Thomas Helwig, a teacher and gifted artist, taught for 34 years at the Art Institute of Pittsburgh. He was known for his barn paintings and his talent with watercolors. Much loved by his students from 1959 through 1993, he kept in touch with hundreds of them even after their graduations.

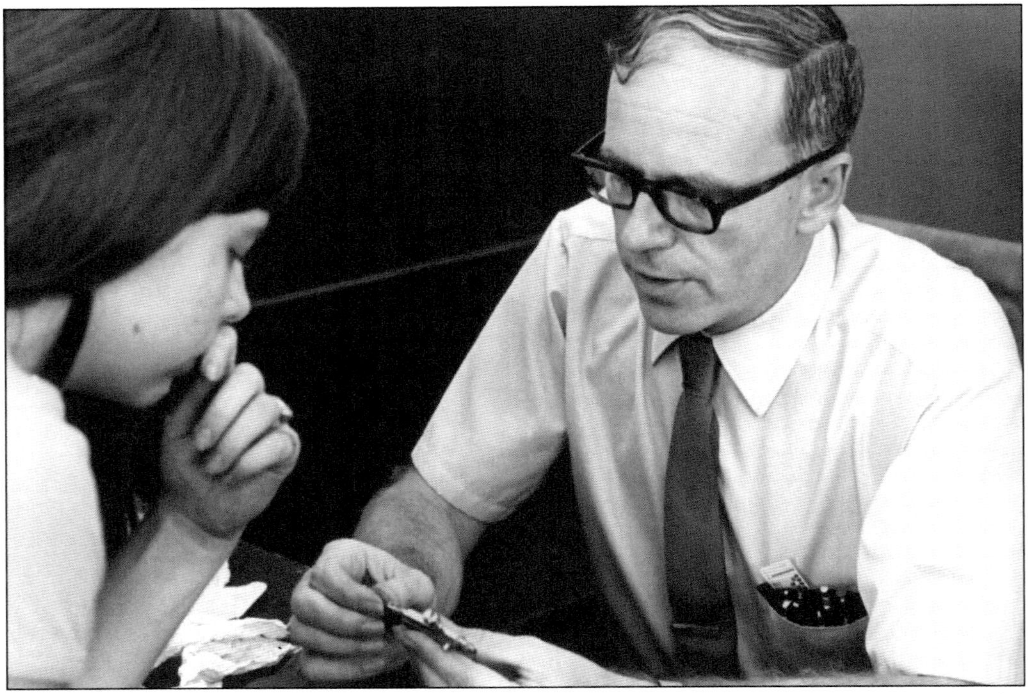

Before there was a major in photography, Bill Cockrell taught photography. Later he taught airbrush to the visual communications students. He joined the staff in 1960 with considerable industry experience, having worked as art director for KDKA-TV and Duquesne Light.

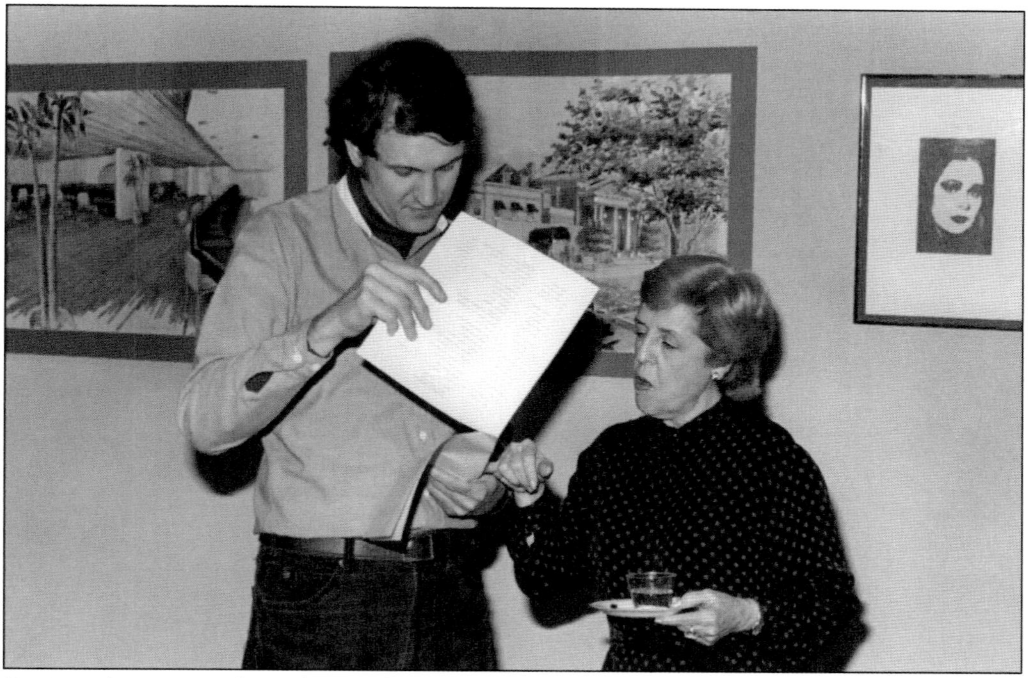

During the 1970s, the school offered a European tour to students. Angelo Ciotti and Florence "Pete" Munn organized the trips. Ciotti is an environmental reclamation artist who restores the natural in urban and industrial spaces. He has traveled and studied extensively. In 1970, he joined the visual communications faculty, approaching teaching art as an opportunity to instill change. Pete Munn was the director of fashion illustration at this time.

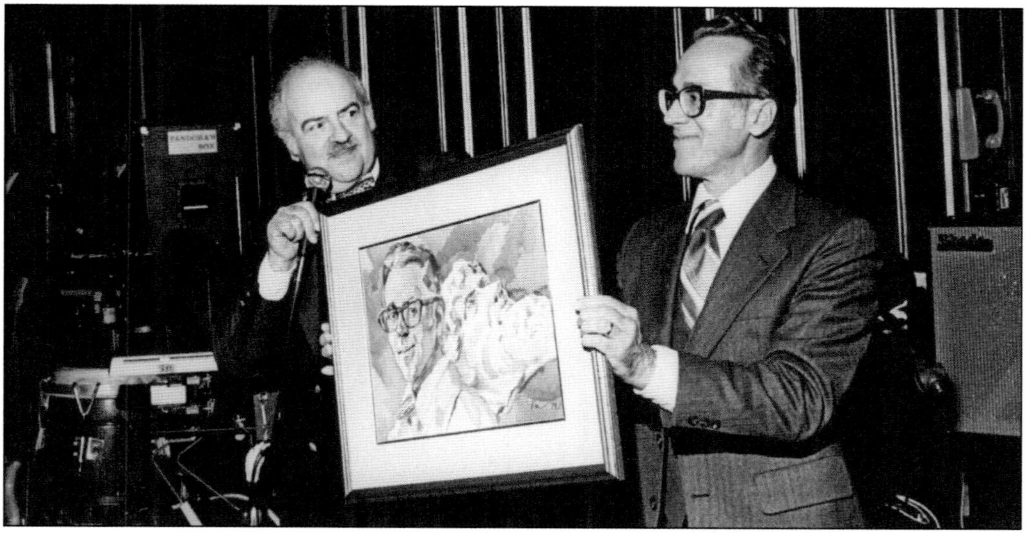

John Johns presents faculty member Thomas Kouris with a portrait by Henry Koerner. Kouris retired in 1991, after teaching life and figure drawing for 35 years. In addition to his paintings and teaching, Kouris was well known for his pencil sketches on his daily trolley commute to Pittsburgh. With the passengers around him as his subjects, Kouris created over 20,000 of these sketches and often gave copies to them. There were times that his focus was so much on his sketching that on the way home he missed his stop.

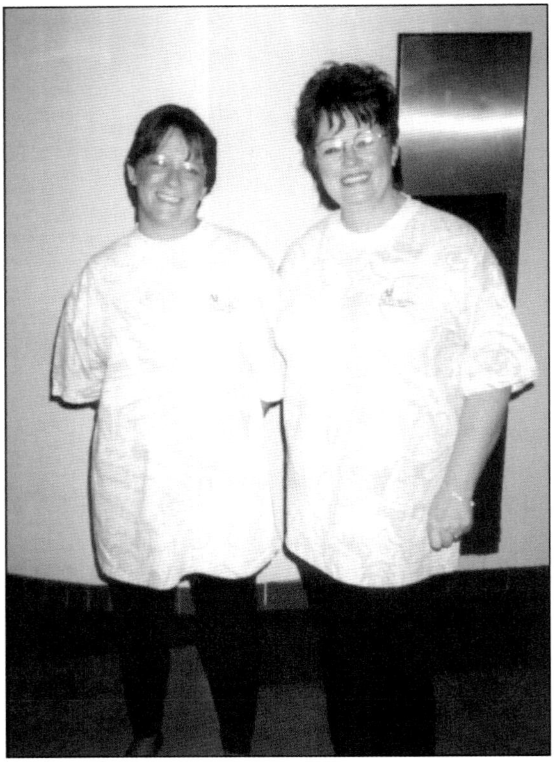

The Art Institute of Pittsburgh building on Penn Avenue was one of the last buildings in Pittsburgh to use manual elevators with elevator operators. Following their father who worked as an elevator operator at the school, Hazel Fischer (left) and her sister Debbie, along with Hazel's son Jim, are fondly remembered by everyone who worked and studied in that building. Hazel was well known for her Halloween antics, when the elevator became a haunted ride, complete with cobwebs and spiders and Elvira as the driver.

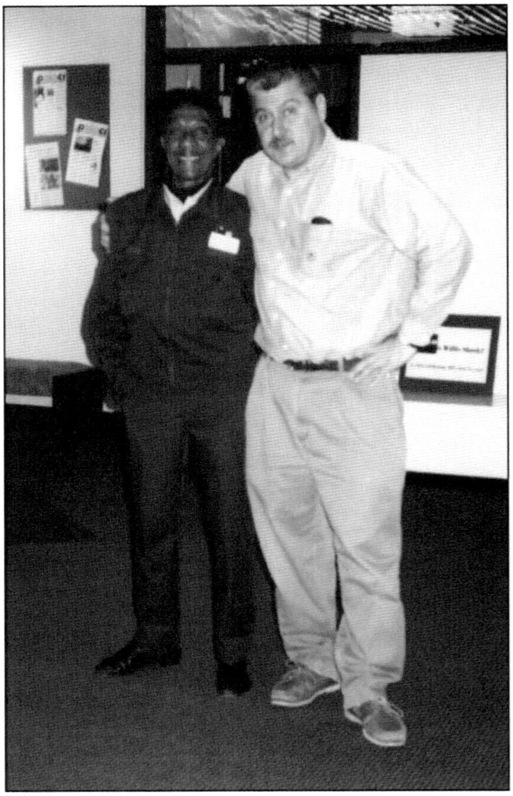

Sam Lane (left) is remembered for his many years of service to the Art Institute of Pittsburgh. Here with Allen Kuchinick, director of facilities, Lane worked at the Art Institute of Pittsburgh for 40 years, starting in the maintenance department and serving most of his career at the Art Institute as a security guard.

Preparing for the faculty show in 1981 are Inez Hall and Ann Ferguson. This juried exhibition in the gallery of the Penn Avenue building is an annual event to display the works of the talented faculty. Ann Ferguson was a faculty member in the visual communications and graphic design departments from 1965 to 2002.

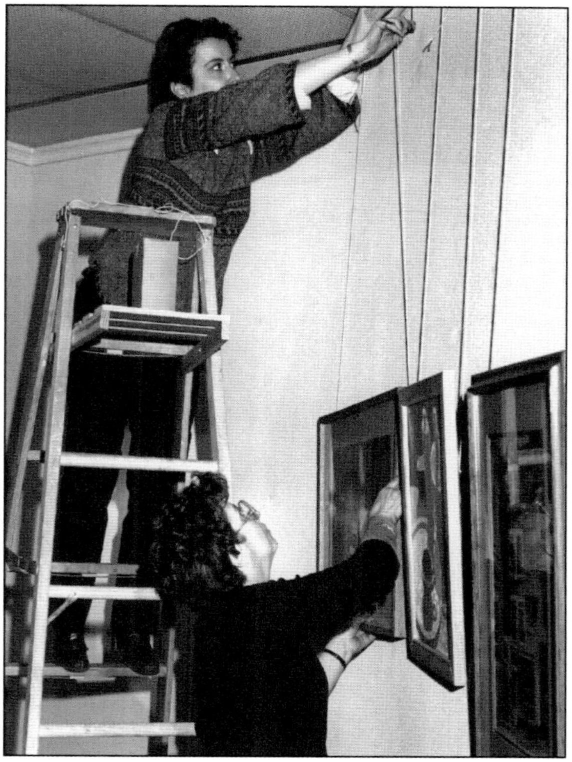

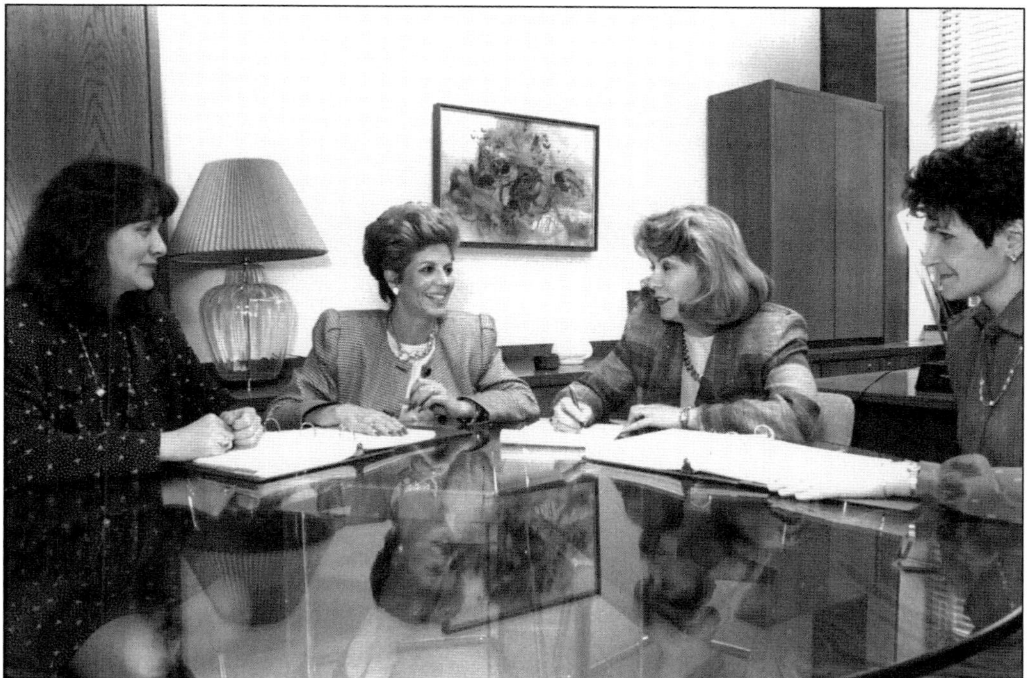

From left to right, Nadine Josephs, Miryam Drucker Knutson, Saundra Van Dyke, and Diane Carney work together to plan curriculum and student events in the early 1990s. Van Dyke, president during the 1990s, was the school's first female president.

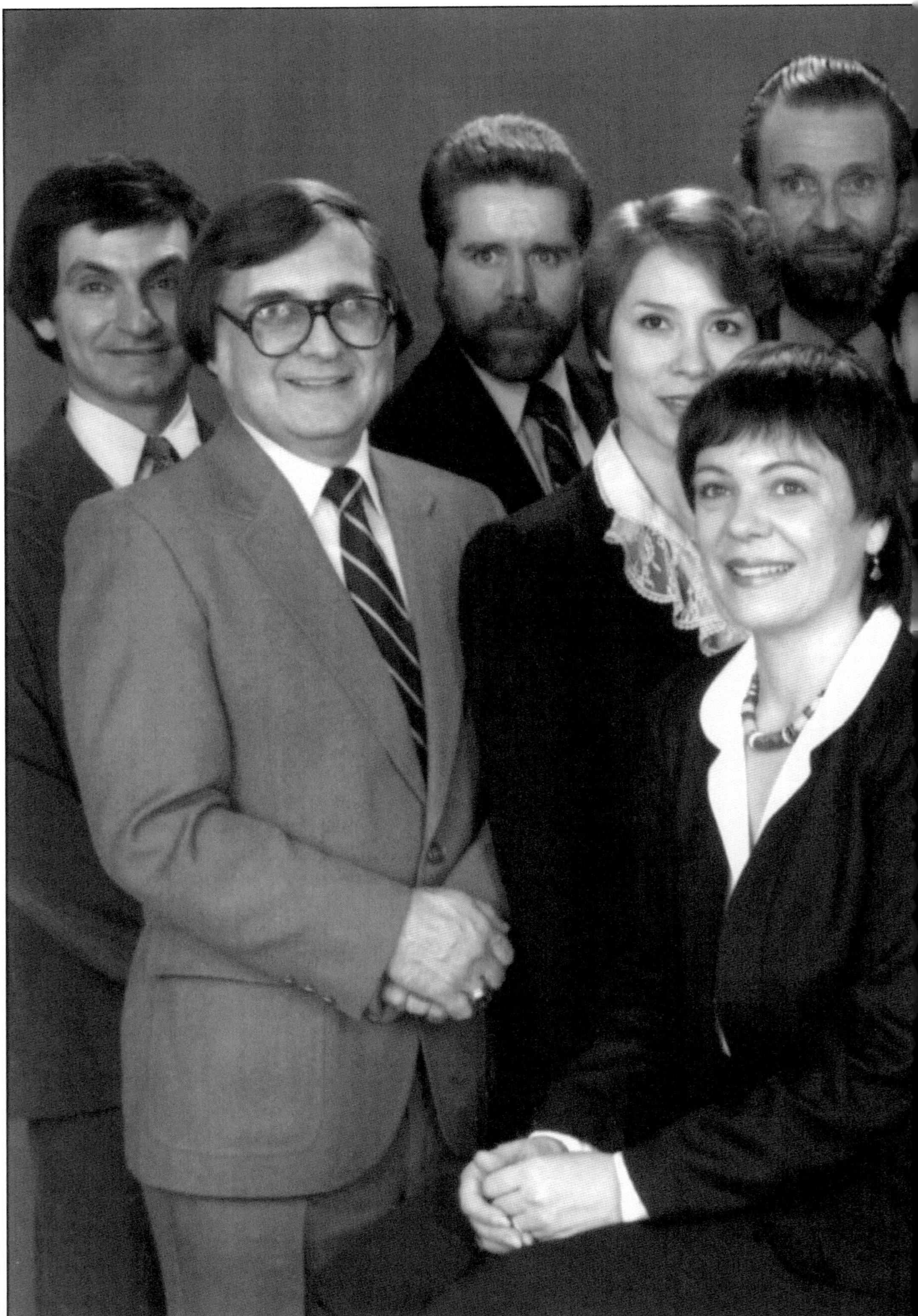

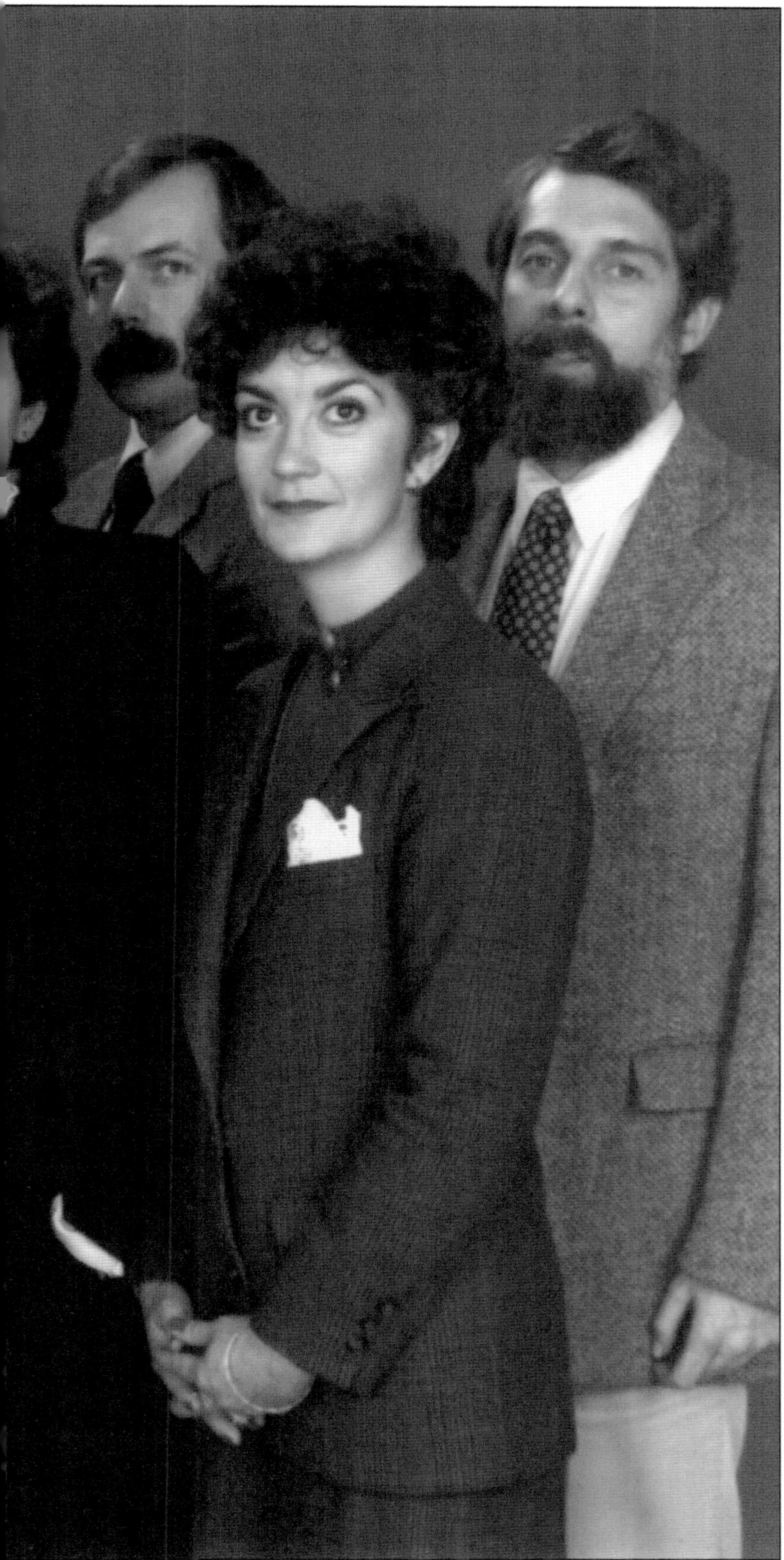

This formal portrait captures department directors and administrators for the 1982–1983 school year. Pictured are Alan Assad, assistant director of industrial design; Steven Frye, assistant director of photography; John Winberg, director of education; Bill McAnulty, director of visual communications; Barry Lavery, director of photography; Matt Krajnak, assistant director of visual communications; Diana Frye, administrative assistant; Mary Jean Stabile, evening director; Roz Woodall, director of fashion merchandising; and Nancy Ruttner, director of interior design. (Courtesy of Bill McAnulty.)

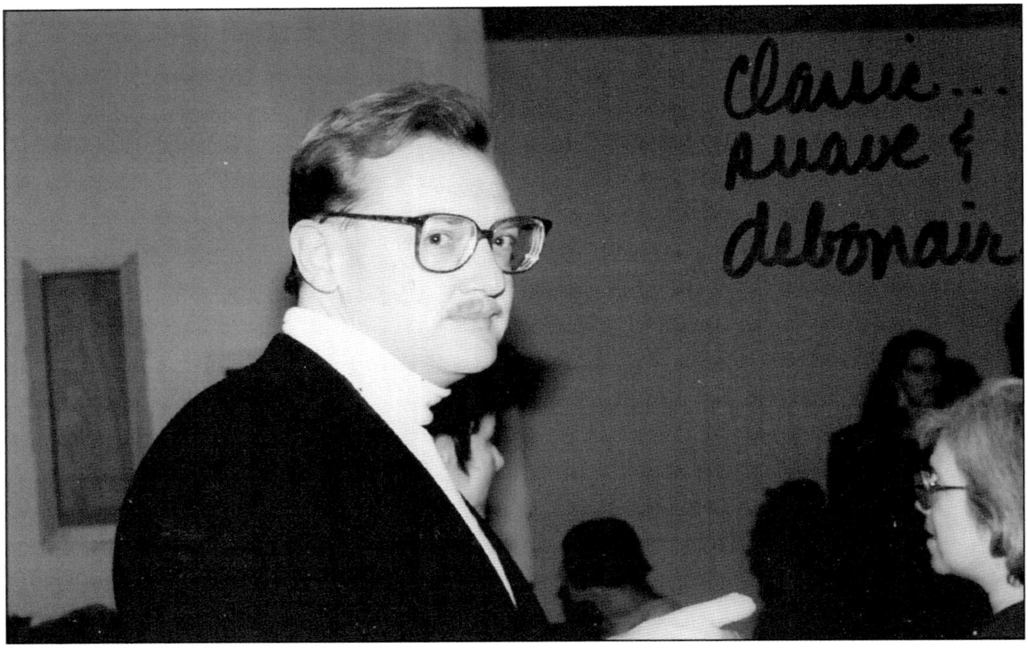

John Franke, so aptly described in the writing on this 1980s photograph as "classic . . . suave & debonair," is the school's resident expert on fashion and decorating trends. Franke has taught in the fashion retail programs for 25 years and is the guide to the ever-popular thrift shop tours. During Franke's suave and debonair days, students too were on top of the fashion trends. Franke recalls his fashion students gathering on the seventh floor of the Penn Avenue building, equipped with large cans of Adorn, VO5, and White Rain, to create the required big hairstyles.

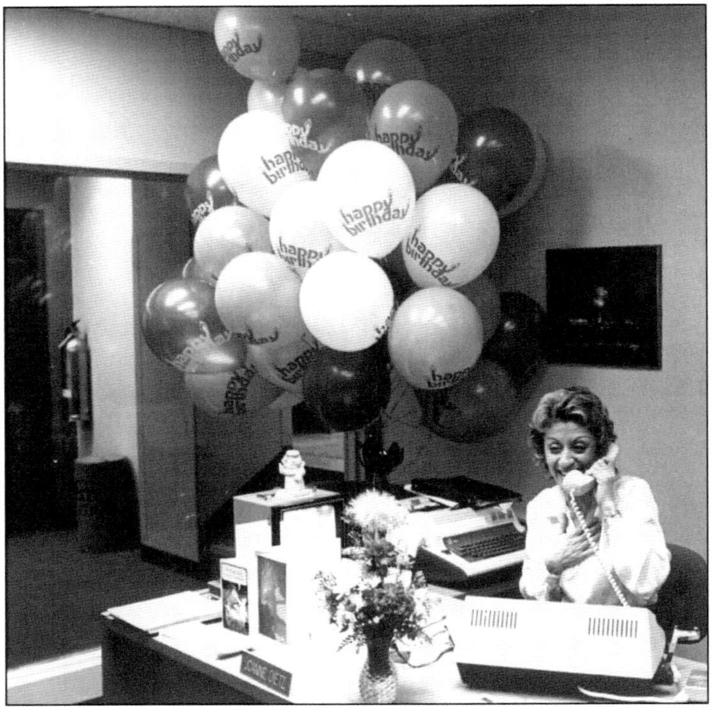

Joanne Dietz, receptionist and switchboard operator throughout the 1980s, was the first voice on the other end of the telephone and the first face many people saw in the morning. She could be counted on for a big smile, like the one she has in this photograph, taken on her birthday. (Courtesy of Bill McAnulty.)

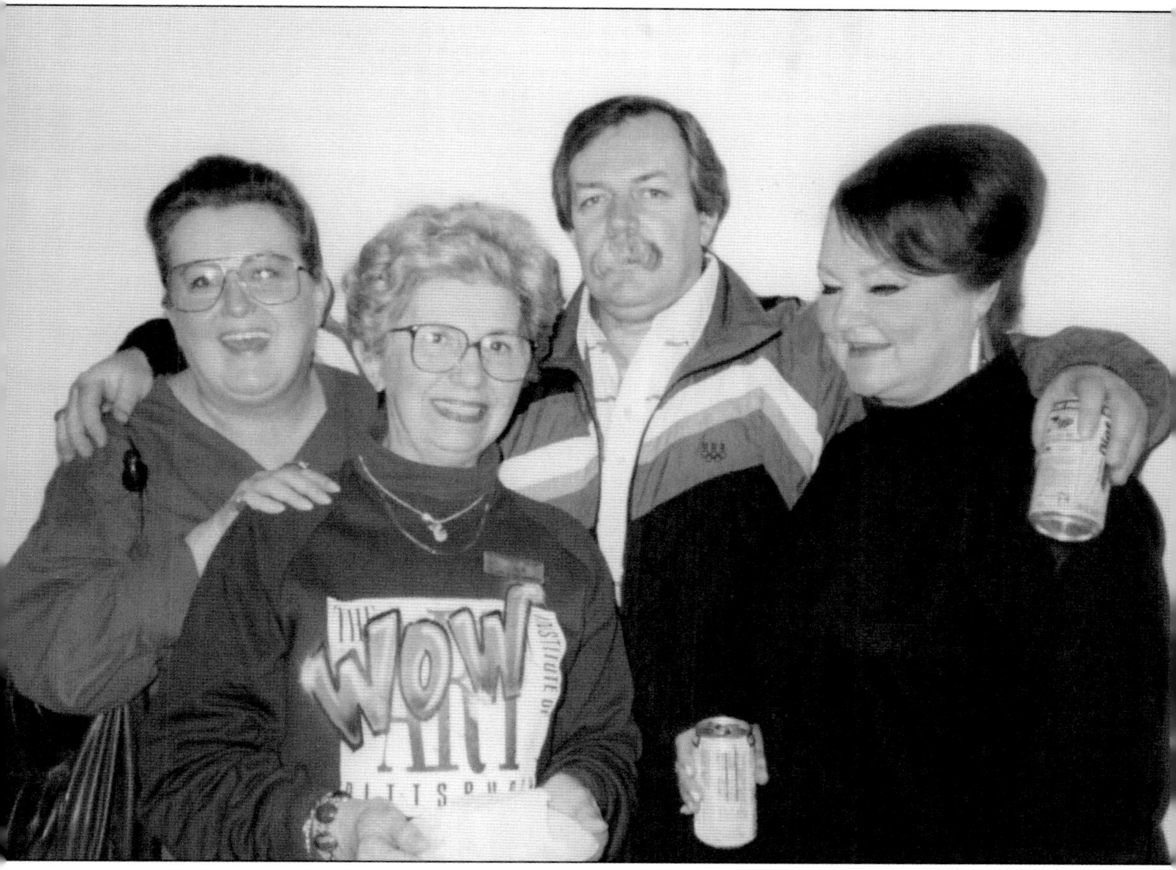

Ann Ferguson, Bill McAnulty, and Rita O'Brien celebrate with Inez Hall (center) at her retirement. Hall joined the visual communications faculty in 1969, teaching fashion illustration and layout design. She was considered by many to be the ideal instructor: patient, classy, and with the student's best interest in mind. As described by many of her colleagues, Hall is fondly remembered as a beautiful lady, impeccably dressed, perfectly coiffed, always immaculate but always understated, dedicated to her work and her students. She is the namesake of an annual award that recognizes outstanding faculty. Recipients of this celebrated award have been Helen Webster (1997), Angelo Ciotti (1998), Alan Hassinger (1999), Ron A. Miller (2000), Mary Jean Stabile (2001), Jim Allan (2002), Una Charlene Langer (2003), James Hudson (2004), Stephen Butler (2005), Angela Love (2006), Lars Nyquist (2007), and Mark Bender (2008). (Courtesy of Bill McAnulty.)

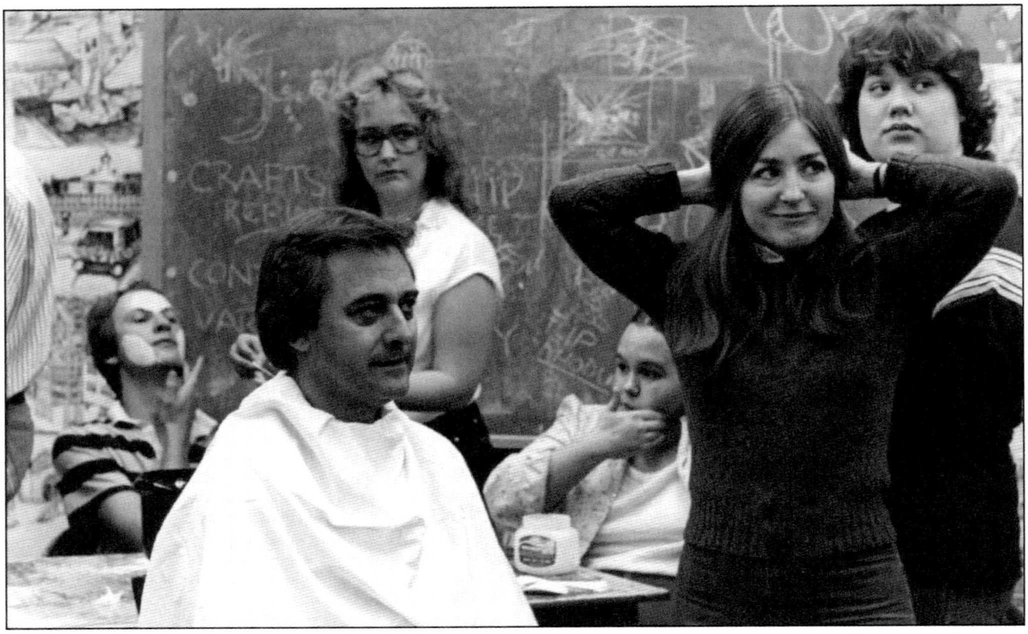

Una Charlene Langer posed Jack Etzel of WPXI-TV as a model in her art history class in the 1980s. This class on mask-making proved so popular that it grew into an elective and eventually into the industrial design department. Langer started teaching at the school in 1976 and has taught an impressive array of courses, including marketing, life drawing, and art history.

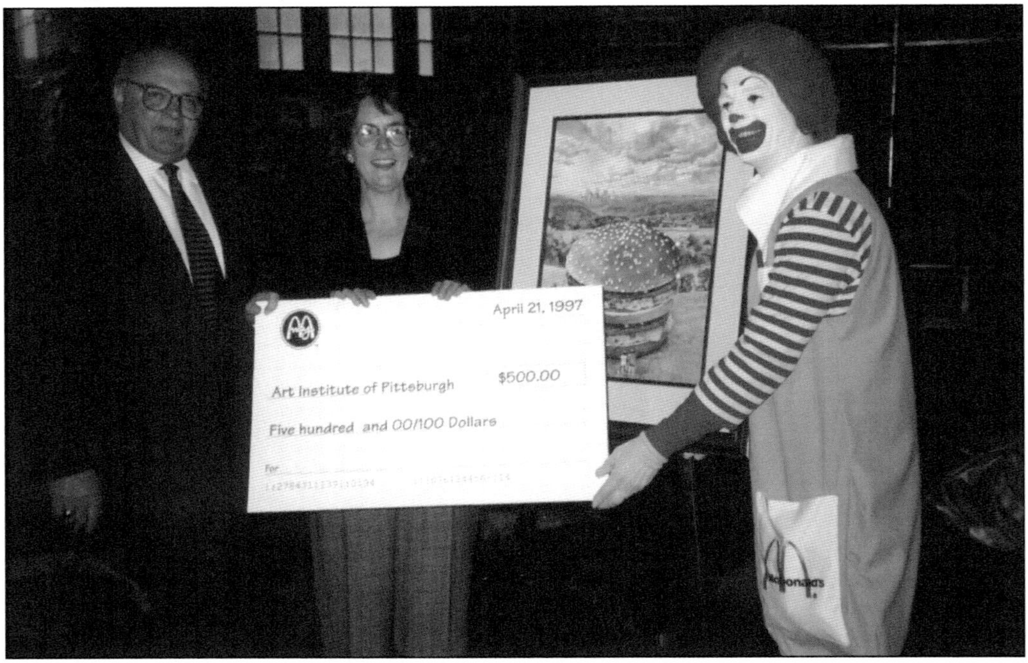

Helen Webster began her teaching career at the Art Institute of Pittsburgh in 1971. She received her bachelor of fine arts degree from Carnegie Mellon University. In 1997, she put her artistic talents to work for McDonald's, painting a watercolor portrait of the Big Mac to help celebrate the burger's 30th birthday.

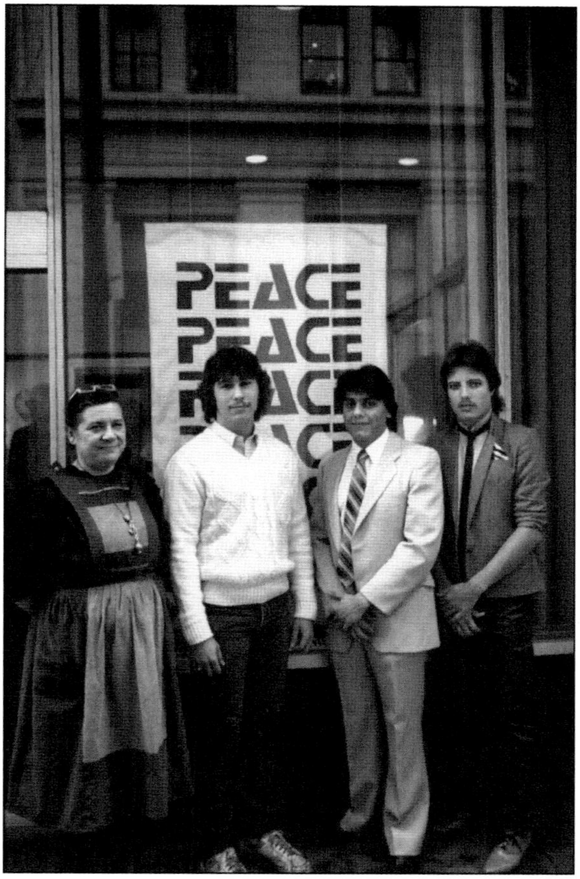

Her adoring students compared Flavia Zortea to Yoda. And like him, her small stature belied a big personality and a huge artistic talent. Zortea worked in the visual communications department. She worked hard to inspire her students and give them the confidence to create. Zortea poses with her students to celebrate their accomplishments. (Below, photograph by Stanley L. Franzos.)

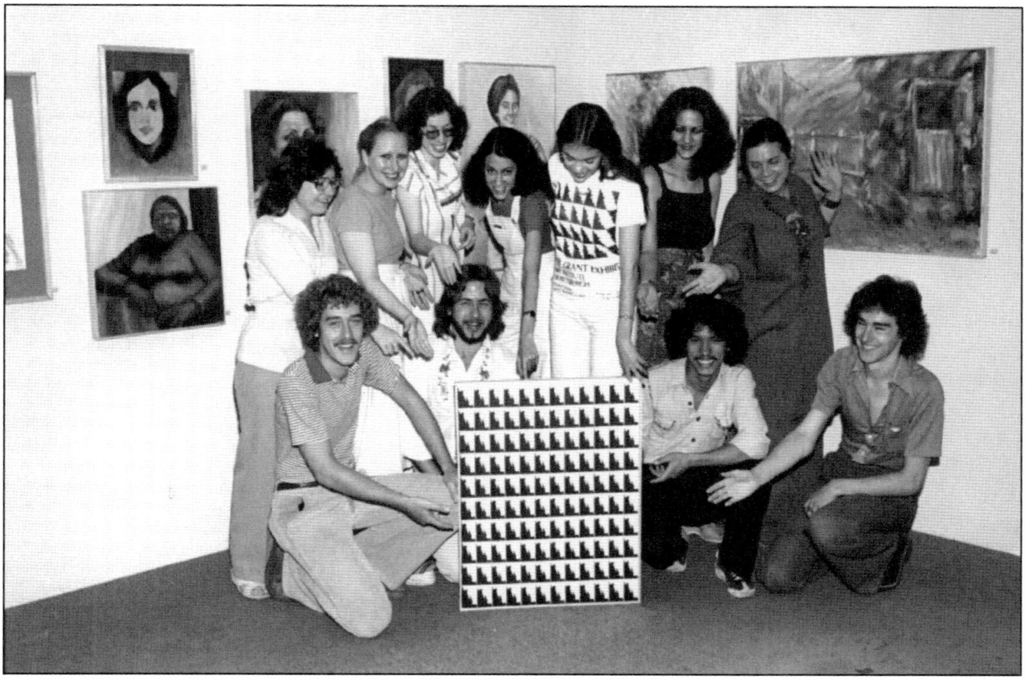

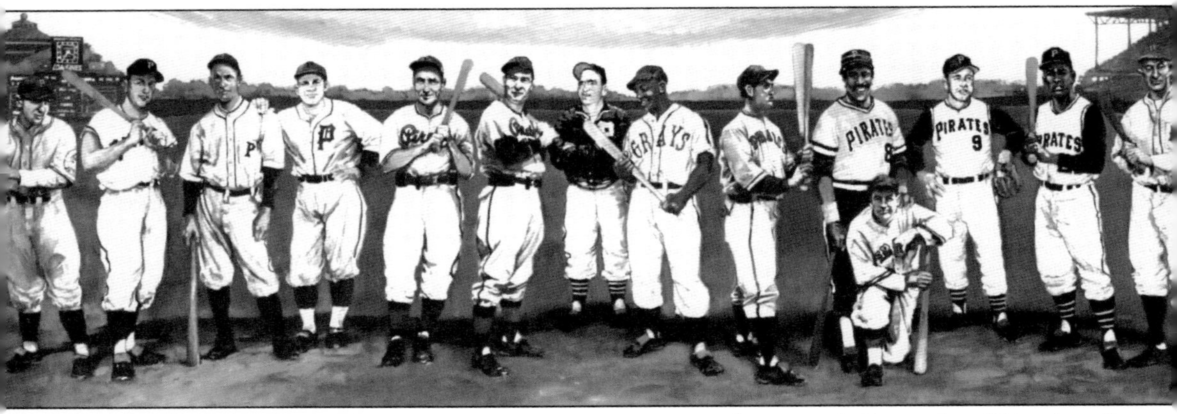

At the Boulevard of the Allies ramp at Ross Street is this mural, *Legends of Pittsburgh*, created by faculty member Michael Malle. The mural depicts some of the most infamous Pittsburgh Pirates from the past: (from left to right) Kiki Cuyler, Ralph Kiner, Fred Clarke, Max Carey, Lloyd and Paul Waner, Danny Muratugh, Josh Gibson, Arky Vaughn, Willie Stargell, Pie Traynor, Bill Mazeroski, Roberto Clemente, and Honus Wagner. The mural is actually a copy of a painting that Malle spent three years researching and implementing. It is an example of the attention to detail that Malle insists upon from his students. He has been a member of the graphic design faculty since 1982 teaching life drawing and illustration classes.

George L. Pry's career with the Art Institutes began in 1977 as a counselor. He moved on to become president of Art Institutes in Houston and Seattle, then returned to Pittsburgh in a leadership role at EMDC, the Art Institute of Pittsburgh's parent company. In 1999, Pry returned to the Art Institute of Pittsburgh as president and has guided the school into a new era of academic maturity. With Pry's leadership, the school achieved collegiate status and accreditation of the Middle States Commission on Higher Education. Over the past decade, the college redefined its role in the Pittsburgh community with relocation to the Boulevard of the Allies and renovation of three student housing facilities, designed to infuse the downtown neighborhood with student residents. Pry's vision continues to unfold as the college prepares for a future that remains true to its mission forged long ago of preparing students for creative careers, while fulfilling the needs of tomorrow's student and employer. Pictured here with Pry are students Alex Rebele, Jackie McClelland, Caitlin Wyckoff, and Catrina Enders, where Pry accepted an award in 2009 on behalf of the college, bestowed by a consortium of leaders for its contributions to the development and future of downtown Pittsburgh.

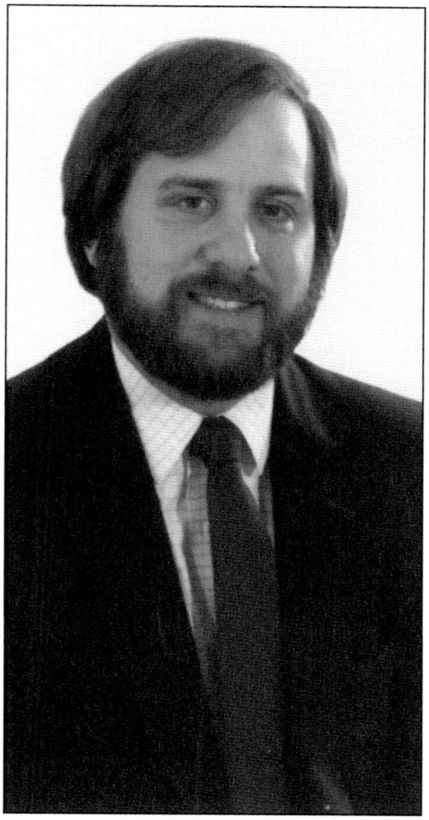

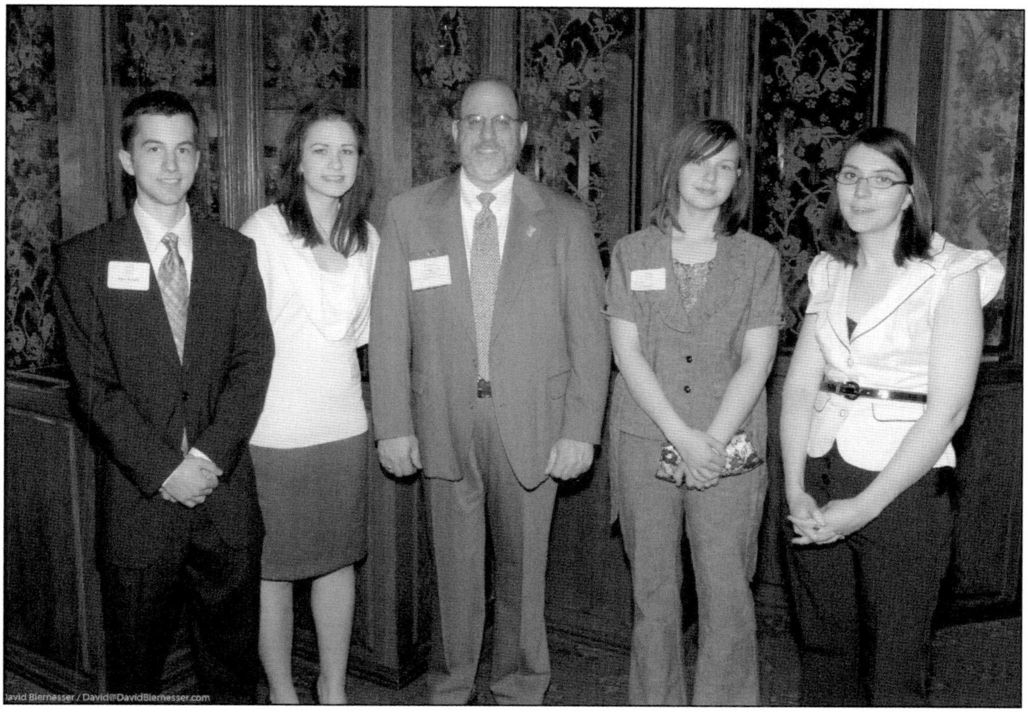

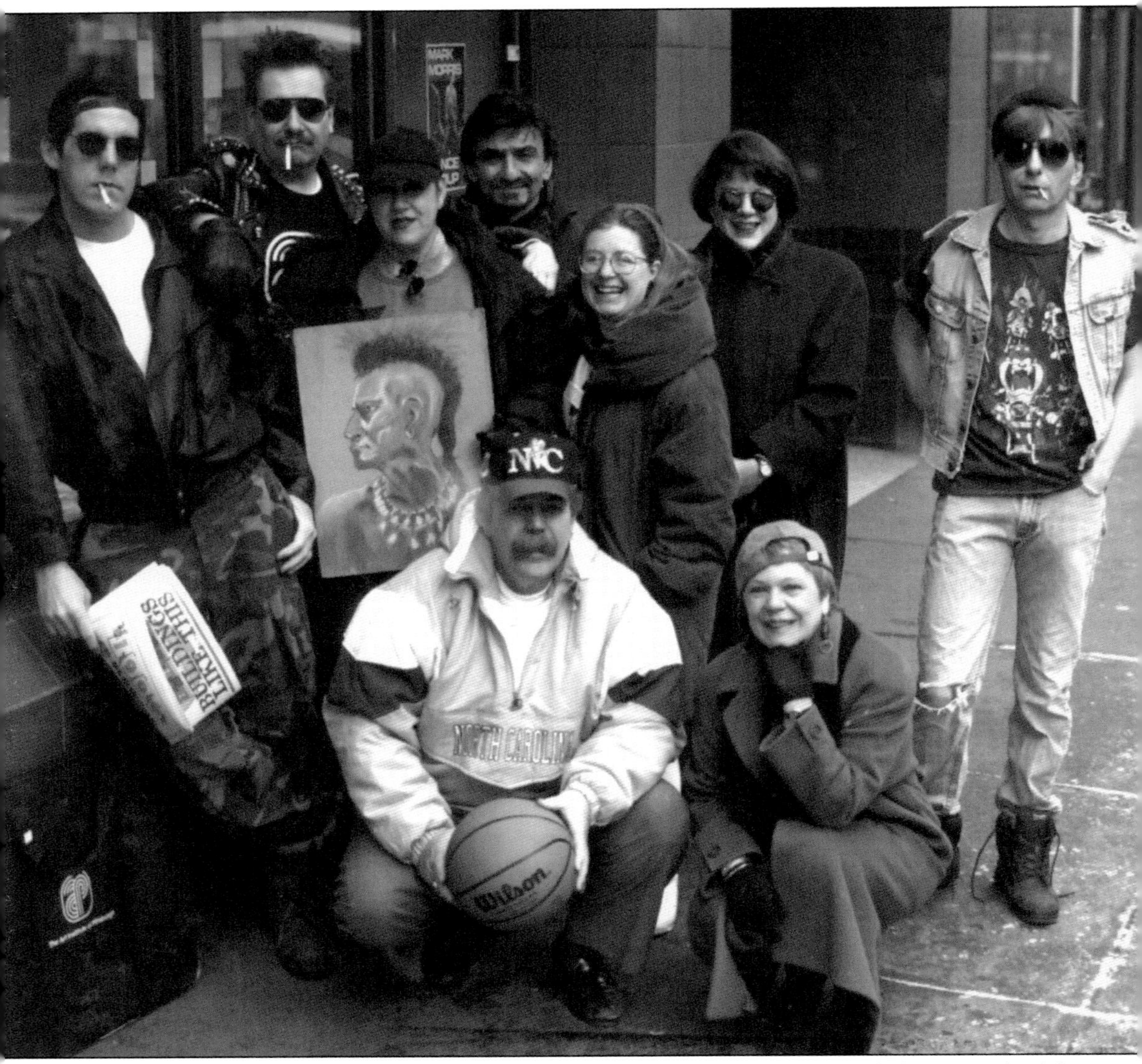

Do not mistake this crew for students—this was dress-up day, and directors had fun dressing as their students in 1996. From left to right are (first row) Bill McAnulty, director of visual communications and fashion illustration; and Nancy Ruttner, director of interior design; (second row) Brad Janis, director of media arts and animation; Rich Rybas, director of video production and photography; Mary Jean Stabile, director of continuing education; Allan Assad, director of industrial design; Una Charlene Langer, assistant director of visual communications and fashion illustration; Connie Moore, director of music video; and Rich Moore, director of technology.

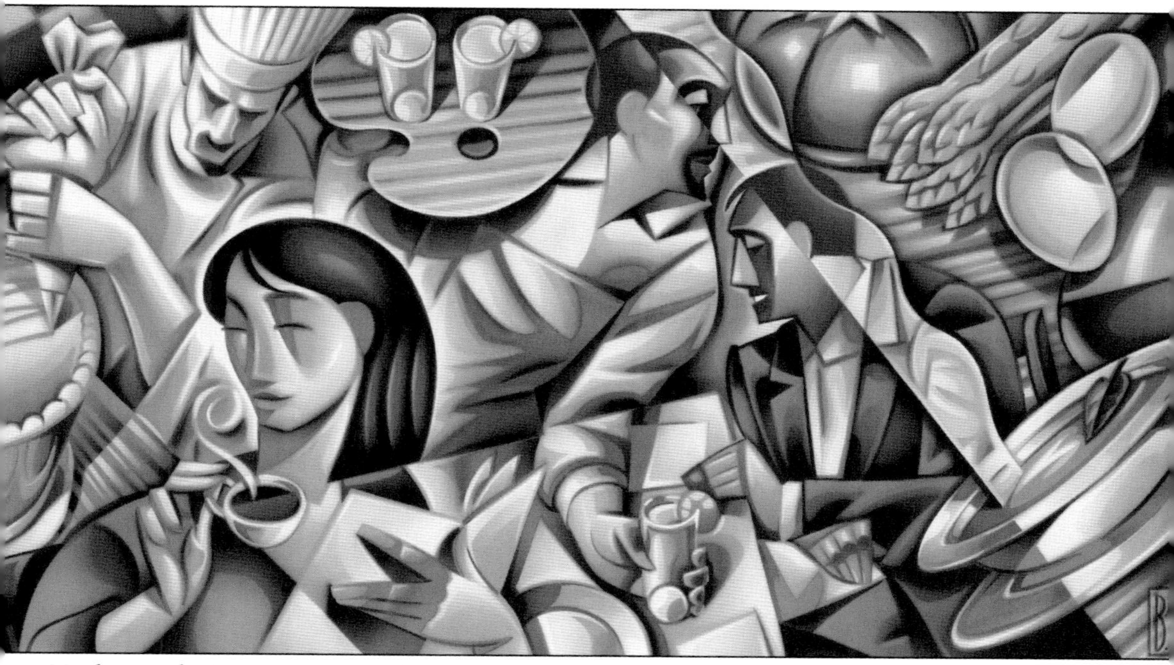

Mark Bender's extensive industry experience inspires and reassures his students. He is a member of the Pittsburgh Society of Illustrators and the New York Society of Illustrators and has received numerous awards and honors, including a silver medal from the New York Society of Illustrators. Bender's style includes references to folk art, cubism, constructivism, and surrealism, as well as the advertising posters of the 1920s and 1930s. Bender painted this mural in the school's own restaurant, Taste of Art.

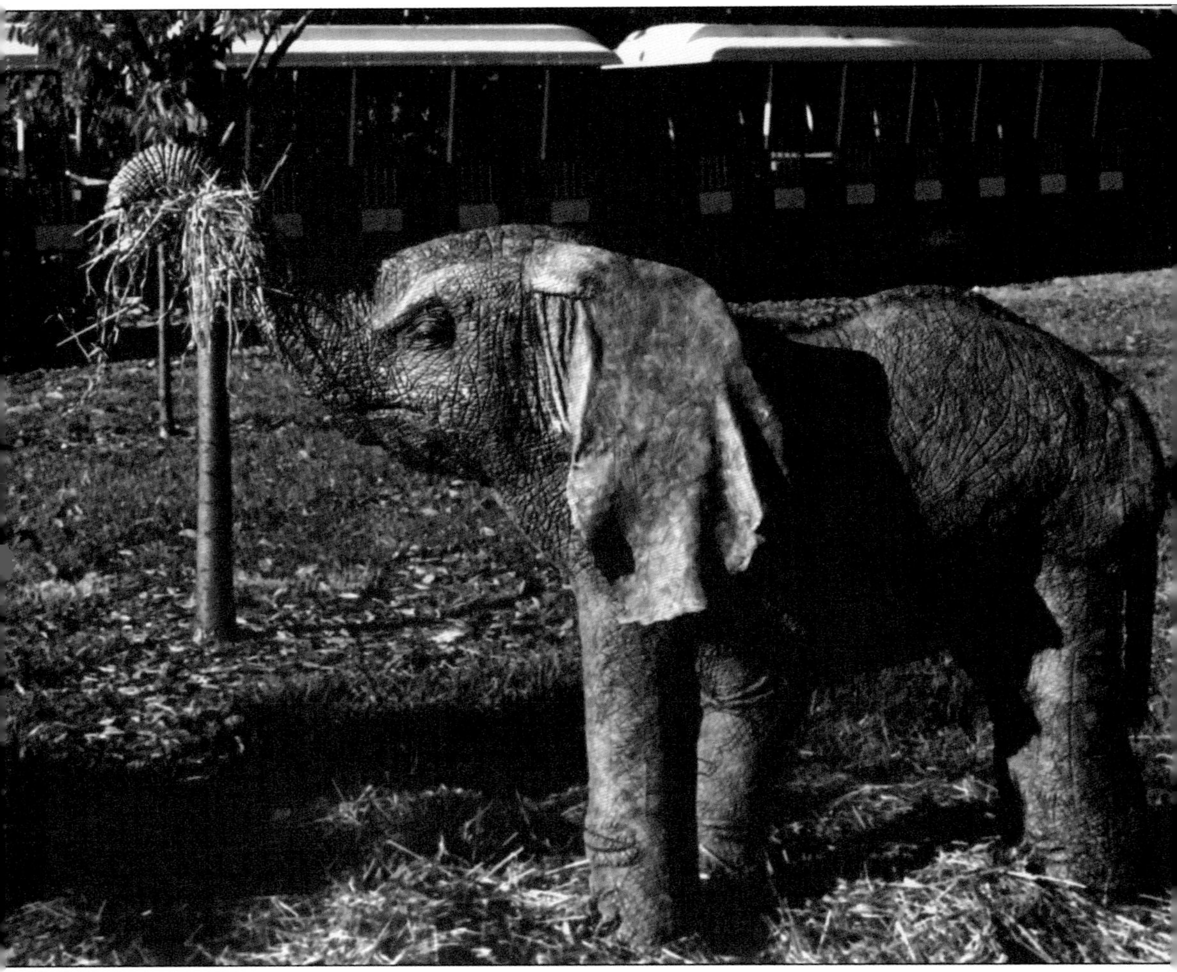

This baby elephant looks so realistic he even fooled a member of his own species. When the elephant sculpture was brought to the Pittsburgh Zoo and Aquarium, zoo officials were amazed at the real female elephant's curiosity, then her bewilderment at the strange creation, which did not behave or move like a real elephant. The sculpture was part of the Sumatran Express. On this train ride through the zoo, riders learn about endangered species by passing a series of sculptures of the animals, like this elephant. Bill Farrell, a member of the industrial design technology faculty since 1988, worked with the zoo and students in his department to create these sculptures. Farrell is an active member of the community, teaming with numerous organizations for student projects. He received a Pennsylvania Association of Private School Administrators Award for Community Service in 1998 for this project.

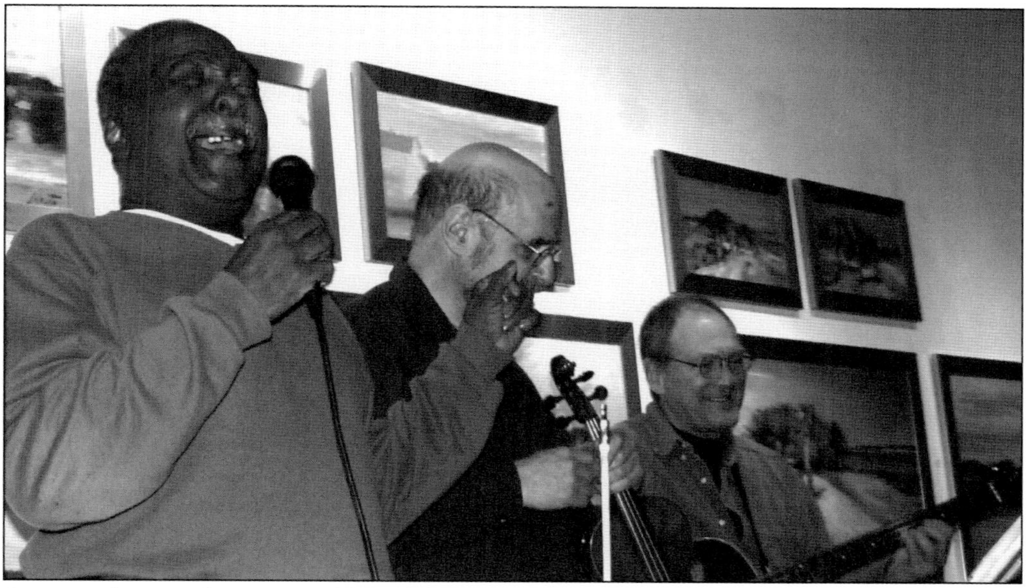

Steve Jackson is known and loved for his ever-smiling face, which greets everyone at the security desk. At many Pittsburgh jazz events, students are often surprised to see Jackson and especially to hear him as he displays his own artistic talents through his lifelong love of music, vocal and instrumental. At Phil Salvato's Third Street Gallery in Carnegie, Jackson (left) sings with Roy Sonne and Phil Salvato, a 1965 graduate. (Photograph by Amy Haller.)

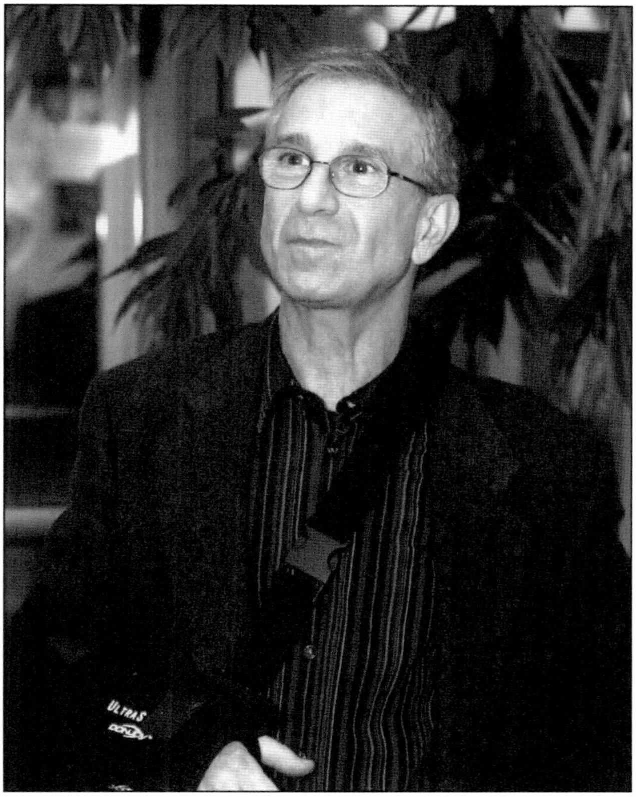

In 2008, after 31 years at the Art Institute of Pittsburgh, Dave DiBella retired as the school's alumni coordinator and gallery show coordinator. DiBella joined the Art Institute in 1977 as an admissions representative, and within a few years, he became the alumni coordinator, where he devoted the majority of his 31-year career. Known for his encyclopedic memory and his awe-inspiring tales of swimming the Chesapeake and competing in the Iron Man competition, DiBella left an indelible mark on those who knew him.

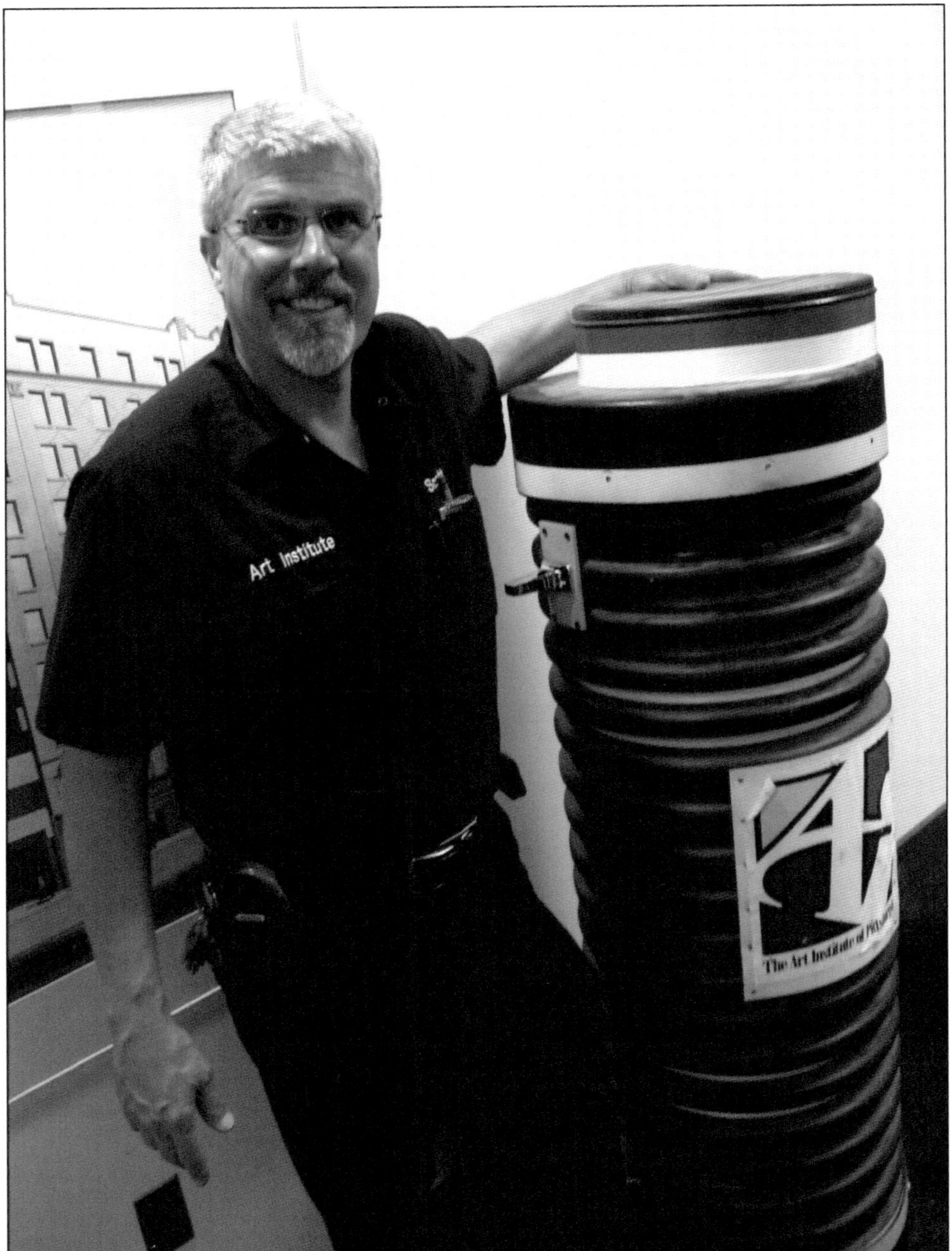

How could something this big be misplaced? Scott Lansing poses here after his heroic discovery of the 1996 time capsule. During the discussions for writing this book, the authors learned that the 75th-anniversary celebration included filling a time capsule to much fanfare. However, just 13 years later, the location of the time capsule seemed to elude the memories of the current faculty and staff. For several weeks, the search was on, and just as it appeared that it may have been lost forever, Scott Lansing rescued the forgotten time capsule in an out-of-the-way storage closet. The next time capsule, for the 100th anniversary, will have its location published in the newspaper so that future generations can find it!

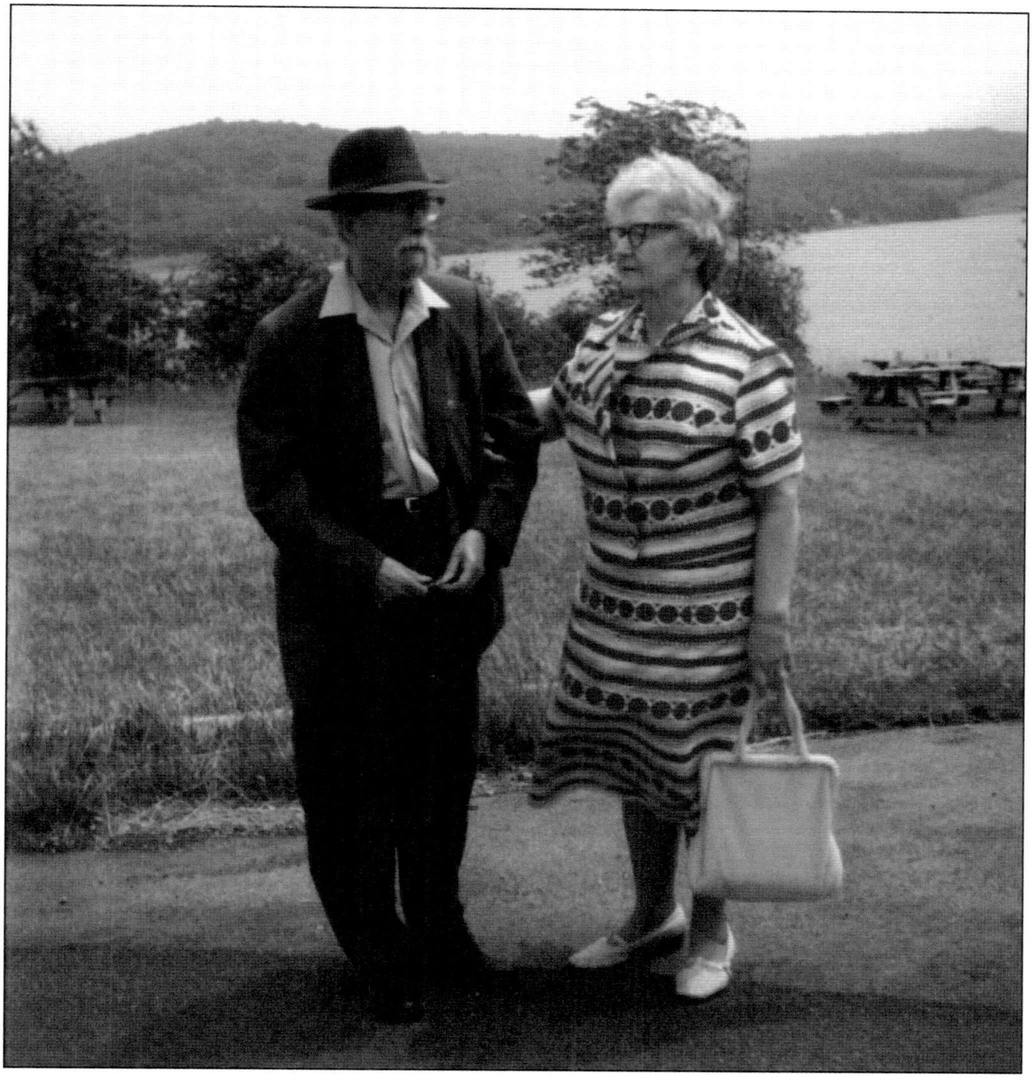

In this photograph, taken in the 1980s, Willis Shook with his wife Elizabeth, whom he called his "99 44/100 percent perfect wife," walked near their home in Lawrence County. It was six decades after the founding of the Art Institute of Pittsburgh. After their retirement from the Art Institute of Pittsburgh in 1962, the Shooks traveled and enjoyed time at their home at Muddy Creek Falls, Lawrence County. The authors are grateful for their forethought in writing their memoirs *My First Twenty One Years (1894–1915)*, written in 1969 by Willis Shook; *Genesis of the Art Institute of Pittsburgh (1921–1962)*, written in 1972 by Willis Shook; and *Muddy Creek Falls, The Early Years (1950–1952)*, diaries written by Willis and Elizabeth Shook. These documents have added to the history where memories have failed. Let this book remind future generations of the proud heritage that is part of the Art Institute of Pittsburgh.